Savage Economics

This innovative book challenges the most powerful and pervasive ideas concerning political economy, international relations, and ethics in the modern world.

Rereading classical authors including Adam Smith, James Steuart, Adam Ferguson, Hegel, and Marx, it provides a systematic and fundamental cultural critique of political economy and critically describes the nature of the mainstream understanding of economics. Blaney and Inayatullah construct a powerful argument about how political economy and the capitalist market economy should be understood, demonstrating that poverty is a product of capitalism itself. They address the questions:

- Is wealth for some bought at the cost of impoverishing, colonizing, or eradicating others?
- What benefits of wealth might justify these human costs?
- What do we gain and lose by endorsing a system of wealth creation?
- Do even "savage cultures" contain values, critiques, and ways of life that the West still needs?

Opening the way for radically different policies addressing poverty and demanding a rethink of the connections between political economy and international relations, this thought-provoking book is vital reading for students and scholars of politics, economics, IPE and international relations.

David L. Blaney is Professor in the Department of Political Science at Macalester College, USA.

Naeem Inayatullah is Associate Professor in the Department of Politics at Ithaca College, USA.

RIPE Series in Global Political Economy
Series Editors: Louise Amoore (*University of Durham, UK*),
Jacqueline Best (*University of Ottawa, Canada*), Paul Langley
(*Northumbria University, UK*) and Leonard Seabrooke
(*Copenhagen Business School, Denmark*)

Formerly edited by Randall Germain (*Carleton University, Canada*), Rorden Wilkinson (*University of Manchester, UK*), Otto Holman (*University of Amsterdam*), Marianne Marchand (*Universidad de las Américas-Puebla*), Henk Overbeek (*Free University, Amsterdam*) and Marianne Franklin (*Goldsmiths, University of London, UK*)

The RIPE series editorial board are:

Mathias Albert (*Bielefeld University, Germany*), Mark Beeson (*University of Birmingham, UK*), A. Claire Cutler (*University of Victoria, Canada*), Marianne Franklin (*Goldsmiths, University of London, UK*), Randall Germain (*Carleton University, Canada*) Stephen Gill (*York University, Canada*), Jeffrey Hart (*Indiana University, USA*), Eric Helleiner (*Trent University, Canada*), Otto Holman (*University of Amsterdam, the Netherlands*), Marianne H. Marchand (*Universidad de las Américas-Puebla, Mexico*), Craig N. Murphy (*Wellesley College, USA*), Robert O'Brien (*McMaster University, Canada*), Henk Overbeek (*Vrije Universiteit, the Netherlands*), Anthony Payne (*University of Sheffield, UK*), V. Spike Peterson (*University of Arizona, USA*) and Rorden Wilkinson (*University of Manchester, UK*).

This series, published in association with the *Review of International Political Economy*, provides a forum for current and interdisciplinary debates in international political economy. The series aims to advance understanding of the key issues in the global political economy, and to present innovative analyses of emerging topics. The titles in the series focus on three broad themes:

- the structures, processes and actors of contemporary global transformations;
- the changing forms taken by governance, at scales from the local and everyday to the global and systemic;
- the inseparability of economic from political, social and cultural questions, including resistance, dissent and social movements.

The series comprises two strands:

The *RIPE Series in Global Political Economy* aims to address the needs of students and teachers, and the titles will be published in hardback and paperback. Titles include

Transnational Classes and International Relations
Kees van der Pijl

Gender and Global Restructuring:
Sightings, sites and resistances
Edited by Marianne H. Marchand and Anne Sisson Runyan

Global Political Economy
Contemporary theories
Edited by Ronen Palan

Ideologies of Globalization
Contending visions of a new world order
Mark Rupert

The Clash within Civilisations
Coming to terms with cultural conflicts
Dieter Senghaas

Global Unions?
Theory and strategies of organized labour in the global
political economy
Edited by Jeffrey Harrod and Robert O'Brien

Political Economy of a Plural World
Critical reflections on power, morals and civilizations
Robert Cox with Michael Schechter

A Critical Rewriting of Global Political Economy
Integrating reproductive, productive and virtual economies
V. Spike Peterson

Contesting Globalization
Space and place in the world economy
André C. Drainville

Global Institutions and Development
Framing the world?
Edited by Morten Bøås and Desmond McNeill

Routledge/RIPE Studies in Global Political Economy is a forum for innovative new research intended for a high-level specialist readership, and the titles will be available in hardback only. Titles include:

Also available in paperback

Savage Economics

Wealth, poverty, and the temporal walls of capitalism

David L. Blaney and Naeem Inayatullah

Routledge
Taylor & Francis Group

LONDON AND NEW YORK

First published 2010
by Routledge
2 Park Square, Milton Park, Abingdon, Oxon OX14 4RN

Simultaneously published in the USA and Canada
by Routledge
270 Madison Avenue, New York, NY 10016

*Routledge is an imprint of the Taylor & Francis Group,
an informa business*   .

© 2010 David L. Blaney and Naeem Inayatullah

Typeset in Times by
RefineCatch Limited, Bungay, Suffolk
Printed and bound in Great Britain by
TJ International, Padstow, Cornwall

British Library Cataloguing in Publication Data
A catalogue record for this book is available
from the British Library

Library of Congress Cataloging-in-Publication Data
A catalog record has been requested for this book

ISBN10: 0–415–54847–0 (hbk)
ISBN10: 0–415–54848–9 (pbk)
ISBN10: 0–203–86495–6 (ebk)

ISBN13: 978–0–415–54847–2 (hbk)
ISBN13: 978–0–415–54848–9 (pbk)
ISBN13: 978–0–203–86495–1 (ebk)

Contents

Preface

Our first book together[1] was a long and necessary detour. Neither of us imagined that book; it appeared suddenly in front of us. *Savage Economics*, due to its direct focus on political economy, and given our graduate training in development studies, is closer to what we had imagined writing. Today, of course, we are finding it difficult to distinguish between our central concerns and detours. Travel changes one's view of home, away and of travel itself.

At the fifth Pan-European International Relations Conference at The Hague, we presented a draft of what is now Chapter 2. Those few who knew our previous work on culture and international relations (IR) were surprised by our move towards economics and political economy. We in turn were surprised by their surprise, thinking that we had never left home. Part of the audience for this book are those who, intrigued by the project of IR as heterology[2] or ethnography,[3] wish to bring heterological and ethnographic concerns to economics, international political economy, and global capitalism.

The inspiration for this book finds its source in teachers, particularly David Levine and James Caporaso. We also want to give special thanks to those who made our entry into the field of IR less painful and whose work continues to inspire us: Rob Walker, Mike Shapiro and Nick Onuf. We are grateful to Sara-Maria Sorentino, Robbie Shilliam, Nick Onuf, Patrick Jackson, Siba Grovogui, and Charles Santiago for reading large parts of the manuscript and for their valuable comments and critique. We thank Janice Bially Mattern for organizing a panel at International Studies Association-Northeast dedicated to this manuscript and two workshops on culture and political economy organized, respectively, by Christina Rojas, and by Mat Paterson and Jacquie Best. We thank Jacquie Best, Mat Paterson, Beate Jahn, Ritu Vij, Mustapha Pasha, Matt Davies, Randall Germain, Xavier

1 Naeem Inayatullah and David L. Blaney, *International Relations and the Problem of Difference*, New York: Routledge, 2004.
2 We advocated re-imagining IR as the study of difference. We draw the term from Michel de Certeau, *Heterologies: Discourse on the Other*, Minneapolis: University of Minnesota, 1986.
3 Wanda Vrasti, "The Strange Case of Ethnography and International Relations," *Millennium*, 2008, vol. 37, 279–301.

Guillaume, George Lawson, Rob Aitken, Sandra Halperin, Arjun Guner-atne, Khaldoun Samman, Clay Steinman, Naren Kumarakulasingam, Isaac Kamola, Zillah Eisenstein, and Chris Brown for reading parts of this manuscript. We also acknowledge the unfailing support of Chip Gagnon, Peter Mandaville, Patrick Jackson, Edward Weisband, John Agnew, Arlene Tickner, Janice Bially Mattern and Himadeep Muppidi. Naeem whole-heartedly thanks Rod Beers, Jim Best, James Davie, Ben Hogben, Thersa Scaffidi, Kim Yaple, Karen Johnson, Laurie Wasik, Lynda Walters, Lynn Tordella, and especially Gail Belokur for the necessary support and good cheer that made his work possible. Naeem is grateful to his extended family as well as to Shahid, Kamal, and Sorayya for their inspiration, faith and love. David thanks his colleagues at Macalester College for helping to create a wonderful work environment and his students who continue to inspire and impress. He also thanks a group of students – Andy ver Steegh, Anna Waggener, Corey Simon, Amanda Wilson, Amanda Peterson, and Mary Liu – for their work on the bibliography. Finally, David especially thanks Sherry for the life partnership that makes all this work possible and meaningful.

As with all our work this is a joint product. Hardly a paragraph, sentence, or word passes without negotiation. The minor exception to that rule is that David took the lead in researching and drafting Chapters 3 and 4, though these too have become joint products through successive revisions.

Some of the work of this book appears elsewhere in different forms. A substantially different version of Chapter 1 appears as "Undressing the Wound of Wealth: Political Economy as a Cultural Project," in Jacqueline Best and Matthew Paterson (eds.) *Cultural Political Economy*, New York and London: Routledge, 2009. An earlier and shorter version of Chapter 2 appears as "The Savage Smith and the Temporal Walls of Capitalism," in Beate Jahn (ed.) *Classical Theory in International Relations*, Cambridge: Cambridge University Press, 2006, 123–55. A shortened version of Chapter 5 appears as "Shed No Tears: Wealth, Race, and Death in Hegel's Necro-Philosophy" in Ritu Vij (ed.) *Hegel Encounters: Subjects of international relations*, London: Palgrave, forthcoming.

Introduction

I. Wealth, Poverty and the Real of Political Economy

The promise of abundance continues to attract and elude us. The market correction of 2008 (and beyond) has led some to consider the possibility of living more simply; many more do so by necessity. But most citizens of modern states seem drawn by the hope that our leaders will somehow restore the reign of abundance.[1] Of course, modern abundance or affluence has never been for all. More than a billion inhabitants of this planet experience an acute form of scarcity—poverty. We have been asked to turn our eyes (and good intentions and actions) toward those for whom abundance is unrealized. How should we think about poverty, abundance, and scarcity?

This question is one of the gravitational centers of this book. Our graduate training in the early 1980s focused on reducing Third World poverty by creating additional wealth. At the time, the basic human needs approach was waning and being replaced by one that aimed to "restore" market sovereignty. Today, poverty has been elevated once again to a central place on the official international agenda; exhortations to attend to our fellow citizens who live on less than some unimaginably small amount per day continue to engage our belief in abundance. The unabated hope is that economic growth will generate reductions in rates of immiseration. This unchallenged assumption, cultivated from the crib for most modern individuals, directs us to believe that poverty can be solved by various wealth-creating techniques. The continued presence of poverty, we moderns aver, is an incidental anachronism in the face of wealth creation—a temporary and minor deformity for which additional wealth creation is the antidote.

Jeffrey Sachs, for example, points us to an original, pre-growth era in which the gap between rich and poor was small; indeed, this was a time, Sachs claims, in which most people lived in poverty. Past economic growth has brought prosperity to some, but too many remain on the lowest "rung" of the

---

1 The appeal of abundance is suggested by the recent book by William M. Dugger and James T. Peach, *Economic Abundance: An Introduction*, Armonk: M. E. Sharpe, 2009.

"ladder of economic development," untouched by the reign of modern abundance. Sachs traces these ideas about poverty and growth to Adam Smith. He references Smith's famous claims that an expanding and complex division of labor produces economic growth and affluence. Where a simple division of labor limits the possibilities for economic growth, people remain in that condition of scarcity we call poverty.[2] In a similar call to action against poverty, Benjamin Friedman attributes our usual understanding of the relation of economic growth and poverty reduction to Enlightenment thinkers like Smith. Friedman uses Smith to deliver a clear moral message: if the question is poverty, then the "answer"—both "immediate and obvious"—is "economic growth."[3] Amartya Sen is more sophisticated. He departs from these thinkers by suggesting that poverty is not an absence of things per se, but a lack of functionings or capabilities. Though this move relativizes the idea of poverty somewhat, since what counts as functioning is conditioned by particular times and places, the abundance of resources produced by market structures nonetheless remains a central feature of any anti-poverty strategy. Sen legitimates his claims by linking them to Adam Smith.[4]

Sachs, Friedman, and Sen appropriately emphasize that growth and poverty reduction are central to what many call "classical political economy"—a "tradition" that we represent in this book through three figures from the Scottish Enlightenment (Adam Smith, James Steuart, and Adam Ferguson) as well as by G. W. F. Hegel and Karl Marx.[5] Nevertheless, we wish to argue that Sachs and company rely on a rather narrow interpretation of Smith. What such narrow readings ignore is that these thinkers worried that *poverty might be intrinsic to wealth creation*. And, that they grasped the devastating implication of this possibility: wealth leaves a wound in modern

2 Jeffrey Sachs, *The End of Poverty: Economic Possibilities for Our Time*, New York: Penguin, 2005, pp. 18–20, 27–38.

3 Benjamin M. Friedman, *The Moral Consequences of Economic Growth*, New York: Knopf, 2005, pp. 3, 19–52.

4 Amartya Sen, *Development as Freedom*, New York: Anchor, 1999.

5 Speaking of "a tradition" is controversial. On the role of "traditions" in IR discourse, see Renée Jeffery, "Tradition as Invention: The 'Traditions Tradition' and the History of Ideas in International Relations," *Millennium*, 2005, vol. 34, 57–84, and Daniel Deudney, *Bounding Power: Republican Security Theory from the Polis to the Global Village*, Princeton: Princeton University, 2007, p. 265. We are less concerned with establishing the existence of a "tradition" of classical political economy than counterpoising these thinkers to those claiming to be heir to a distinctively liberal (or Marxist) tradition. The figures we have chosen often speak directly to each other, an interweaving of conversations amongst the Scots that had influences on Hegel and Marx. More importantly, we demonstrate that these thinkers address common questions and that their answers intersect in revealing ways. Surely the thinkers themselves would have repudiated some of the associations we locate, but they are dead. Other thinkers, especially those in the utilitarian "tradition," are important, but they appear to us as ancestors of marginalist economics, which teaches us much less on the issues we survey here and may be the subject of a future project. We can only apologize for our relative ignorance of the French Enlightenment.

society.[6] Specifically, additional wealth creation, rather than solving poverty, only exacerbates the pathology of the wealth/poverty nexus. We believe that classical political economy's intellectual vibrancy results from how honestly they wrestled with this wound of wealth. Reading Smith and the tradition of classical political economy more carefully reveals alternative ways of thinking about poverty (and wealth), about the character of modern civil or market society, and about the nature of historical progress itself.

The claim that wealth and poverty are indissolubly fused opens up capitalism for debate. We do not mean the polemics of entrenched opposition between free-market capitalists and anti-capitalists, where enemies are given no quarter or voice. We imagine something quieter and deeper—a debate internal to modern capitalist society in which both the advantages and disadvantages of capitalism as a form of ethical life are directly confronted. Such an opening has a further benefit. If poverty is a necessary component of capitalist modernity, then it cannot merely be ascribed to a pre- or nonmodern age untouched by modern abundance. Modern capitalist societies are forced to account for poverty not as an archaic characteristic of an external other, but as internal to the contemporary self. And, if modern capitalism is not the exclusive and final solution to the human condition, then we can begin to admit, what perhaps we knew all along, that other forms of life have valuable insights for us. Suddenly, those alternative modes of living existing on the margins of modern society have a claim on life that may be acknowledged even by the dominant. In this way, the debate internal to capitalist modernity expands outwards to include others as potential participants—a dialogue in which the modern does not fix the terms of debate, nor have the final word. We have advocated such a dialogue elsewhere and have found Karl Polanyi's work an inspiration.[7] We will reference Polanyi's work repeatedly in this book.

If modernity fails to resolve the problem of poverty, then we are freed from the conversation-closing insistence that modern market-generated growth is *the* solution. Having shed this moral blackmail, we can reconsider additional and interconnected questions about the nexus of wealth and progress addressed by classical political economists: about the relationship of wealth and the fragility of social order; about wealth, inequality and uneven development; and about wealth and modern violence, especially colonial conquest. Whatever the achievements of modern capitalism in wealth creation and its attendant benefits, and it is not our intention to deny those achievements, they come with massive and often hidden costs. Classical political economy is at its worst when, in attempting to preserve the purity of modern progress,

6 We will elaborate this notion of a "wound" later in this preface.
7 David L. Blaney and Naeem Inayatullah, "Prelude to a Conversation of Cultures in International Society? Todorov and Nandy on the Possibility of Dialogue," *Alternatives*, 1994, vol. 19, 23–51. On Polanyi, see Naeem Inayatullah and David L. Blaney, *International Relations and the Problem of Difference*, New York: Routledge, 2004, ch. 5.

it masks these wounds—first, by discounting and diminishing those costs and, then, projecting them onto supposedly temporally superseded ways of life. This defense of purity involves the construction of what we call a temporal wall around modern capitalism. But at its best, the political economy tradition exposes, lingers upon, and wrestles with these costs, making them, as do Marx and Polanyi, central to their analysis.

Exposing, exploring, and wrestling with these costs also casts doubt on a set of assumptions about modern capitalism and human progress. It leads us to ask: what justifies modernity's impositions? The figures we examine all struggle directly with this issue and they recognize the role that imposition invariably plays in the advance of modern capitalism. They acknowledge the colonial moment in capitalism (or the capitalist moment in colonialism). To its credit, classical political economy's response is *not* simply that the benefits outweigh the costs and that we therefore can move forward without ethical regret. They understand that something deeper about the human condition is at stake: ways of life are displaced and values are lost in this imposition. Our cast of theorists sense that material progress by itself is not enough to justify the violence (both internal and colonial) that accompanies it. They discern that capitalist modernity sacrifices nothing less than the values and human goods provided by different ways of life. As we shall see, classical political economy *does* produce an implicit or explicit theodicy—an explanation and rationalization of persistent malevolence in a world inexorably destined, so the story goes, to produce the human good.[8] Nevertheless, their progressive optimism retains an element of tragedy. In the chapters that follow, we document how they express this tragedy.

Perhaps our training in political economy sensitizes us to the tragedies of human progress.[9] We are moved to acknowledge that the tragic elements of human existence bring forth a potentially productive humility. Our polemical energy is focused on nothing so grandiose as utopian visions that might somehow convert the world—the world being so big and complex and we so small and limited—whatever the appeals of such utopias. Our rage at the state of the world has been transformed over the years into the belief that, at best, we can only encircle what Lacan and others call the "real." Lacanian-influenced scholars use the term "real" to point to the impossible but necessary gestures constitutive of the modern symbolic order—gestures that must be hidden as modern thinkers desperately attempt to hide or suture these

8 We argue that the modern symbolic order, including its political economic variant, does engage the problem of justifying evil, even if it does worse in helping the victims understand their suffering. See Ashis Nandy's *The Romance of the State and the Fate of Dissent in the Tropics*, New Delhi: Oxford University, 2008, p. 123.

9 It is also important that our training countered neoclassical economics, where optimal solutions arrived at against a backdrop of a universal/individual standard of utility wash away any ethical loss. We have more or less utility, but no moral goods are sacrificed.

cracks or wounds.[10] Or, similarly, the "real" is used to point to an "antagonism" that "prevents closure of the social field, the totalization that is always already impossible."[11] "Encircling" is required when life's impossibilities are too difficult to approach directly. Put differently, we can only gesture towards that which resists adequate symbolization.[12] As one commentator put it, if you move toward life's problems in a straight line, they will kill you.[13] Agreed, and even our attempt to encircle the "real" with a gesture to tragedy may be too painful and difficult to sustain. The pleasures of an orthodoxy that erases doubt and pain tempt us. Indeed it may be, as Lacan suggests, that the devotion to the fanciful promises of modernity—a faith in wealth that refuses to acknowledge doubt—sustains pleasures that are difficult to forgo.[14]

Our investment in classical political economy is not, we hope, merely academic. Compared to most contemporary commentary, the classical tradition of political economy has been far more instructive, resourceful, and honest in its depiction of the cracks or antagonisms of modernity than usually credited. Despite protecting this wound behind temporal walls, the classical tradition's ability to resist the pleasures of devotion at important points, to encircle the "real," and uncover the wound of wealth has encouraged us to tighten our own orbit. More than this we dare not ask.

II. On Method and History: Freeing the Captive Soul[15]

In his generous but probing critique of our previous book, Edward Weisband implored us to be explicit about our "method." We resisted his suggestion because we believe that most readers, rather than searching for method, look for the work that a method produces. For those who insist on also grasping our method, we believe it can be gleaned from the work itself. Nevertheless, Professor Weisband's voice is not completely lost on us and we recognize that our silence may contribute to undue confusion. We hope that what follows might pass as a statement of method.

Quentin Skinner suggests that scholars return to thinkers of an earlier era

10 We draw on A. Kiarina Kordela, *Surplus: Spinoza, Lacan*, Albany: SUNY, 2007, p. 17. See also Slavoj Zizek, *On Belief*, New York: Routledge, 2001, pp. 13, 18; Bruce Fink, *The Lacanian Subject: Between Language and Jouissance*, Princeton: Princeton University, 1995, p. 143.

11 Jenny Edkins, *Poststructuralism and International Relations: Bringing the Political Back In*, Boulder: Lynne Rienner, 1999, p. 113. See also her *Trauma and the Politics of Memory*, Cambridge: Cambridge University, 2003, pp. 14–15.

12 Slavoj Zizek, *The Plague of Fantasies*, London: Verso, 1997, pp. 213–18.

13 Henry Kariel, "Becoming Political," in Vernon Van Dyke (ed.) *Teaching Political Science*, Humanities Press, 1977, p. 129.

14 A. Kiarina Kordela, "Capital: At Least it Kills Time (Spinoza, Marx, Lacan, and Temporality)," *Rethinking Marxism*, 2006, vol. 18, p. 554.

15 We draw this title from a phrase in Claude Lévi-Strauss, *Structural Anthropology*, New York: Basic Books, 1963, p. 199.

in order to "grasp *their* concepts," "follow *their* distinctions," and "appreciate *their* beliefs." Such retrieval, he claims, helps us understand that our current values and visions, and the social practices they inform, cannot be taken for granted, but "reflect a series of choices made at different times between different possible worlds." In Skinner's view, this re-reading involves nothing less than an intellectual "exorcism" that "restores a broader sense of possibility" by returning to the "battlefield" of political and ethical discourse.[16] Thus, this act of traveling in time, a theme we will revisit, is not an end in itself. Rather, we return to these thinkers so that we might heal ourselves in the present.[17]

This is not the way scholars usually speak. Exorcism is a practice of a different set of times and places, healing attributed to different professions. Skinner's invocation of exorcism and our invocation of healing involve what Mary Louise Pratt calls an "unseemly comparison."[18] Yet it is precisely such a comparison that, in Ashis Nandy's terms, opens us up to the past as a resource—as "an open-ended record of the predicaments of *our* time,"[19] as a comparison that focuses our attention on a process of "recovery of the *other* selves of cultures and communities, selves not defined by the dominant global consciousness."[20] As Nandy sees it, it is exactly the figure of the shaman—a critical voice standing at once outside the modern but also lurking uncomfortably within—that opens us to the resources of those pasts that lie, often repressed, within ourselves.[21]

As Claude Lévi-Strauss explains, the shaman might be understood interestingly in parallel to the psychoanalyst.[22] The shaman, like the psychoanalyst, locates or provides a "*language*, by means of which unexpressed, and otherwise inexpressible, psychic states can be immediately expressed." "In both cases the purpose is to bring to a conscious level conflicts and resistance

16 Quentin Skinner, *Visions of Politics. Volume I: Regarding Method*, Cambridge: Cambridge University, 2002, pp. 3, 6–7. Emphasis added.

17 Though the work done by thinkers like Quentin Skinner, John Pocock, Andrew Skinner, Christopher Berry and Donald Winch is beyond our skills and aspirations and we give their interpretations a Nandyan/Lacanian twist that they might well refuse, we feel a debt to those who dig deeply into the times and intellectual debates that shaped the thinkers that interest us. See also Chakrabarty's reflections on Pocock and Skinner in Amitav Ghosh and Dipesh Chakrabarty, "A Correspondence on *Provincializing Europe*," *Radical History Review*, 2002, vol. 83, pp. 163, 169. We consciously deploy the "imperial we" here.

18 Mary Louise Pratt, "Arts of the Contact Zone," *Profession*, 1991, vol. 91, 33–40.

19 Ashis Nandy, *Time Warps: Silent and Evasive Pasts in Indian Politics and Religion*, New Brunswick: Rutgers University, 2002, p. 10.

20 Ashis Nandy, "Shamans, Savages and the Wilderness: On the Audibility of Dissent and the Future of Civilizations," *Alternatives*, 1989, vol. VIV, p. 264 (emphasis added).

21 Ibid., pp. 265–7. That the other lies uncomfortably within (both author and text) is a key theme of Nandy's work. See also *The Intimate Enemy: Loss and Recovery of Self Under Colonialism*, Delhi: Oxford University, 1983, and *Traditions, Tyranny, and Utopias: Essays on the Politics of Awareness*, Delhi: Oxford University, 1987.

22 See Lévi-Strauss, *Structural Anthropology*, pp. 198–9.

which have remained unconscious, owing [often] to their repression . . . ." In the "shamanistic cure," as for the modern healer, "it is about provoking an experience . . . [that] establishes a direct relationship with the patient's conscious and an indirect relationship with his unconscious." "[B]oth succeed," says Lévi-Strauss, "by recreating a myth which the patient has to live or relive."

While we can pass neither for shamans nor as psychoanalysts, we can confront international political economy with a myth of its own origins; a myth that encircles the "real" by pointing to those impossible gestures that both constitute and disable political economy as an ethical vision. We follow Zizek's suggestion that "philosophy needs the recourse to myth . . . to 'suture' its own conceptual edifice." But this mythic edifice of a universal history of human material and social progress also exhibits a *"symptomal* mode, in which the ideological lie which structures our perception of reality is threatened by symptoms qua 'return of the repressed,' cracks in the fabric of the ideological lie."[23] The task is to reveal "the 'internal alterity' of thought, its failure to be identical with itself, or what since Freud we can call its unconscious."[24] This interpretive task of encircling the "real" of political economy leads us to some of the key (and tragic) moments in the mutual construction of modernity and colonialism of which international political economy (IPE) is a specific effect. Exploring that myth takes us "back" to the classical political economy tradition, back to an intellectual "battlefield" in which the wound of wealth was less healed than it was dressed, covered, and paraded; and it brings us again to the present where the wound continues to fester, infecting our very souls and producing a pathology that spurs the restless desire of modern global citizens to conquer "problems" of instability, poverty and inequality by inflicting (or is it re-inflicting?) the same abundance—the same wound of wealth—on others.[25]

Confronting IPE with the myth of its origins requires, as Nandy makes clear, an ability to move between the past and the present, a capacity to travel in time.[26] Or, put differently, the past does not appear as external to the present.[27] Our claim to travel in time entangles us in a paradox constructed along with the very doctrine of historical progress. History, Constantin

---

23 Zizek, *On Belief*, pp. 11, 13.

24 Kordela, *Surplus*, p. 50. Since the focus is on thought itself more than the internal states of thinkers, the evidentiary requirements of a psychoanalytic approach to political theory are really no greater than other approaches despite Terrence Ball, "History and the Interpretation of Texts," in Gerald Gaus and Chandran Kukathas (eds.) *Handbook of Political Theory*, London: Sage, 2004, p. 23, and Patrick Jackson's recent comments on this manuscript.

25 Kordela, *Surplus*, p. 19, follows Freud in highlighting the need to continue to repeat or reproduce the original repression. We connect this idea to Zizek's point in *On Belief*, p. 132, that disavowing the wound involves reproducing it by projecting it onto others.

26 Nandy, *Time Warps*, p. 5.

27 Kordela, "Capital," pp. 556–7.

Fasolt reminds us, is a "bulwark against ignorance and lies"—the key to any claim about progressive enlightenment or advance. But its capacity to serve this function of putting the past behind us depends on constantly policing the boundary between the past and present. The idea that "the past is gone forever" allows us to construct what counts as (present) evidence of the past: those "things existing in the present that carry traces of information about the past" that make up the "evidence," "sources," or "data" from which theories of history may be formulated. This boundary also informs the key methodological principle guiding the writing of history: "thou shalt place everything in the context of its time." This principle, Fasolt suggests, "keeps historians from committing anachronism"—a kind of "chronological pollution" that "profanes the past by mixing the past and present."[28] It also potentially profanes our understanding of the present as different from (and thereby potentially better than) the past. Attention to this boundary (whether conscious or not) allows the historian to formulate convincing (or at least plausible) accounts of the past, the present, and possible futures. So it is with us.

Our task is to construct historical stories that disrupt the usual, though sometimes barely conscious, use of Adam Smith and the Scottish Enlightenment as foundational in the formation of a supposedly coherent liberal political economic tradition—a tradition that trumpets closure on issues surrounding wealth, order, human progress and freedom. The point is not simply, as Quentin Skinner and John Pocock would emphasize, that "liberalism" as a tradition is a later invention.[29] Rather, we tell stories that disrupt contemporary claims about a coherent liberal political economic tradition; we want to expose its lurking internal others—poverty, violence, disorder— and its unresolved and deeply fraught tensions surrounding time and place. Such tensions remain alive and open even when they are said to be closed. Doing this sort of history—even in the form of the counter-mythmaking that we do in the chapters that follow—appears to require the separation of past and present that Fasolt argues is elemental to an historical consciousness. It is to police the very boundary between the past and present that we want to challenge, though we quite consciously commit the sin of anachronism or chronological pollution and therefore expose our own histories as mythmaking. We are forced to ask ourselves: how can we tell a coherent historical story that disrupts the historical consciousness itself?

We locate our alternative myth in relation to the intellectual constructs of

28 Constantin Fasolt, *The Limits of History*, Chicago: University of Chicago, 2004, pp. ix, xiii, 3–6.

29 Quentin Skinner, *Liberty Before Liberalism*, Cambridge: Cambridge University, 1998, and J. G. A. Pocock, *Virtue, Commerce, and History: Essays on Political Thought and History, Chiefly in the Eighteenth Century*, Cambridge: Cambridge University, 1985. By contrast, Deudney, in *Bounding Power*, pp. 6–7, 86, 198–9, treats Scottish Enlightenment figures as direct ancestors of various forms and features of what is called "liberal" international relations.

Smith, the other Scottish Enlightenment figures we survey, and the resonances of Scottish political economy that we find in Hegel and Marx. The Scots themselves are usually seen as a *point of arrival* in establishing an historical consciousness and then wielding such a consciousness *against* superstition and *for* progressive human enlightenment. The universal history of the Scots was built on early modern Europe's experience of a vast revolution in time, where, as Reinhart Kosselleck suggests, human history was gradually separated from sacred time. Europeans could then look back on "the past" as prior to and distinct from the present and the future; the "philosophy of progress" was now conceivable.[30] The division between present and past is necessary, says Fasolt, to show that the modern era has broken from the bounds of tradition. The division also shows that history—knowledge of times now past—is a privileged vantage point from which to assess human capabilities for future progress.[31] The figures we survey assume this privileged vantage point as they construct a universal history and as they justify the violent imposition of modern capitalism.

Early modern Europe is also marked by the emergence of what Le Goff calls "bourgeois time."[32] Clock time becomes the basis for organizing not only thought but also working life. As time becomes a measure of work, it also becomes something not to be wasted; "the first virtue" for the new humanism, Le Goff suggests, "is a sense of time and its proper use."[33] Thus, along with the process of defining a "difference" between the past and the present and future, time begins to move at a new and faster pace linked to the idea of human progress, particularly to what Koselleck calls "techno-industrial progress." We might think of this as the progress of modern capitalism. But this pace of capitalist development is not constant; it varies across space, across different peoples or nations, and across groups within societies. This "coexisting plurality of times" opens up a new temporal space for the powerful intellectual practice of comparison.[34] It also poses a question of how to account for these temporal differences—a problem of comparison with which Adam Smith and his fellow Scots struggled.

The Scottish Enlightenment, Andrew Skinner suggests, was "above all the age of history."[35] The modern era of commerce is understood against the past—as a product of human progress. As we develop at length in the chapters that follow, Smith, his Scottish contemporaries, and the extension of

---

30 Reinhart Kosselleck, *Futures Past: On the Semantics of Historical Time*, New York: Columbia University, 2004, pp. 12, 16–17.

31 Fasolt, *The Limits of History*, pp. xiii–xiv, 4.

32 Jacques Le Goff, *Time, Work, and Culture in the Middle Ages*, Chicago: University of Chicago, 1980, pp. xii–xiii, 24–30.

33 Ibid., pp. 48–51.

34 Kosselleck, *Futures Past*, pp. 247–9, 251, 282–3.

35 Andrew Skinner, "Natural History in the Age of Adam Smith," *Political Studies*, 1967, vol. XVI, p. 32.

classical political economy in Hegel and Marx, explicitly disallow challenges to modernity from the diverse forms of human society. They translate the diversity of social forms into a series of progressive sequential stages—from savagery to commerce. The Scots, as Jonathan Friedman emphasizes, turn space into time.[36] This move secures a neat separation of past and present, so that others elsewhere are not merely different but temporally prior and backward. In addition, modern capitalist progress turns on appreciating and managing time as a resource—the emergence of what Marx would later call an "economy of time."[37] Indeed, Smith believes that human material progress is about conserving time via the application of the division of labor; the savage and barbarous past is poor precisely because it lacks substantial division of labor and consequently wastes time. History is seen, then, as a linear process of human progress in which scarcity is replaced by abundance and tragedy is excised from the human story.[38]

But we also recover a different, if recessive, story. In Smith, we find a hint, more fully expressed by his peers, Adam Ferguson and James Steuart, as well as by Hegel (and arguably Marx), that modern progress also produces scarcity. This is a "symptomal" moment where the repressed returns—where abundance creates scarcity instead of alleviating it. This inversion signals a lack at the center of the confident historical story. Despite claims that the Enlightenment turns on unquestioned theories of progress, we can also discover in all these thinkers moments of conscious doubt and unconscious slippage, where the neat separation of stages (and, by implication, the distinction of past and present) is disrupted. The savage past of scarcity, violence, and disorder continues to haunt the commercial present of the Scots as well as our own. Tragedy cannot be excised from modern human existence, however difficult this wound is to face. The task of this book is to encircle this wound so that we may better face it.

Our pursuit depends, as we have hinted, on the contention that even texts written in a confident age of history speak with multiple voices. They contain not only dominant themes but also recessive elements that transgress the temporal boundaries explicitly or implicitly set.[39] In this case, the very doing

---

36 Jonathan Friedman, "Civilizational Cycles and the Theory of Primitivism," *Social Analysis*, 1983, no. 14, pp. 37–8.

37 Karl Marx, *Grundrisse: Foundations of the Critique of Political Economy*, New York: Vintage, 1973, pp. 172–3.

38 Nicholas Xenos, *Scarcity and Modernity*, London and New York: Routledge, 1989, p. 35. For Xenos, pre-modern scarcities are transformed into scarcity as an ontological condition. Theories of progress are, as Kordela, "Capital," pp. 549–50, suggests, a "totality on a mission." Stages are all connected into a single logical progression, in which the spaces designated as past and future are not allowed to be truly other, but serve as an expression of universal laws of development that justify the present.

39 The language is from Nandy, *Traditions, Tyranny, and Utopias*, p. 17. A more conventional reader of texts, J. G. A. Pocock, argues that texts contain "a complex internal structure" and can be understood "as a diversity of acts performed by an author that cannot be understood

of history itself reveals its own partial undoing: the founders of our contemporary framing of political economic issues open up debates about abundance and poverty, order, and peace to which they are supposed to have given clear and uncontestable answers. But in doing so, they disrupt the very historical understanding they are thought to have secured. That the doctrine of progress is thrown into doubt is hardly surprising. That scarcity is the twin of, rather than superseded by, abundance should be less surprising to us than it is. What is perhaps most surprising is the challenge this disruption poses to the clear separation of past and present, a separation upon which our styles of science and political/ethical reasoning depend.

III. An Overview of the Chapters

Seven chapters and an epilogue follow this introduction. Their order respects chronology to the extent that we establish the influence of the Scots on the later work of Hegel and Marx. However, we treat Smith first, because of his canonical status. We read Steuart and Ferguson alongside and against Smith, though their major works appeared before *Wealth of Nations*. Successive chapters also progressively encircle the wound of wealth. They build and deepen our confrontation with problems of poverty and the violence of capitalist modernity. We chart the attempts by these political economists to suture or symbolize the cracks that inevitably appear as they build a theory of progressive time. These cracks increasingly emerge in our reading as a recovery of alternative possibilities for political economy. In an initial chapter we provide a tentative explanation for the failure of contemporary political economy to treat cultural difference as a key category, an explanation we hope is made plausible also by our readings of Smith, et al.

Chapter 1 explores the language of culture that we use in this book. Following Michel-Rolph Trouillot, we argue that if the savage slot within the field of the modern symbolic order is filled by the discipline of anthropology, then the utopian slot is filled by political economy. We regard political economy as an effect of the Western self's desire to differentiate the West from what it deems as savage or barbarous others. Trouillot's assertion inspires us to argue that culture and economy have been bifurcated in the scholarly literature. We find it telling that neither the economically minded nor the culturally attuned ask why a culture might create a seemingly asocial, technical economics. In avoiding this question neither economists, nor their critics, are required to engage the form of cultural life created by the advent of economic logic. We then show how Richard Ashley's criticism of economic logic sustains the bifurcation of economics from culture and how this bifurcation allows him (and IPE more generally) to ignore the larger

as a result of a single intention." See "Intentions, Traditions and Methods: Some Sounds on a Fog-Horn," *Annals of Scholarship*, 1980, vol. 1, pp. 57–8.

questions that emerge when economics itself is seen as a cultural project. We end by offering a serious reading of classical political economy as one route to recovering a cultural political economy.

Chapter 2 emphasizes the role "savage" Amerindians play in Adam Smith's work. Reading Smith against the theme of "savagery" allows us to recover a neglected intellectual influence on Smith—the Jesuit Father Lafitau. Lafitau's lumping of ancient peoples and modern savages into a single category forms the basis for Smith's "universal history." We then examine Smith's deployment of a comparative ethnological strategy to develop a stage theory of human progress that displaces "savage" others into the past, thereby building a temporal wall that insulates commercial society, the pinnacle of human progress, from ethical critique by other ways of life. Finally, we expose inversions in Smith's texts—breaches in the temporal wall. Here the repressed other—the savage—returns as a critical mirror for the present, allowing us to recover potential ethical resources for assessing the present state of global capitalism, a theme we develop at greatest length in Chapter 7.

James Steuart more openly explores the wound of wealth and demonstrates far less confidence in the great and harmonious economic and historical machines than Smith. As we show in Chapter 3, Steuart sees commerce as progressive but also as disordered and fractured. The natural operations of the market do not secure the economic prospects of countries and individuals. For Steuart unregulated markets connect abundance to scarcity and life to death. Providence does not promise order, nor do economic wounds necessarily serve a higher good. He hopes, however, that artful and persistent economic management can keep the forces of disorder in check. Steuart's relative comfort with disorder may be partly explained by the fact that he is more attuned to difference—a world of multiple and varied political economies. He repudiates Smith's picture of political economy as a simple science and discounts Smith's insistence on the presence of natural laws to which states and peoples are utterly subject, even to the point of their very destruction. For Steuart, international political economy appears as a limited *intercultural* political economy and it points us beyond itself to something closer to Karl Polanyi's ethnological IPE.

Adam Ferguson's work reveals a scholar with a clearly divided self. As we see in Chapter 4, Ferguson speaks not only for modern commerce but also with the voice of the "backward" Highlander who is immersed in an order of manly virtues, strong social connections, and active citizenship. His analysis of the wound opened up by a commercial age is powerful and in some respects darker even than Marx's. Ferguson's trepidations about the modern heighten his perception of the contingencies in *all* polities. For Ferguson, modern civil societies emerge from the historical tensions and conflicts of international (or intercultural) relations. Despite Smith's assurances that the rise of an interest-driven way of life will calm the passions, Ferguson believes that civil society remains vulnerable to a combination of external geo-economic competition fueled by greed and vanity, the complacency of a citizenry dominated by commercial concerns, and an ostensibly liberal but highly militarized polity that threatens liberty. He exposes the "real," instead of displacing his doubts about civil society behind the temporal walls of the past (as does Smith) or the future (as does Marx). Consistent with this less optimistic picture, Ferguson reveals a more complicated temporal understanding; he undercuts the privilege of the modern, recognizing that the time of the modern overlaps with that of the past, though he falls short of Polanyi's effort to make the past co-eval with the present—a move essential to a cultural political economy.

Though commentators rarely foreground Hegel's racial constructions, in Chapter 5 we place Hegel's racializing moves at the center of our reading and, by extension, at the center of the modern project of political economy. Hegel's *Philosophy of Right* is at once a philosophical reconstruction of modern political economy and an historical account that demonstrates how modern European culture is *the* product of a long historical evolution. It is Western Europeans who embody modernity's possibilities through the realization of freedom, while non-Europeans remain outside the modern world. In pronouncing this judgment, Hegel maps racial categories onto continents such that racialized non-European peoples are deemed irrelevant to the tasks of "world history" and condemned to extinction, enslavement, or colonialism. Colonialism is also crucial to Hegel's account of the problem of poverty in modern civil society. Colonial expansion serves as both a solution to the problem of the internal disintegration of civil society and as an extension of modern civilization to undeveloped areas. For Hegel, as for Smith, the machine of history often achieves its nobler ends through death and destruction. Though this admission stands in serious tension with Hegel's vision of modernity as the universal actualization of freedom, we appreciate his unequivocal depiction of the costs of modernity. We show that Hegel's denigration of non-Europeans and his necro-philosophy are crucial and necessary to his suturing of the wound of wealth.

In Chapter 6, we explore both dominant and recessive themes in Marx's account of colonialism and the rise of capitalism. Though his dominant treatment of modern capitalism follows Smith in temporally displacing others, Marx also displays more generosity towards colonial resistance than is usually understood. The bulk of this chapter shows that his complex attitude towards colonialism reflects methodological ambiguities in his work. The most difficult section of the chapter examines the temporal assimilationism of Marx's method as laid out in *Grundrisse*. We then present this picture of Marx's temporal displacements against Dipesh Chakrabarty's effort to find a space for historical difference within Marx's *Capital*. Finally, we offer a more powerful strategy for opening up such space in Marx. In *Capital*, we demonstrate that Marx violates his own methodological stipulations, revealing the presence of an alternative working method—a moment of perspectivism that preserves difference instead of assimilating alternative historical forms within a progressive temporal schema. We close the discussion by drawing a parallel between Marx's method of "alternative temporal forms" and Karl Polanyi's critique of the economistic fallacy—a parallel that opens up capitalism to critique from temporally displaced others.

We apply Polanyi's ethnological mode of ethical critique in Chapter 7. International political economy speaks of the globe mostly in terms of the universal laws of economics. This understanding of political economy rests on classical political economy's temporocentrism. Modern, civilized society is understood and ethically justified in relation to alternative forms of life that are rendered as backward and temporally superseded. Difference in this vision serves only to confirm and never to challenge the institutions and practices of modern social life. The "savage" acts as a "constitutive other" for political economy: an oppositional but nevertheless necessary category to the theory and practice of political economy. However, the repressed category of the savage returns and reappears as a source for critical reflection on a modern capitalist society. For the savage to play this critical role—not merely as the return of a repressed but explicitly as a critical resource—we are required to undo the temporal displacement that makes the savage an anachronism. Drawing on the ethnographic archives, we treat the savage (or, more properly, hunter-gatherer societies) as temporally co-eval. This co-evality removes liberal capitalism's presumptive naturalness and inevitability. Beyond this denaturalizing move, we argue that the savage may also provide us with ethical resources for envisioning alternatives to the prescriptions of political economy. In the end, we examine the implications of "savage times" for contemporary thinking about time, space, and economic life.

A short epilogue returns us to the question of poverty and the use of scarcity as a moral blackmail, threatening us with savagery. We then briefly turn to the major challenge facing IPE: our own complicity.

1 The cultural constitution of political economy

The "West" constructs itself, in part, through the discipline of political economy. Political economy as theory and practice comes into being through a self-idealization of the West as wealthy, modern, and civilized. This idealization splits the West from others who are deemed poor, backward, and savage. One effect of this split between the West and its others is to hide troubling questions about wealth, modernity, and civilization. Is wealth for some bought at the cost of impoverishing others? What benefits of wealth might justify such immiseration? More generally, what do we gain and lose by embracing modern wealth creation? Do other, even "savage," cultures offer values, modes of critique, and institutional forms that the West still needs?

Standard economists rarely pose such questions because they assume the vast benefits of wealth creation. Few would be surprised by economists' implicit commitment to wealth creation, or by their disregard of larger issues. What we may find surprising is that today's social and cultural critics rarely engage these questions about economy. Interestingly, economists and their critics tend to share an understanding of economics as an acultural domain whose logic operates regardless of the particularities of space and time. Economics' purported universalism serves both economists and their critics: economics can present itself as science, while critics can dismiss economics as a mode of inquiry devoid of cultural and ethical meaning. Both ignore the emergence of political economy as a cultural project and, therefore, neither really engages the ambiguities of wealth.

Contemporary studies are impoverished by this bifurcation. This impoverishment appears all the more striking in contrast to the relative richness of classical political economy. Figures like Smith, Steuart, Ferguson, Hegel, and Marx help restore our sensitivity to the political and ethical content of modern economic life. Their work helps us specify how wealth production inflicts a wound upon the West *and* the world. Festering within this wound is the problem of modern poverty: the social deformities created by wealth creation when some are subjected to others in the name of such values as freedom, equality, and individuality. Retrieving the complexity and intractability of modern poverty may permit us to revive international political economy as a domain of ethical contestation and, perhaps, to better encircle the wound of wealth.

I. Political Economy and the Utopian/Savage Slot

Michel-Rolph Trouillot has noted that "the savage is an argument for a particular kind of utopia."[1] The West, Trouillot explains, constructs itself in relation to a complex other.[2] On one side, "the savage" serves as exemplary of an early state of humankind, against which modern progress is measured and vindicated. On the other, the savage is only possible as set against the "West" as a "utopian projection," a "universalist" and "didactic" project. If anthropology came to fill "the Savage Slot" in the "field of significance" that constitutes the "West," as Trouillot emphasizes, we suggest that what might be called the "Utopian Slot" comes to be filled mostly by political economy.

Political economy serves to articulate our greatest ambitions and values—for wealth, social stability, ethical refinement, peace, (in)equality[3] and freedom, to draw a list from Adam Smith and his Scottish Enlightenment fellows. David Hume is exemplary. For Hume, "*industry, knowledge*, and *humanity*, are linked together by an indissoluble chain, and are found, from experience as well as reason, to be peculiar to the more polished, and, what are commonly denominated, the more luxurious ages."[4] "Law, order, police, discipline: these can never be carried to any degree of perfection, before human reason has refined itself by exercise, and by an application to the more vulgar arts, at least, of commerce and manufacture. Not to mention," Hume continues, "that all ignorant ages are infested with superstition, which throws the government off its bias, and disturbs men in the pursuit of interest and happiness."[5] For Hume and the Scots, wealth accumulation moves humans to a refined or civilized society.

Political economy, as Hume hints and as we explore at length in this book, emerges from a cultural partitioning where others serve as a negative benchmark against which Europe is wealthy, civilized and rational. These others, the developmentally anachronistic—the non-modern—are appropriately poor, barbaric, and irrational. The savage is precisely what the modern European self is not. The non-Western or non-modern appear, then, not

---

1 Michel-Rolph Trouillot, "Anthropology and the Savage Slot," in Richard G. Fox (ed.) *Recapturing Anthropology: Working in the Present*, Santa Fe: School of American Research, 1991, p. 27.

2 Ibid., pp. 18, 26–9.

3 Modern accounts of equality are simultaneously accounts of necessary and justified inequality.

4 David Hume, "Of Refinement in the Arts," in *Essays: Moral, Political, Literary*, Indianapolis: Liberty Fund, 1985, p. 271.

5 Ibid., p. 273.

merely as outside of political economy, but also as the excluded other against which the West and the modern are defined. The savage serves, in Timothy Mitchell's terms, as the "constitutive outside," so that the identity of the modern West can be seen as a product of the colonial and neocolonial management of difference.[6] We might say that political economy's role within the field of significance of the "West" reveals it to be less a discipline analyzing the commonality and variety of human experience and more a particular political/cultural project that is an effect of this splitting of self and other; a kind of splitting where, nevertheless, the disowned elements of the self remain essential to its very construction.[7] In this sense, political economy is always a global project, encompassing a universal vision though imagined in relation to certain repressed but constitutive others.

The splitting of the West and the savage is achieved temporally.[8] The rigorous observation and systematic comparison of Scottish political economy is transmuted into a stadial scheme in which the West is located at the apex of development. The savage, while an historical curiosity, is ethically relevant only as a superseded moment of an heroic tale of social progress that culminates in the modern commercial self. Still, the splitting of the savage from the West, and the savage slot from the utopian slot, is not so easily accomplished. Though the savage may serve as the negative marker that continues to give a globalized or internationalized political economy its ethical purpose as theory and practice, the idealized self of the West and the savage have multiple, overlapping, and intimate relations. As Mitchell points out, modernity "depends upon, even as it refuses to recognize . . . forces that escape its control."[9]

The Scots themselves sense this difficulty. They deploy a stage-theory of social development to secure this splitting, erecting a "temporal wall" between the West and the savage other.[10] But this architectural metaphor simply conceals an overlap of the utopian and savage slots.[11] Though separated and pushed backward, the other nevertheless returns and finds life within the self. The modern cannot eradicate the values and visions of the imagined savage. Nor, more strikingly, can modern commercial beings do without the savage, since we continue to require those superseded values and visions as a mirror to the idealized self and as a corrective for the deficiency

6 Timothy Mitchell, "The Stage of Modernity," in Timothy Mitchell (ed.) *Questions of Modernity*, Minneapolis: University of Minnesota, 2000, pp. 4–5, 12–13.

7 See Jessica Benjamin, *The Bonds of Love: Psychoanalysis, Feminism, and the Problem of Domination*, New York: Pantheon, 1988, pp. 25–31, 62–3, 218. This claim was presented in an expressly Nandyan/Lacanian form in the Introduction.

8 We have developed an earlier version of this argument in Naeem Inayatullah and David L. Blaney, *International Relations and the Problem of Difference*, New York: Routledge, 2004, ch. 2.

9 Mitchell, "The Stage of Modernity," pp. 12–13.

10 See ch. 2.

11 We are reminded of the power and fragility of architectural metaphors by Kojin Karatani, *Architecture as Metaphor: Language, Numbers, Money*, Cambridge: MIT, 1995, pp. 6–9.

of modernity.[12] Jonathan Friedman argues that because modern theories of civilizational progress turn on the suppression of the primitive, they consistently bring us back to the primitive as a moment of protest or as an alternative vision of the ideal.[13] Further, this uneasy juxtaposition of an idealized image of self and its backward other provides an opportunity for the West to tame its most obtrusive anxieties and doubts. Where better to bury doubts than in the richest source of dreams and fantasies—a domain that seems to vindicate the West and represent its greatest historical achievements? Perhaps the separation of self and other is most faithfully defended in political economy because that is where their overlap appears most dangerous.

An investigation of the cultural constitution of political economy involves exploring an identity formation that splits self and other. It also requires articulating the transgressive vision that lies within the necessary overlap of self and other. We find in this space the modern "West's" most sacred and enduring social and political ideals, its greatest fears and anxieties, and potentially powerful alternative visions of social and political life. Exploring this terrain also means recognizing that political economy is a cultural encounter.

II. The Bifurcation of Culture and Economy

Economy and culture are often set in opposition. The difficulty of the relationship of economics and culture results because, as Philip Crang notes, "the economic and the cultural have long been cast as 'self' and 'other,' each defined by what the other is not."[14] Cultural critics usually blame conventional economists for their imperial reach despite the limited relevance of their categories. For example, Pierre Bourdieu suggests that economic concepts are inappropriately applied "outside of any reference to the work of historians or social anthropologists."[15] Stephen Gudeman pits his cultural analysis of economic life against the "widely accepted view" that "an economy comprises a separate sphere of instrumental or practical action."[16] William Jackson's reflections on the economics discipline indicate that "mainstream economists never stray beyond core theoretical assumptions which eschew cultural ideas."[17] "Positing a set of individual motives and

12 As Bruno Latour, *We Have Never Been Modern*, Cambridge: Harvard University, 1993, suggests, the very purifying moves that construct the modern also proliferate hybrids.

13 Jonathan Friedman, "Civilizational Cycles and the History of Primitivism," *Social Analysis*, 1983, no. 14, pp. 39–42.

14 Philip Crang, "Cultural Turns and the (Re)Constitution of Economic Geography: Introduction to Section One," in Roger Lee and James Willis (eds.) *Geographies of Economies*, London: Arnold, 1997, p. 4.

15 Pierre Bourdieu, *The Social Structures of the Economy*, Cambridge: Polity, 2005, p. 3.

16 Stephen Gudeman, *Economics as Culture: Modes and Metaphors of Livelihood*, New York: Routledge, 1986, p. xii.

17 William A. Jackson, "Culture, Society, and Economic Theory," *Review of Political Economy*, 1993, vol. 5, p. 453.

capacities as universal" eliminates any possibility of seeing cultural difference, as Rhoda Halperin explains.[18] Daniel Miller argues that the construction of "algorithms that model particular relationships within capitalism"
render it a "general and ideal system," bearing little resemblance to an
"holistic" view that considers "behaviors . . . within the larger framework of
people's lives and cosmologies."[19] "Economy," claims Timothy Mitchell, is
thought to refer to a "realm with an existence prior to and separate from
its representations, and thus to stand in opposition to the more discursive
constructs of social theory."[20] Cristina Rojas and Craig Murphy suggest
that the field of international political economy universalizes "the categories
of capitalism and of the application of laissez-faire principles" in defiance
of history and "cultural, racial or gender differences."[21] The complaint is
that contemporary economics sets itself in opposition to culture in order to
establish its scientific status as a singular and universal truth.

Most economists dismiss this protest. Contemporary neoclassical economists proudly insist that economic laws operate regardless of the specificities
of space and time or the particulars of cultural landscapes. Thus, to speak of
a *culturally constituted* political economy is to invoke a tension. The modifier
"culture" threatens to undermine the nomothetic elegance of general laws;
it seems to make an aesthetic and logical mess of efforts to get beyond intentions and towards unintended consequences that appear as natural laws or
structural regularities. Culture seems to align itself in our imagination as one
with the ideographic; culture stands in for culture*s* and culture*s* suggest
multiple systems meaningful interaction. Crang notes that the language of
culture points us to a " 'generic' fact of human life, bound up with the human
competencies to make the world meaningful and significant." But it also
points us towards a " 'differential' quality, marking out and helping to constitute distinctive social systems."[22] To give in to the cultural is to be newly
sensitive to cultural variation, seemingly downgrading economics from its
status as natural law. It is to confront different meanings and purposes than

18 Rhoda H. Halperin, *Cultural Economies Past and Present*, Austin: University of Texas, 1994,
    p. 14.
19 Daniel Miller, *Capitalism: An Ethnographic Approach*, New York: Berg, 1997, pp. 8, 17.
20 Timothy Mitchell, "Fixing the Economy," *Cultural Studies*, 1998, vol. 12, p. 84.
21 Craig N. Murphy and Cristina Rojas de Ferro, "Introduction: The Power of Representation
    in International Political Economy," *Review of International Political Economy*, 1995, vol. 2,
    p. 67. That IPE is particularly resistant to any questioning of rational actor assumptions
    is suggested by Deborah Kay Elms, "New Directions for IPE: Drawing from Behavioral
    Economics," *International Studies Review*, 2008, vol. 10, pp. 240–3. Benjamin J. Cohen's
    account of the field confirms this: *International Political Economy: An Intellectual History*,
    Princeton: Princeton University, 2008.
22 Crang, "Cultural Turns," p. 5. We have made a parallel presentation of the use of the
    language of "culture" in Inayatullah and Blaney, *International Relations*, ch. 4. See also
    Raymond Williams, "Culture is Ordinary," in Robin Grable (ed.) *Resources of Hope: Culture,
    Democracy, Socialism*, London: Verso, 1989, pp. 2–18.

those central to contemporary economic analysis, transforming economics into a branch of ethnography.

We assume that economy is culturally constituted in some deep sense, and we share the critics' concerns about contemporary studies of "economy." However, our purpose here is somewhat different. Our ethnological posture requires that we take seriously the conventional economist's universalistic stance. We bank on the idea that understanding the social meanings and ethical purposes created by a supposed *a*cultural economics is a project with some merit. If political economy tries to establish itself as the nomothetic or utopian self in contrast to which culture embraces the savage slot or the ideographic other, we wonder why it does so. What work is enabled and produced by this bifurcation for both sides of the divide? To ask this question is not necessarily to absolve economics of its imperial pretensions. Rather, we probe how and why the bifurcation enables both (international) political economy and ethnologically oriented scholars to naturalize the mutually constituting utopian and savage slots. In order to destabilize the utopian/savage slot, we ask: what meanings and ethical purposes are brought into social life through the pursuit of an acultural political economy? What meanings and purposes are highlighted by a nomothetically oriented economics? Which remain hidden? How does deploying a culturally constituted political economy help us retrieve important, but repressed, themes? Our project is not, then, a wholesale rejection of modern economics or modern capitalism, though it does require that we construct, as Linda McDowell suggests, "an understanding of the conflicts and contradictions, the doubts and uncertainties in the multiplicity of practices that constitute 'the economic.' "[23] It involves recognizing that contemporary economics, despite some protest, necessarily engages, even surreptitiously constructs, a "moral economy"—a domain of "moral sentiments and norms."[24]

We are wary, then, of arguments that drive a wedge between culture and economy. If the economic stakes a claim to the natural and the universal, and the cultural finds its modus vivendi in the particular and in difference, then an embrace of the cultural may simply reproduce the economic/cultural divide. As Nigel Thrift warns, an emphasis on culture has led many thinkers to take "remarkably little . . . note of economics." Or, more strongly, he claims that this opposition is constitutive of elements of the cultural turn itself: "Culture was culture because it had been purified of the taint of the

---

23 Linda McDowell, "Acts of Memory and Millennial Hopes and Anxieties: The Awkward Relationship Between the Economic and the Cultural," *Social and Cultural Geography*, 2000, vol. 1, p. 22.

24 See Andrew Sayer, "(De)commodification, Consumer Culture, and Moral Economy," *Environment and Planning D: Society and Space*, 2003, vol. 21, p. 341. Amartya Sen, *Development as Freedom*, New York: Anchor, 1999, ch. 5, makes roughly the same point, as does Deidre N. McCloskey, *The Bourgeois Virtues: Ethics for an Age of Commerce*, Chicago: University of Chicago, 2006.

economic."[25] This purification of culture might be seen as necessary to secure for the cultural turn its critical distance and bite. But it also reproduces the bifurcation, re-inscribing the boundary, so to speak, even as commentators hope to recover the cultural for critical social inquiry.

Some critics of postcolonial studies have pointed to a similar stalemate. Sumit Sarkar argues that the effort to recover an authentic voice independent of Enlightenment modernism or to identify cultures of resistance to Eurocentrism has led many postcolonial thinkers to construct an "autonomous world" of culture ("literature, art, education, domesticity" and "religion") set in opposition to the "material," where the material is associated with the West. But the effect of claiming the cultural for the postcolonial is to surrender the definition of the material to the modern West and its economists.[26] Arif Dirlik pointedly suggests that postcolonial critics have relieved themselves of the necessity of facing their own role in "contemporary capitalism" by "repudiating a foundational role of capitalism in history." However, where Eurocentrism is "built into the very structure of . . . capitalist culture," it is difficult to imagine any serious decentering or provincializing of the West that does not confront directly political economy.[27] If a critical posture to modernity is purchased by purifying culture of the economic, then a productive confrontation with modernity's utopian slot remains unlikely.

III. Ashley's Economization of the Economy

A cautionary tale may help us to see how secure the bifurcation between economics and culture remains.[28] Richard Ashley is acclaimed for his work

25 Nigel Thrift, "Pandora's Box? Cultural Geographies or Economies," in G. Clark, M. Gerther and M. Feldman (eds.) *The Oxford Handbook of Economic Geography*, Oxford: Oxford University, 2003, pp. 692, 698–9. Peter Jackson, "Commercial Cultures: Transcending the Cultural and the Economic," *Progress in Human Geography*, 2002, vol. 26, p. 4, makes a similar formulation of the problem. Nancy Fraser, *Justice Interruptus: Critical Reflections on the "Postsocialist" Condition*, New York: Routledge, 1997, ch. 1, turns this claim to a political/ethical critique of identity politics, though, as Jacinda Swanson, "Recognition and Redistribution: Rethinking Culture and the Economic," *Theory, Culture and Society*, 2005, vol. 22, 87–118, demonstrates, Fraser simply reproduces this boundary.

26 Sumit Sarkar, "The Decline of the Subaltern in *Subaltern Studies*," in Vinayak Charurvedi (ed.) *Mapping Subaltern Studies and the Postcolonial*, London: Verso, 2000, esp. p. 309. This bifurcation in postcolonial studies is striking, since *Subaltern Studies* was often grounded in a Marxist historiography. See Dipesh Chakrabarty, *Provincializing Europe: Postcolonial Thought and Historical Difference*, Princeton: Princeton University, 2000, p. 47, and Eiman O. Zein-Elabdin and S. Charusheela, "Introduction: Economics and Postcolonial Thought," in Zein-Elabdin and Charusheela (eds.) *Postcolonialism Meets Economics*, New York: Routledge, 2004, pp. 4–6.

27 Arif Dirlik, "The Postcolonial Aura," *Critical Inquiry*, 1994, vol. 20, pp. 331, 350.

28 See our earlier paper: Naeem Inayatullah and David L. Blaney, "Economic Anxiety: Reification, De-reification, and the Politics of IPE," in Kurt Burch and Robert Denemark (eds.) *Constituting International Political Economy*, Boulder: Lynne Rienner, 1997, 59–77.

challenging orthodox interpretations of international relations theory. His ideas on "economism" are less well known even if, in our view, they are amongst his most important and stimulating work. In his "Three Modes of Economism" Ashley's purpose is precisely to de-reify economic logic.[29] However, his argument constructs economy as an "other," over and against a "lifeworld" of social meaning and ethical purpose, thematic ambiguity, and creative contestation. Though Ashley does not use the language of culture, preferring to talk about restoring the role of the "political," his embrace of the "lifeworld" as a domain of alternative views and social/political action parallels the role that "culture" plays for some contemporary critics of the economy.

For Ashley the economy presupposes a distinction between "social system" (society) and "environment" (nature). Relations within the social system are distinctly political, concerned with key social purposes and relations of domination and contestation. The economy is defined by relations between the social system and the environment, but these (economized) relations are treated as distinctly asocial in their logic. The environment serves society as a source of objects subject to "manipulation and control" for social reproduction—a relation of "work and production," but not meaning or purpose. This relationship is conceived as purely technical or instrumental, a system of inputs and outputs in which the system transforms the environment so that it can obtain what it values, requires, or needs in order to maintain or reproduce its given structures. The definition of the economy is thus imbued with familiar neoclassical propositions of scarcity and efficiency that complete the economy's insulation from a world of cultural meanings and purposes.[30]

Ashley thus fears that the logic of economy is "an abstract theoretical contrivance" that has led—with the rise of the modern capitalist economy—to the "conscious contemplation" of all choices in instrumental terms. "Economic behavior" has become "self-consciously understood by women and men in just these transparent terms, i.e., in terms of a logic of economy."[31] Where "a logic of economy" has a hold on the mind, people are led to accept the social world as "given" or "politically neutral."[32] We might add "culturally neutral," and note that Bourdieu speaks of the supposedly natural as involving the inculcation of individuals to the habit of calculation, as a "conversion" experience.[33] In Ashley's modern economy, technical rationality prevails. As "the premier justificatory framework for human action," it presupposes

---

29 Richard K. Ashley, "Three Modes of Economism," *International Studies Quarterly*, 1983, vol. 27, 463–96.
30 Ibid., pp. 474–5.
31 Ibid., p. 475.
32 Ibid., p. 473.
33 Bourdieu, *Social Structures*, pp. 5–6.

the essential givenness and internal consistency of the decisionmaker and his values or goals, by regarding as given the definition of a problem (the gap between desirable and actual system conditions) to be solved, and by treating as unproblematic a distinction between values to be served and options to be taken[;] the algorithm exactly reproduces the logic of economy's presupposition of given boundaries between (a) fixed and apolitically defined system structures to be reproduced ... and (b) a manipulable environment to be objectified and controlled in the interest of reproducing those structures. Like the logic of economy, technical rationality reflects not at all on the truth content of values or ends, and never on the structures or boundaries of the agent, but only on the efficiency of means. In short, technical rationality is the unreflective logic of economy *par excellence.*[34]

Technical rationality appears to displace all (other?) social and political content from the economy. Thus, the logic of economy embedded in existing capitalist societies is especially debilitating to human political and ethical purposes and "the period of historical economism we are now experiencing is a very dangerous time."[35]

Although we share Ashley's concern that technical rationality often over-rides substantial political/ethical concerns, we find it somewhat puzzling that he unproblematically characterizes existing capitalist societies as completely dominated by "technical rational logic." At one point he admits that "even within bourgeois culture, conformity to the model [of the logic of economy] has its definite limits," but this admission does not deter the weight of his argument: the internalization of the logic of economy is the "social path-ology of advanced capitalist society," the escape from which is "the political task of our time."[36] In the end, Ashley remains satisfied to depict the economy as a social practice that is reducible to and reified as the logic of technical rationality. To use Ashley's own language, we see this as an *economism of the economy* (a fourth mode of economism) and a continued bifurcation of the economy from culture. Treated in this way, the economy becomes a special source of anxiety for Ashley against which a picture of the "lifeworld" pro-vides hope for "salvation."[37] Political logic is "intrinsically dialectical," cap-able of "calling into question the dominant social order on which it depends." It possesses "generative power" that can override the merely technical and apolitical logic that governs our participation in the economy.[38] Thus, a

34 Ashley, "Three Modes," pp. 475–6.
35 Ibid, p. 490.
36 Ibid., pp. 476, 492.
37 Gillian Youngs, "The Knowledge Problematic: Richard Ashley and Political Economy," Nottingham: Trent University manuscript, 1994, p. 15, uses this term to characterize Ashley's conception of the political possibilities of the lifeworld.
38 Ashley, "Three Modes," pp. 478–80.

crucial part of this bifurcation of danger/salvation turns on the opposition between an *asocial* economy and a *social* lifeworld rich with the ethical ambiguity, reflexive questioning, the creative energies of cultural life, and the restorative possibilities of political action.

IV. Towards Cultural Political Economy

This view of the logic of economy and capitalist society works to stunt our theorizing. First, in accepting a technical characterization of economy we are turned away from richer, more nuanced accounts of economic life (such as those provided by classical political economy, as we shall see). To put it starkly, since Ashley reduces economic practice to the asociality of technical rationality, the economy is left devoid of *social* practice. However, political economy remains fitted into Trouillot's utopian slot and thereby points to an entire way of life. What is missing in Ashley's vision is that the imperial imposition of economic rationality is motivated and vivified by broader social goals, namely an expansion of wealth that is a precondition for freedom and individuality. The economy expresses these meanings and purposes, even if it does so in limited, complicated and contradictory ways: the unleashing of naturally "orderly" processes that undercut social stability for many; a thin understanding of freedom that produces freedoms for some at the expense of others; a realized formal equality that is substantively denied; the creation simultaneously of wealth and poverty; and an expansion of human capacities alongside a degradation of civic potentials. Thus, Ashley misses that the instrumental elements of economic logic—a kind of asociality at the heart of the social practice of economy—are integral to and a consequence of a rich structuring of *social* meaning and purpose.

Second, Ashley's bifurcation of the logic of economy and lifeworld produces an equally stunted notion of the possibilities of cultural/political life. Though classical political economy envisions the economy as a distinct domain, it does not imagine that other domains of the social whole are somehow insulated or separated from the social meanings and purposes that sustain the economy. It is only by purifying society of the logic of economy that Ashley can find in the modern lifeworld the pure motivations, creative energies, and recursive questioning required for our salvation from the logic of economy. However, our modern cultural energies, critical reflexivity, and political and social action do not spring from some place completely free of the operation of technical rationality or insulated from capitalist notions of freedom, equality, and individuality. There is no generative power or creative questioning that *simply* stands outside of and opposed to economy.[39]

---

39 We find a similar conclusion in various theorists of the modernity/coloniality nexus that stake out an oppositional stance to modern capitalism. See Boaventura de Sousa Santos, "*Nuestra America:* Reinventing a Subaltern Paradigm of Recognition and Redistribution,"

Third, Ashley does not consider the possibility that his anxiety about the economy is less a challenge to the political economy tradition than a symptom of fears deeply rooted in that tradition itself. Indeed, political economy shares the very anxiety that Ashley sets in opposition to a complacent economic logic. Classical political economy comes to us laced with uncertainty about ourselves as social beings. That the individual's role in the economy is narrowly self-regarding may be thought to produce certain social goods, but there is also recognition that our civic and familial roles may demand something other than self-interest narrowly conceived. How can we protect and cultivate a broader self-interest or ethicality from the narrow self-regard induced by the alienation of a capitalist economy? As we will see, such worries are central to a whole range of political economists, from Smith, Ferguson, and Steuart to the resonances of the Scots in Hegel and Marx. Likewise, anxieties surrounding the advantages and purposes of wealth, the possibilities of both national and international (dis)order, the meaning of equality where some are poor, and the character and preconditions of freedom all pervade the political economy tradition.

Finally, we find it telling that both the contemporary economist and Ashley share a common view of the distinctiveness of the logic of economy. Even more revealing is that both deploy this claim to justify the purity of their scholarly pursuits. For economists, the economy is purified of a cultural content that might vitiate claims about the universality and naturalness of this distinct economic logic and plunge them into political/ethical debate. For Ashley, enclosing this economic logic allows him to purify the lifeworld so that it might be a privileged site of critical activity in relation to an ethically inert economic analysis. Each needs a certain and fixed boundary to champion their domain and to avoid the rich sources of ambiguity within the overlap.

Seeing political economy as culturally constituted exposes the wound that is overlooked when social theory occupies the utopian/savage slot, as either utopian project or abstract criticism. Political economy as a cultural project reveals what both economists and cultural critics hide, that wealth creation creates a tenacious wound. With a cultural political economy we can face the ethical claim that cultural critics such as Ashley obscure and economists treat as given by nature: that the institutionalization of technical rationality is central to the creation of wealth and thereby a vital means of promoting freedom, equality, and individuality; and that the apparently asocial practice of instrumental reason is not separable from a wider system of social meaning and purpose. Economists and cultural critics share an interest in hiding this ambiguity, but they do so for different reasons. The economists resist

Theory, Culture and Society, 2001, vol. 18, 188–93 and Arturo Escobar, "Worlds and Knowledges Otherwise: The Latin American Modernity/Coloniality Research Program," *Cultural Studies*, 2007, vol. 21, 184–90.

because of their mostly unquestioned commitment to the net benefits of capitalist practices; the critics because of their refusal to debate the possible virtues of capitalism. The absence of this debate, as well as its unacknowledged and necessary persistence, is part of the wound of wealth. The pain of holding this debate is the "real" of modern life—both what it cannot avoid and cannot seem to face.[40]

Our elaboration of this critique strives to show that the resources needed to address this wound are *not* scarce. In the following chapters, we locate these critical resources through a direct confrontation with major figures of classical political economy. We take some measure of reassurance from a few endorsements of this project. Matthew Watson, in calling for a re-visioning of international political economy, suggests that classical political economy does not share the contemporary tendency to see " 'the economy' as an enclosed and self-contained entity." Rather, Smith and others see economic life as enmeshed in a web of social relationships drawing us to questions of moral psychology, philosophy, politics, and law.[41] Similarly, but from a self-proclaimed post-capitalist perspective, J. K. Gibson-Graham argues that, in the face of what we have called an economism of the economy, classical political economy is one among many sources providing "conceptual resources for different languages of economy"—for alternative imaginations of economic life and, in our view, international political economy.[42] We have already suggested that the savage other lurks within political economy. In the Introduction, we asserted that our representatives of classical political economy display a relative, if sometimes begrudging, acknowledgement of the wound of wealth and an inability or unwillingness, finally, to treat this wound as somehow transcended, either historically or dialectically. The continuing presence of the figure of the savage in political economy is central to that acknowledgment of this wound. It remains so today, as we explore in Chapter 7.

40 See the introduction for a fuller discussion.
41 Matthew Watson, *Foundations of International Political Economy*, Houndsmill: Palgrave, 2005, pp. 18–19. See also Colin Hay and David Marsh, "Introduction: Towards a New (International) Political Economy," *New Political Economy*, 1999, vol. 4, pp. 15–16.
42 J. K. Gibson-Graham, *The End of Capitalism (as we knew it): A Feminist Critique of Political Economy*, Minneapolis: University of Minnesota, 2006, p. xi.

2 The savage Smith and the temporal walls of capitalism[1]

In the standard literature in international political economy (IPE), Adam Smith serves as the marker for a "classical liberal school of economics." Built on a "shared and coherent set of assumptions" about the human drive to truck and barter, leading to inevitable material improvement, this "economics" claims to derive from Smith a set of "inviolable laws" of economic life that mandate free markets internally and free trade internationally.[2] Others within IPE and international relations have complicated this view,[3] even if their efforts have failed to dislodge the standard reading. Nonetheless, additional readings may be useful for those who are sensitive to the historicity of economics and its richly debated propositions.

Our reading of Smith emphasizes the role that Amerindians play in his work. Reading Smith against the theme of "savagery" allows us to: (1) focus on an often neglected intellectual influence on Smith—the Jesuit Father Lafitau; (2) critically examine how Smith uses comparative ethnology and a theory of human progress to insulate commercial society from ethical critique; and, perhaps most fruitfully, (3) recover mostly repressed ethical resources that help us assess the present state of global capitalism.

1 The title is a play on Ashis Nandy's article, "The Savage Freud," in *The Savage Freud and Other Essays on Possible and Retrievable Selves*, Princeton: Princeton University, 1995, 81–144.
2 Robert A. Isaak, *Managing World Economic Change: International Political Economy*, Upper Saddle River: Prentice Hall, 2000, p. 4, makes the claim about the existence of a liberal "school." Many texts begin with this same assumption. The account of liberalism as possessing "shared and coherent" assumptions can be found in Robert Gilpin, *The Political Economy of International Relations*, Princeton: Princeton University, 1987, pp. 26–31, 44, 81. It is worth noting that Gilpin's later book, *Global Political Economy: Understanding the International Economic Order*, Princeton: Princeton University, 2001, gives Smith much less space, but this may be attributed to the fact that Gilpin no longer treats IPE as a domain of debate among schools. Apparently, the major issues have been decided.
3 See especially Matthew Watson, *Foundations of International Political Economy*, Houndsmill: Palgrave, 2005. See also Craig N. Murphy's interesting use of Smith in *Industrial Organization and Industrial Change: Global Governance Since 1850*, New York: Oxford University, 1994, and Justin Rosenberg's use of the language of civil society in *The Empire of Civil Society: A Critique of the Realist Theory of International Relations*, London: Verso, 1994.

Linking comparative ethnology and Adam Smith may seem surprising, since neither Smith nor any of the key Scottish social thinkers made the voyage to the New World.[4] Nonetheless, their encounters with the Indians were no less profound than those of earlier adventurers, missionaries, and scholars whose reports they inherited. It was in and through these reports that the Scots journeyed. Their travels were "cognitive," a "travel in the mind's eye," as Anthony Padgen puts it.[5] By locating the Indians' place in history, the Scots identify the Indians as travelers on a common human path. For Smith and his fellow Scots, cultural contact with Europeans launched the Indians on a great developmental journey towards Europe—a journey that took the Indians from their past life towards Europe's present.

The need to locate the Indians had a prior history. Since the "discovery" of the Americas, Europeans struggled to make sense of continents and peoples that were difficult to place alongside scriptural and classical authority.[6] Many European thinkers treated the New World peoples' physical and social distance from the singular moment of Edenic creation as proof of their degeneration from Christian faith and civilized behavior. Reports of cannibalism, human sacrifice, and deficient arts and sciences confirmed the distance and degeneration of the Amerindians from the norms of human (i.e. European) practice. Numerous thinkers sought to contain the disorder the Indians represented thereby by placing them below the threshold of humanity, justifying enslavement or extermination. Or if their humanity was accepted, Indian difference was translated into a form of infancy that European tutelage might steer. Thus, imperialism's pedagogical component was deployed quite early. Over the next century or more, European thinkers conjectured that the distance and degeneration of Amerindians meant they lived in the earliest state of human existence.

By the middle of the eighteenth century, the fear of cannibalism and human sacrifice had receded somewhat and Amerindians were no longer the novel puzzle of social theory. For most Enlightenment thinkers the demands of a scientific theory of humankind replaced the imperative to preserve scriptural and/or classical authority. Indians continued to represent difference in emerging theories of moral and civic philosophy, but the key problem became how to account for their low levels of development. The temporal separation of the Indians and Europeans became in the hands of Smith and the Frenchman Turgot a theory of historical development with four ages or stages: from hunting and gathering, shepherding, and agriculture, to commerce. The movement from one stage to another results from processes

---

4 Adam Ferguson is a partial exception. He visited the American colonies in the spring of 1778 as an emissary to the rebel forces, but was not allowed behind American lines.

5 Anthony Pagden, *European Encounters with the New World: From Renaissance to Romanticism*, New Haven: Yale University, 1993, p. 30.

6 See Naeem Inayatullah and David L. Blaney, *International Relations and the Problem of Difference*, New York: Routledge, 2004, ch. 2.

internal to each stage; history appears in Smith's words, "a great, an immense machine, whose regular and harmonious movements produce a thousand agreeable effects."[7] The temporal distance between Indians and Europeans, previously bridged only by the activities of missionaries, could now be understood within an "abstract and philosophical" scheme that locates the American Indian at the very beginnings of human society.[8] Indian differences were benignly rendered as superseded ways of life.

Smith's knowledge of the Amerindians came largely from Father Joseph François Lafitau's *Customs of the American Indians*. Smith and others gave Lafitau's work a "special role" because it "provided a convincing demonstration of the fact that contemporary American society could be regarded as a living model—conveniently laid out for study, as if in a laboratory—of human society in the first or earliest stage of its development."[9] Lafitau's decisive impact might be thought surprising since his principal aim—to reassert a Christian eschatology—was far from the minds of Smith and other Scottish Enlightenment figures. Nonetheless, his work provided the kind of cognitive travel the Scots needed for their comparative history. And as we will note, Lafitau's characterization of his travels as movement through time foreshadows that the past can threaten Europe's present. Smith was aware that Rousseau used "savagery" to critique emerging commercial societies[10] and that "cognitive travel" can disturb the meanings and purposes that constitute contemporary societies. To shield the European present from such disturbances, Smith protectively encased commercial society behind temporal walls.[11]

I. Lafitau: To the Indians and Back

Like earlier travel writers, Father Joseph François Lafitau's most famous work, *Moeurs des sauvages Ameriquains comparées aux moeurs des premiers temps* [*Customs of the American Indians Compared with the Customs of Primitive Times*] (1724), struggles to incorporate the presence of the Americans with the scriptural claim about the singular origin of the human species.[12]

---

7 Adam Smith, *The Theory of Moral Sentiments*, Indianapolis: Liberty Fund, 1976, p. 316.

8 Ibid.

9 Ronald L. Meek, *Social Science and the Ignoble Savage*, Cambridge: Cambridge University, 1976, p. 57.

10 See Adam Smith, "A Letter to the Authors of the *Edinburgh Review*," in *Essays on Philosophical Subjects*, Indianapolis: Liberty Fund, 1980, pp. 250–4.

11 This suggests that Fasolt's claims that the Enlightenment historiography decisively established the distinction "between past and present" needs to be qualified. See Constantin Fasolt, *The Limits of History*, Chicago: University of Chicago, 2004, p. 32.

12 Joseph François Lafitau, *Customs of the American Indians Compared with the Customs of Primitive Times, Volumes I and II*, Toronto: The Champlain Society, 1974, pp. 33–4, 327–30. See also Michel de Certeau, "Writing vs. Time: History and Anthropology in the Works of Lafitau," *Yale French Studies*, 1980, issues 59–60, p. 54.

Lafitau (1681–1746) is recognizably an Enlightenment thinker, however, help-ing to explain his considerable influence on the Scots.[13]

Consistent with this picture of Lafitau as an Enlightenment figure, Fenton and Moore speculate that his early life in the busy port of Bordeaux stimu-lated his "dreams of the New World" and spurred interest in missions in North America as well as his later scholarly vocation.[14] In this way, Lafitau is easily associated with a spirit of scientific curiosity, akin to that embraced by the Enlightenment. Others highlight Lafitau's own description of his book as an attempt to refute the work of skeptics, like Pierre Bayle, in order to associ-ate Lafitau more with an earlier period of dogma.[15] We might see Lafitau as a liminal figure, occupying a pivotal space between religious debate and secular and scientific history. While this characterization accurately captures some-thing about Lafitau, it perhaps anachronistically overdraws the distinction between religious authority and scientific history. Lafitau regards science and religion as overlapping categories; for Lafitau a move towards a scientifically precise history serves and enhances religious authority.[16]

By the eighteenth century, questions about the status and origins of the Amerindians were far from over, though these controversies flowed along now familiar contours. Scholars usually accepted the idea of a single creation and assumed that Amerindians had migrated from Asia to the Americas.[17] Jesuit José de Acosta's *Historia natural y moral de las Indias* (1590) had shaped the debate by insisting that, since barbarism existed in multiple forms, comparisons among peoples could be given a firm empirical basis and that "all the peoples of the world could be graded for civility."[18] This claim merely spurred argument, including the important late seventeenth/early eighteenth-century "Quarrel between the Ancients and the Moderns." Do the Ancients represent a "golden age" in relation to which the rest of human history appears degenerate? Or does the modern era promise social and scientific

---

13 Meek, *Ignoble Savage*, ch. 4, makes the strongest case for this influence. See also Anthony Pagden, *The Fall of Natural Man: The American Indians and the Origins of Comparative Ethnology*, Cambridge: Cambridge University, 1982, p. 205.

14 William N. Fenton and Elizabeth L. Moore, "Introduction," Joseph François Lafitau, *Cus-toms of the American Indians Compared with the Customs of Primitive Times*, Toronto: The Champlain Society, 1974, p. xxxi.

15 See Pagden, *Fall*, pp. 200–5; Meek, *Ignoble Savage*, p. 58, and Margaret T. Hodgen, *Early Anthropology in the Sixteenth and Seventeenth Centuries*, Philadelphia: University of Pennsylvania, 1964, p. 491.

16 See Carl L. Becker, *The Heavenly City of the Eighteenth-Century Philosophers*, New Haven: Yale University, 1971, ch. 1.

17 This is not to ignore the persistence of various polygenist theories of dual or multiple cre-ations and their importance for theories of "scientific" racism in the nineteenth century. See George W. Stocking, Jr., "Scotland as the Model of Mankind: Lord Kames' Philosophical View of Civilization," in Timothy H. H. Thoresen (ed.) *Toward a Science of Man: Essays in the History of Anthropology*, The Hague: Mouton, 1975, pp. 85–6.

18 Pagden, *Fall*, p. 198.

advance beyond all other forms of human society, including the Ancients? This dispute was at its height when Latifau studied at seminaries in Pau and Paris.[19] This debate's frame allowed him to cast " 'Antiquity' as a single category" applicable to both contemporary Amerindians and dead Ancients.[20] By Lafitau's time, drawing extensive parallels between ancient and contemporary paganism was well established, underpinning his effort to locate "conformities" across various "heathen" peoples.[21]

In *Customs of the American Indians*, Lafitau defends the scriptural account of the unity of creation in the face of the discovery of new and different lands and peoples. This defense required translating the myriad differences offered by the peoples of the New World into recognizable similarities and differences.[22] On the one hand, Lafitau explains similarities via migratory diffusion, by tracing "the origins of these peoples in the dark ages of antiquity."[23] As Pagden puts it, "new and troubling peoples" can be seen as descendents of Eurasians; the unknown thereby emerges from the known.[24] Various parallels between ancient religiosity, government, and marriage practices vindicate the picture of the Old World origins of the Americans.[25] Differences, on the other hand, are explained with a familiar claim about decay or degeneration.[26] Movement across time and space (and thereby away from the perfection of creation and the centers of continuing revelation) produces a degeneration of religious practice, moral belief, and linguistic structures. Amerindian decay seems obvious in relation to Christian moral and religious truths and Eurasian languages. The similarities between Amerindians and the ancients are explained by common origins; differences and decay as movement away from those origins.

Lafitau struggled with a second issue that profoundly shaped his text. Along with establishing a singular creation, he worked to demonstrate the presence of a common religious experience based in an original revelatory

---

19 Fenton and Moore, "Introduction," pp. xxxi and xliii.
20 Pagden, *European Encounters*, pp. 92–3. See also Certeau, "Writing vs. Time," pp. 45–6, on the creation of "antiquity" as a category.
21 Frank E. Manuel, *The Eighteenth Century Confronts the Gods*, Cambridge: Harvard University, 1959, p. 19; Hodgen, *Early Anthropology*, pp. 345–6. On the importance of Lafitau's practice for evolutionary theory within anthropology, see George W. Stocking, Jr., *Victorian Anthropology*, New York: Free Press, 1987, pp. 12–13.
22 See Fenton and Moore, "Introduction," p. xlvii, and Hodgen, *Early Anthropology*, p. 268.
23 Lafitau, *Customs I*, p. 25.
24 Pagden, *Encounters*, p. 29.
25 On the Hurons and Iroquois, see Lafitau, *Customs I*, pp. 67–9. The entire text is designed to draw "conjectures" based on comparisons of ancient and Indian practices. The chapter headings give a sense of the range of the comparisons across religion, government, marriage and education, occupations of both men and women, warfare, trade, diplomacy, games, medicine, mourning and burial practices.
26 Lafitau, *Customs I*, pp. 30–1, 34–5. See also Inayatullah and Blaney, *International Relations*, pp. 50–7.

act.[27] Targeting skeptics who defended the conventionality of religious belief,[28] Lafitau placed the universality of religious sentiment on a more secure foundation by arguing that the generative moment of human religiosity was the first social unit formed by Adam and Eve.[29] Though many ancient and contemporary peoples have strayed far from the original path, their religiosity reveals vestiges of that original monotheism imparted at creation. Here Lafitau de-emphasizes customs or practices that are particularly vulnerable to degeneration across time and space, stressing more the commonalities of imagery and myth which he sees as more lasting. He locates the deepest commonalities among peoples in the realm of "symbolic representation," and uses this realm to demonstrate the single and original inspiration for religious faith.[30] In this way, Lafitau places the human experience in its great variety, across both space and time, within what he calls a "symbolic theology."[31]

Enlightenment figures dismissed such "anti-rationalist" conclusions. Voltaire's tone is especially mocking but Adam Smith also finds many of Lafitau's major conclusions unsound. Though they deride some elements of his method and ignore the sections on religion, Lafitau still inspires the Scots.[32] He is noteworthy, if for no other reason, than the near exhaustiveness of his sources. He epitomizes the emerging view, as Certeau explains, that far-flung times and places might be available for the contemporary thinker in the form of collections of material artifacts and archives of written reports.[33] Exhaustiveness alone is insufficient to recommend Lafitau to Smith, however. Collections and archives remain silent unless their secrets are voiced; meaning is revealed only when the accumulated vestiges of ancient times and reports of contemporary peoples are systematically compared. While others also made such comparisons, Lafitau is distinguished by the "wide-ranging character" of his comparisons,[34] his "scrupulously factual account of the evidence,"[35] his "tabularization of ethnographic knowledge into a systematic and comprehensive form,"[36] and that he is the "most sophisticated and explicit as to his method."[37]

---

27 The account in Pagden, *Fall*, ch. 8, is especially good. See also Certeau, "Writing vs. Time," pp. 54–5.
28 Lafitau, *Customs I*, p. 29. See also Pagden, *Fall*, p. 200, and Manuel, *The Eighteenth Century*, p. 146.
29 This is also the generative moment of human sociality in the form of the family. Lafitau, *Customs I*, ch. VI. See also Certeau, "Writing vs. Time," pp. 54–5.
30 The quoted phrase is from Pagden, *Fall*, p. 204. See also Fenton and Moore, "Introduction," pp. lxxvi–lxxvii.
31 Lafitau, *Customs I*, pp. 35–6.
32 Pagden, *Fall*, pp. 205 and 246 (fn. 29).
33 Certeau, "Writing vs. Time," pp. 43–5.
34 Meek, *Ignoble Savage*, p. 63.
35 Pagden, *Fall*, p. 201.
36 Ter Ellingson, *The Myth of the Noble Savage*, Berkeley: University of California, 2001, p. 65.
37 Fenton and Moore, "Introduction," p. xlviii.

Lafitau is careful to avoid the errors of previous authors who rely on "imperfect and superficial records only," resort to "conjectures [that] are so vague and uncertain that they rather give rise to more doubts than clarifying the existing ones," and claim linguistic connections based on poor knowledge of the languages involved.[38] He stresses that his knowledge of Amerindian customs is based on personal experience, mastery of local languages, and reliable eye witness accounts.[39] Most important, he explains the way a comparison of the Ancients and the Indians allows us to understand both much better:

> I have not limited myself to learning the characteristics of the Indian and informing myself about their customs and practices, I have sought in these practices and customs, vestiges of the most remote antiquity. I have read carefully [the works] of the earliest writers who treated the customs, laws and usages of the peoples of whom they had some knowledge. I have made a comparison of these customs with the other. I confess that, if the ancient authors have given me information on which to base happy conjectures about the Indians, the customs of the Indians have given me information on the basis of which I can understand more easily and explain more readily many things in the ancient authors.[40]

Pagden attributes the scientific power of this process of comparison to the capacity and willingness to move back and forth across time:

> The reflective, informed and "sensible" being possesses the ability to be, in this [imaginative] way, literally in more places than one. And it is precisely this capacity for cognitive travel which constitutes his power of scientific understanding. For all scientific knowledge, and the power that that knowledge brings with it, demands just such movement. And all movement follows the same trajectory. It begins as going out and ends as coming back.[41]

Similarly, Ter Ellingson explains that Lafitau's method of comparison involves a form of "time-shifting" that overcomes geographical distance in order to establish a "common kinship" among peoples.[42] Thus, the collections and archives used to document the practices of the Ancients and the Indians (and establish common origins) are understood "without recourse to dates or places."[43] As Certeau explains, Lafitau draws from a "stock of monuments,

38 Lafitau, *Customs I*, p. 26.
39 Ibid., pp. 26–7.
40 Ibid., p. 27. See also the description in Pagden, *Fall*, pp. 198–9.
41 Pagden, *European Encounters*, p. 30.
42 Ellingson, *Myth*, p. 77.
43 Fenton and Moore, "Introduction," p. xlviii.

piled up without chronological order, elements which are susceptible of being *formally* compared and which fit together *symbolically* as general categories."[44]

By placing antiquity and contemporary barbarism within a common "symbolic theology," Lafitau provides a picture of the Amerindians as full members of the human species, "[m]en being everywhere born with the same good or bad qualities."[45] He rejects fanciful descriptions of the Indians that ignore the presence of common features of human society:

> I have seen, with extreme distress, in most of the travel narratives, that those who have written of the customs of primitive peoples have depicted them to us as people without any sentiment of religion, knowledge of a divinity or object to which they rendered any cult, as people without law, social control or any form of government; in a word, as people who have scarcely anything except the appearance of men. This is a mistake made even by missionaries and honest men who, on the one hand, have written too hastily of things with which they were not sufficiently familiar and, on the other, did not foresee the disastrous consequences which could be drawn from the expression of an opinion so unfavourable to religion. . . .
> It results, nevertheless, (from this), that we are prejudiced by the first statement and become accustomed to forming a conception of these Indians and barbarians which scarcely differentiates them from beasts.[46]

Lafitau does not locate the Amerindians in a golden age or natural state; nor does he characterize them as fully degenerated or beastly. He produces instead a series of careful observations about the Indian societies. Some of his reports—on age-grades, kinship relations and the position of women in Indian societies—are considered quite acute and unsurpassed by professional anthropologists until the nineteenth, or perhaps even the twentieth, century.[47] However, Lafitau's aim to defend the possibility of missionary activity places his project at some distance from the central concerns of his Enlightenment contemporaries.

Another implication of his method better explains Lafitau's role in Enlightenment historiography. Certeau's revealing claim, that Lafitau's historical system replaces the Bible, gives us an initial hint of that importance.[48] In the Christian worldview, temporal events or secular history necessarily

---

44 Certeau, "Writing vs. Time," p. 47.

45 Lafitau, *Customs II*, p. 299. See also *Customs I*, pp. 89–91. See our discussion in Inayatullah and Blaney, *International Relations*, pp. 50–7.

46 Lafitau, *Customs I*, pp. 28–9.

47 Fenton and Moore, "Introduction," pp. cvii–cxix; Martha Haroun Foster, "Lost Women of the Matriarchy: Iroquois Women in the Historical Literature," *American Indian Culture and Research Journal*, 1999, vol. 19, pp. 122–4.

48 Certeau, "Writing vs. Time," p. 54.

gain meaning only via "subordination to eschatology," but this "millenarian formula" lacks the "means of explicating the succession of particulars in social and political time"; the emerging imperative is to fill that gap with a natural philosophy rooted in careful observation of human experience.[49] Lafitau might be seen as a transitional figure in relation to this imperative. Despite his ostensive religious motivations, he makes a "scientific gesture," setting himself apart from "his social ties and attachments" and placing himself in the position of an autonomous observer and producer of a system of knowledge. Thus, Lafitau represents an "enticing" image of scientific practice, seducing us with its claim to overcome the diversities and discontinuities of time in order thereby "to produce the formal system of an absolute knowledge."[50]

Lafitau's "scientific gesture" appeals to the Scots. They were drawn to locating the Ancients and contemporary primitives at the beginning of time because it supports the idea "that all human cultures could be interpreted as the working out in time of certain known and stable characteristics of the human mind."[51] Or, as Fenton and Moore explain, though Lafitau "was neither historical nor evolutionary in the strictest sense of these terms," he contributed "documentation to substantiate the 'law' of progress."[52]

Though the Scots treat his work as a substantial achievement, our reading of Lafitau's work foreshadows our critique of Scottish Enlightenment historiography. His practice of "time-shifting" pushes an understanding of the Amerindians (and the Ancients) into terms that are his alone.[53] As Certeau evocatively puts it, Lafitau's comparison "silences" both the Ancients and the savages.[54] His travel outward to the Indians and Ancients and then back to the European self thereby damages our understanding of the particular and distinct histories of both.[55] Or we might say more hopefully that he brings home collections and archives whose secrets wait to be sufficiently voiced.

II. Smith and the Indians: Time, Space and Moral Science

The Scottish Enlightenment is noted for its distinctive variant of the doctrine of progress: Smith's "conjectural history" and the "four-stages theory."[56]

49 J. G. A. Pocock, *The Machiavellian Moment: Florentine Political Thought and the Atlantic Republican Tradition*, Princeton: Princeton University, 1975, pp. 31–2, 47–8. In the Introduction, we discuss this necessity (and impossibility) of filling the gaps in the modern structure of thought as the "real."

50 Certeau, "Writing vs. Time," pp. 53–4, 59–60. See also Fenton and Moore, "Introduction," pp. lxiv–lxv.

51 Pagden, *Fall*, p. 208.

52 Fenton and Moore, "Introduction," p. xliv. See also Meek, *Ignoble Savage*, pp. 54 and 61.

53 Pagden, *European Encounters*, p. 53.

54 Certeau, "Writing vs. Time," p. 63.

55 Hodgen, *Early Anthropology*, pp. 348–9.

56 Ronald Meek's *Ignoble Savages* is the key text.

Though "conjectural history" builds on Lafitau's work, Smith's use of this technique diverges in a crucial respect. Where Lafitau embraces a scientific method to give credibility to a particular eschatological scheme, Smith embraces science as a calling that sets the modern apart from the superstitions of the past. If God remained a concern, it was as the rather distant "author" of creation, constructing a natural order, the laws of which humankind might discern.[57] In that quest to comprehend the natural order, human beings assumed a central place in the creation (if not quite authorship) of their own world.[58] Smith and Lafitau converge at another point, however. For both, the new peoples and continents "discovered" and "explored" by Europeans were sources of some anxiety. The Scots, like Lafitau, needed to make the amazing diversity of peoples and societies consistent with the principles of, in this case, a natural order.[59] For them, managing this diversity requires the kind of travel associated with the scientific practice of comparative or "conjectual history."

For the Scots, as for Enlightenment thinking more generally, a "science of man" was necessarily an empirical science, rooted in experience and evidence. Newton's knowledge of a world of bodies subject to laws inspired a search for similar laws governing human behavior and institutions. Francis Bacon, perhaps more than any other, articulated what was also Newton's intuition— that natural and moral science might advance in step.[60] Since the Scots began with the assumption that humans naturally live in society, the evidence on which to base a science of man might be drawn from numerous sources, reflecting societies far-flung in time and space. The evidence available might be personal, rooted in the thinkers' own contemporary, European experience or it might come to them via written reports of the past or other societies. The latter made available vast amounts of "indirect and secondary" material about "the contemporary 'savage' world of the Americas, Asia and Polynesia and the world described by ancient authors."[61]

The Scots saw a complex picture of amazing diversity in the recorded evidence of human societies but this very diversity stood in potential opposition

---

57 Adam Smith, "The History of Astronomy," in *Essays on Philosophical Subjects*, Indianapolis: Liberty Fund, 1980, pp. 48–53. On the Scots', especially Smith's, placement of religion and science, see D. D. Raphael, "Adam Smith: Philosophy, Science and Social Science," in Stuart C. Brown (ed.) *Philosophers of the Enlightenment*, Atlantic Highlands: Humanities Press, 1979, 77–93, and Andrew Skinner, "Economics and History—The Scottish Enlightenment," *Scottish Journal of Political Economy*, 1965, vol. 12, p. 22.

58 Robert Wokler, "Anthropology and Conjectural History in the Enlightenment," in Christopher Fox, Roy Porter, and Robert Wokler (eds.) *Inventing Human Science: Eighteenth-Century Domains*, Berkeley: University of California, 1995, pp. 33–4.

59 The importance of the problem of diversity for the Scots is discussed especially well by Christopher J. Berry, *Social Theory of the Scottish Enlightenment*, Edinburgh: Edinburgh University, 1997, ch. 4.

60 Ibid., pp. 52–3.

61 We draw here on Berry, *Social Theory*, pp. 52–4, 61; the quotation is from p. 61.

to a moral or civic science.[62] Part of the solution was to locate recurring patterns in human societies. Following the example of Montesquieu perhaps, the *social* thinker would identify the common chains of cause and effect that explained these patterns.[63] The assumption, as we noted above, "was that everything in society and history, just like everything in the physical realm, was bound together by an intricate concatenation of causes and effects which it is the main task of the student of man and society—i.e. the social scientist—to unravel."[64]

Thus, for the Scots a science of man required the telling of tales and the writing of historical narratives, so as to incorporate all this disparate material into a truly "philosophical account."[65] Travel narratives, including Lafitau's, could serve as no more than "raw material" or perhaps inspiration. Even the noted chains of cause and effect do not alone produce a moral science of the kind envisioned by Smith. Rather, the social thinker must build on these causal chains in order to tell a story with a clear moral point. Minimally, this requires finding a kind of constant that explains the great uniformity they see (and seek) in human societies. As Andrew Skinner notes: "The key to this problem was found, as Hume had insisted it must be, in the constant and universal principles of human nature."[66] With a given set of characteristics of human nature—"Hume lists ambition, avarice, self-love, vanity, friendship, generosity and public spirit"—the Scots could identify patterns that operate regardless of context. In this way, "[a]ll human behavior . . . is explicable because it is governed by regular springs which have uniform effects."[67]

Against this desire to locate causal constants stood evidence of great human diversity. This diversity might be *explained* as the consequence of placing a fixed human nature in varying physical settings (i.e., variations in climate and fertility of the soil), but the Scots resisted this move because of its relativistic implications. They wished to go beyond saying that differences in geography produce different forms of society.[68] For Smith and the Scots, a

62 Berry, *Social Theory*, pp. 74–5 and Michael J. Shapiro, *Reading "Adam Smith:" Desire, History, and Value*, Lanham: Rowman and Littlefield, 2002, p. 48, remark on the potentially paradoxical relationship of the evidence and the scientific ambition.

63 See Berry, *Social Theory*, ch. 3; David Carrithers, "The Enlightenment Science of Society," in Christopher Fox, Roy Porter, and Robert Wokler (eds.) *Inventing Human Science: Eighteenth Century Domains*, Berkeley: University of California, 1995, pp. 243–4.

64 Meek, *Ignoble Savage*, p. 1.

65 Pagden, *European Encounters*, pp. 84–5. The narrative character of the Scottish "science of man" is noted by Berry, *Social Theory*, pp. 54–5; and Roger Smith, "The Language of Human Nature," in Christopher Fox, Roy Porter, and Robert Wokler (eds.) *Inventing Human Science: Eighteenth Century Domains*, Berkeley: University of California, 1995, p. 102.

66 Andrew Skinner, "Natural History in the Age of Adam Smith," *Political Studies*, 1967, vol. XVI, p. 41.

67 Berry, *Social Theory*, p. 69.

68 Montesquieu's employment of physical causes—climate, geography—might well reduce the clutter of empirical evidence, identifying and explaining the persistence of a small number of forms of society and government, but the Scots believed that Montesquieu's scheme failed to provide a basis for making clear enough *moral distinctions* among forms of society. See Fania

moral science produces practical guidance about the direction of human society; about where, reflecting the Scottish Enlightenment's teleological moment, human society must *necessarily* and *appropriately* go.[69] This would be, as Becker puts it, "philosophy teaching by example."[70]

Thus, the Scots add a crucial element: the idea that human nature itself contains an impetus to progress. As distinct from (other) animals, humans seek to improve their condition and capabilities—a condition Smith believes "comes with us from the womb."[71] Though variable climate and geography might be of some importance, the key differences in the environment are those humans themselves create. The Scots argued that

> man, following his natural propensities, inevitably produces results well beyond his original intentions; that man, in reacting to a particular situation, must ultimately produce a qualitative change thus creating a new situation within which the same forces must operate.[72]

All human action generates progress and the diversity of social forms is variation in human achievement. Whereas in Lafitau difference means spatial distance from a Christian center, here difference is seen as temporal distance from the apex of progress. Differences across societies, whether ancient or contemporary, may be thought of as products of, to insert a contemporary usage, uneven development.[73] History is given a new moral reading—as "a repository of exemplars, for good or for evil."[74]

Oz-Salzberger, "The Political Theory of the Scottish Enlightenment," pp. 170–1, and Murray G. H. Pittrock, "Historiography," pp. 260–1, both in Alexander Broadie (ed.) *The Cambridge Companion to the Scottish Enlightenment*, Cambridge: Cambridge University, 2003; Skinner, "Natural History," p. 38.

69 On Smith as moralist and practical commentator, see Donald Winch, *Adam Smith's Politics: An Essay in Historiographic Revision*, Cambridge: Cambridge University, 1978; Richard E. Teichgraeber, III, *"Free Trade" and Moral Philosophy: Rethinking the Sources of Adam Smith's Wealth of Nations*, Durham: Duke University, 1986; Jerry A. Muller, *Adam Smith, in His Time and Ours*, Princeton: Princeton University, 1993; Charles L. Griswold, Jr., *Adam Smith and the Virtues of Enlightenment*, Cambridge: Cambridge University, 1999; and Samuel Fleischacker, *On Adam Smith's Wealth of Nations: A Philosophical Companion*, Princeton: Princeton University, 2004.

70 Becker, *Heavenly City*, p. 88.

71 Adam Smith, *An Inquiry into the Nature and Causes of the Wealth of Nations*, Chicago: University of Chicago, 1976, p. 362 [II.iii]. See Berry, *Social Theory*, pp. 69–70; Skinner, "Natural History," pp. 42–4.

72 Skinner, "Economics and History," p. 5.

73 See Paul Smith, "Conjecture, Acquiescence, and John Millar's History of Ireland," *The European Legacy*, 1996, vol. 1, p. 2233. J. G. A. Pocock, *Machiavellian Moment*, pp. 486–7, also notes that this move translates the components of cyclical theories of history into theories of progress.

74 Knud Haakonssen, *Natural Law and Moral Philosophy: From Grotius to the Scottish Enlightenment*, Cambridge: Cambridge University, 1996, p. 6.

Smith regards progressive time as stadial, involving movement though clearly discernable and ascending stages. He famously describes those stages in his lectures of 1762–3, identifying four: "1st, the Age of Hunters; 2dly, the Age of Shepherds; 3rdly, the Age of Agriculture; and 4thly, the Age of Commerce."[75] Key to these stages is Smith's understanding of property rights. He rejects the idea that property is among those things considered as "naturall rights." The most powerful cause "from which property may have its occasion" is occupation, "by which we get any thing into our power that was not the property of one before."[76] But the means by which we create and acquire property vary according to the form of society. Smith explains this principle at some length:

> In Tartary, where as we said the support of the inhabitants consist[s] in herds and flocks, *theft* is punished with immediate death; in North America, again, where the age of hunters subsists, theft is not much regarded. As there is almost no property amongst them, the only injury that can be done them is depriving them of their game. Few laws or regulations will [be] requisite in such an age of society, and these will not extend to any length, or be very rigorous in the punishments annexed to any infringements of property . . . . In the age of agriculture, they are not so much exposed to theft and open robbery [as are herds and flocks], but then there are many ways added in which property may be interrupted as the subjects of it are considerably extended. The laws therefore tho perhaps not so rigorous will be of a far greater number than amongst a nation of shepherds. In the age of commerce, as the subjects of property are greatly increased the laws must be proportionately multiplied. The more improved any society is and the greater length the severall means of supporting the inhabitants are carried, the greater will be the number of their laws and regulations necessary to maintain justice, and prevent infringement of the right to property.[77]

In addition, variations in "law"—the rules governing occupation of land, ownership of houses, forms of exchange, and inheritance practices—correspond to the modes of subsistence that characterize the successive "Ages" of man.[78]

The Scots are hardly the first to deploy the idea of "Ages" of human progress, but the distinctiveness of Smith's "four-stages theory" is worth emphasizing.[79] First, each stage corresponds to a particular mode of acquiring

75　Adam Smith, "Report of 1762–3," in *Lectures on Jurisprudence*, Indianapolis: Liberty Fund, 1982, p. 14 (para. 27).

76　Ibid., p. 13 (paras. 25–6).

77　Ibid., p. 16 (paras. 33–5).

78　Ibid., pp. 14–49 (paras. 27–115).

79　Meek, *Ignoble Savage*, chs. 1 and 2, gives a good account of the influences on the Scots and suggests Turgot as a co-inventor of the four-stages theory.

subsistence or, in a later language, mode of production. Second, as human societies advance through these successive modes of acquiring subsistence, we can expect corresponding changes (or, generally, improvements) in institutions, laws, and manners.[80] Human society gradually loses its rudeness; as the arts and industry advance so are the individuals in society refined.[81] Some, like Ronald Meek, see in this formulation a precursor of Marx's historical materialism,[82] as we shall see in Chapter 6, but our purpose at this point is less to trace out such influences than to examine the logic of "conjectural history."

"Conjectural history" combines three methodological principles: (1) the use of systematic comparison; (2) conjectures, premised on assimilating ancient peoples and contemporary savages as a single, coeval category; and (3) the equation of human infancy with the category of savagery. We have already noted that careful employment of historical comparisons gave eighteenth-century social thinkers' work the status of science: comparison reveals patterns of commonality and difference. These patterns are then built into causal chains that demonstrate society's orderly advance. Though comparison might, thereby, facilitate ranking of the relative achievements of societies in various areas of human endeavor, it does not yet justify the claims of a *stage* theory. Elaborating human history as a series of stages requires the second and third principles, allowing a series of carefully constructed, albeit "a priori conjectures."[83]

The claim that Scottish Enlightenment thinkers deployed "conjectures" has a long history. It is found first in Dugald Stewart's short biography of Adam Smith (1793).[84] For Stewart, Smith's challenge was to trace the entire history of human progress from its origins to the present. However, this project faces a seemingly insurmountable constraint—an absence of evidence from the early times of human society. This absence must be filled by conjecture, as Stewart explains:

> In this want of direct evidence, we are under a direct necessity of supplying the place of fact by conjecture; and when we are unable to ascertain

---

80 See Meek, *Ignoble Savage*, p. 2; Skinner, "Natural History," pp. 42–5; Berry, *Social Theory*, pp. 93–9.

81 See David Hume, "Of Refinement in the Arts," in *Essays: Moral, Political, Literary*, Indianapolis: Liberty Fund, 1985, 268–80. This language is characteristic of the Scots more generally. See Berry, *Social Theory*, pp. 180–1; Andrew Skinner, "Economic Theory," in Alexander Broadie (ed.) *The Cambridge Companion to the Scottish Enlightenment*, Cambridge: Cambridge University, 2003, pp. 183–4.

82 Ronald L. Meek, "The Scottish Contribution to Marxist Sociology," in J. Saville (ed.) *Democracy and the Labour Movement*, London: Lawrence and Wishart, 1954, 84–102.

83 See Aaron Garrett, "Anthropology: the 'Original' of Human Nature," in Alexander Broadie (ed.) *The Cambridge Companion to the Scottish Enlightenment*, Cambridge: Cambridge University, 2003, p. 81.

84 Dugald Stewart, "An Account of the Life and Writings of Adam Smith, L.L.D." in Adam Smith, *Essays on Philosophical Topics*, Indianapolis: Liberty Fund, 1982, 269–351.

how men have actually conducted themselves upon particular occasions, of considering in what manner they are likely to have proceeded, from the principles of their nature, and the circumstances of their external situation. In such inquiries, the detached facts which travels and voyages afford us, may frequently serve as land-marks to our speculations; and sometimes our conclusions *a priori*, may tend to confirm the credibility of facts, which, on a superficial view, appeared to be doubtful or incredible.

Nor are such theoretical views of human affairs subservient merely to the gratification of curiosity. In examining the history of mankind . . . when we cannot trace the process by which an event *has been* produced, it is often of importance to show how it *may have been* produced by natural causes.[85]

Stewart refers to "this species of philosophical investigation" as "*Theoretical or Conjectural History*."[86]

Smith's conjectural history does not entail a cavalier attitude toward evidence, but conjecture was key to Smith's ability to translate the amazing diversity of "facts" available to him into a stadial theory. He draws heavily on Lafitau's example. Lafitau's assimilation of the contemporary Indians and the Ancients allowed "facts" about each to inform an understanding of the other and Smith turned directly to him for evidence about the nature of early human societies. If the peoples of the ancient world, particularly the various barbarous groups and the contemporary savages, could be seen as at the same level of progress, then Smith could bundle them together in a common stage of human progress (or lack thereof). Thus, the Amerindians became exemplary of the category "savage" and books like Lafitau's became definitive sources on the first stage of human social development.

There was certainly justification for such a move in a time where Locke had declared: "in the beginning all the World was America."[87] Smith himself, as Dugald Stewart noted, provided a philosophical basis for this claim.[88] In "Considerations Concerning the First Formation of Languages," Smith begins with a thought experiment meant to illustrate the origins of language. Imagine two "savages," he asks, somehow isolated from society and without language. The savages "would naturally begin to form that language by which they would endeavor to make their mutual wants intelligible to each other, by uttering certain sounds, whenever they meant to denote certain objects."

85 Adam Smith, *Essays on Philosophical Topics*, p. 293.
86 Ibid.
87 John Locke, *Two Treatises of Government*, Cambridge: Cambridge University, 1988, Book II, p. 301.
88 Stewart, "An Account," pp. 292–3. Pagden, *European Encounters*, pp. 129–40 discusses the key role of conjectural theories of language in placing the Amerindians within Enlightenment historical schemes.

Smith prods the reader to follow his surmise (conjecture) that, as is the case with infants, the beginnings of language would be restricted to a process of nomination, a stream of proper names for "concrete" objects. Only later would our savages begin to learn and apply "a considerable degree of abstraction and generalization."[89] The analogy of childhood and savagery was a powerful one; it allowed Smith and his fellow Scots to treat materials about the Indians as evidence of the "infancy of society."[90] Combined with the historical optimism built into the idea of a progressive human nature, savagery could be seen as the initial stage in human societies' development from infancy to maturity. Where England, France and, potentially, Scotland serve as exemplary of human maturity, human progress also may be read backwards—from a commercial society to its earlier origins.[91]

The savage operates thereby as a null point against which Smith assessed the progress of his own and other commercial societies. In *The Wealth of Nations*, the paltry livelihood of the savage serves as the basis of comparison with the affluence brought by a developed division of labor:

> Among the savage nations of hunters and fishers, every individual who is able to work, is more or less employed in useful labour, and endeavors to provide, as well as he can, the necessaries and conveniences of life, for himself, or such of his family or tribe as are either too old, or too young, or too infirm to go a hunting and fishing. Such nations, however, are so miserably poor, that from mere want, they are frequently reduced, or, at least, think themselves reduced, to the necessity sometimes of directly destroying, and sometimes of abandoning their infants, their old people, and those inflicted with lingering disease, to perish with hunger, or to be devoured by wild beasts. Among civilized and thriving nations, on the contrary, though a great number of people do not labor at all, many of whom consume the produce of ten times, frequently of a hundred times more labour than the greater part of those who work; yet the produce of the whole labour of the society is so great, that all are often abundantly supplied, and a workman, even of the lowest and poorest order, if he is frugal and industrious, may enjoy a greater share of the necessaries and conveniences of life than it is possible for any savage to acquire.[92]

---

89 Adam Smith, "Considerations Concerning the First Formation of Languages," in Adam Smith, *Lectures on Rhetoric and Belles Lettres*, Indianapolis: Liberty Fund, 1985, pp. 203–6.

90 Berry, *Social Theory*, p. 92. See also Pittrock, "Historiography," p. 274.

91 Meek, *Ignoble Savage*, p. 222.

92 Adam Smith, *The Wealth of Nations*, p. 2 [Introduction]. See also Smith, *Wealth of Nations*, p. 16 [I, i] and "Report of 1762–3," *Lectures on Jurisprudence*, p. 338 [VI, 19]. Donald Winch, *Riches and Poverty: An Intellectual History of Political Economy in Britain, 1750–1834*, Cambridge: Cambridge University, 1996, p. 59, comments on this consistent pattern of comparison.

Where the division of labor distinguishes civilized society, savagery is conceived as "the *absence* of division of labor"[93] and, as Smith suggests above, is characterized consequently by a lack of refined manners—a lack of humanity. The savage, the rude, and the barbarous stand in polar opposition to the commercial and the civilized.[94]

Once you "know" the beginning and the end, filling in the intermediate steps of a stadial schema becomes easier. Indeed, it involves noting the finer but distinctive gradations that constitute an orderly creation. As Arthur Lovejoy notes, the principles of "the Great Chain of Being" were adapted to provide a model for Enlightenment scientific practice. If the idea of the "plenitude" of creation suggested nature's fullness or completeness, the principle of "continuity" suggested that the "qualitative differences of things . . . constitute [a] linear or continuous series"—that "all organisms can be arranged in one ascending sequence of forms" or "classes." Thus, nature's plenitude is necessarily presented as a set of scales of being. When the "Great Chain" is "temporalized" in the form of a theory of progress, "the scale of being thus becomes literally a ladder."[95] The task for Smith and others was simply to fill in the gaps or missing links between the origins of human development and its present apex in order to reflect nature's plenitude and continuity.

In this way, Smith and the Scots develop "conjectural history" as a moral science—a "universal history" of stages of human social and moral development.[96] Not only are patterns of social and moral advance visible to scientific inquiry, but scientific inquiry itself is seen to be a product of this process of human development, superceding "superstition, ignorance and dogma."[97]

93 David P. Levine, *Economic Studies: Contributions to the Critique of Economic Theory*, London: Routledge and Kegan Paul, 1977, p. 37.

94 Our emphasis on the savage past simplifies the story somewhat, since the Scots attended also to the distinction between barbarous and civilized societies; Rome's collapse in the face of barbarian invasion was a special preoccupation. See Nicholas and Peter Onuf, *Nations, Markets, and War: Modern History and the American Civil War*, Charlottesville: University of Virginia, 2006, pp. 93–7. Despite this, Smith and others often collapse the distinctions contained in the "four stages theory" to present a binary of civilized and savage/barbarous.

95 See Arthur O. Lovejoy, *The Great Chain of Being: A Study of the History of an Idea*, Cambridge: Harvard University, 1964, pp. 52, 55–6, 247. Lovejoy's account helps us see the "four-stages theory" as less of a mystery than does Pocock, though he does argue that the "concept of barbarism" was crucial to the formation of that theory. See J. G. A. Pocock, *Virtue, Commerce, and History: Essays on Political Thought and History, Chiefly in the Eighteenth Century*, Cambridge: Cambridge University, 1985, pp. 115–16. Why Smith settles on four stages is more difficult to explain.

96 Onuf and Onuf, *Nations, Markets, and War*, p. 27, argue: "Universal histories are conjectural, and conversely conjectural histories tend to be cast in universal terms." The thought experiment involved in conjecture seems to lead us in that direction: deducing from premises about human nature what must by necessity be the case is a recipe for universalistic claims.

97 Roger Smith, "Human Nature," pp. 100–1.

The human sciences diagnose the mysteries of the past and provide an account of their own power to discern those mysteries. And this is done without asserting the role of some external agent in history. All that is required is the gradual but persistent operation of human nature; moral advance is produced without plan or conscious design.[98] The order that social inquiry discerns is spontaneously generated—the "harmonious movements" of an "immense machine."[99]

Our difficulties with Smith's moral science partly parallel those we locate in Lafitau. Like Lafitau, Smith displaces the Indians in time; though contemporaneous, the Indians appear instead as exemplary of some initial age of human society. Relegated to the role of a null point and understood only in contradistinction to modern, civilized society, the Indians do not speak in their own terms; their histories are submerged in the historical constructions of the Enlightenment scientist. Indeed, the Indians do not speak at all. Their views of their own societies or of other, including European, societies are silenced. Thus, Smith's "conjectural history" extends beyond the fundamental religious uniformity posited by Lafitau to incorporate the whole of human social life. Comparison works to subordinate the diversity of human experience so that Smith can tell his universal moral story.

Ernst Cassirer suggests that all Enlightenment thinking struggled with the perennial problem of the relationship between the general and the particular.[100] We have seen the Scots searching for principles that reduce the diversity of experience to general patterns. Indeed, the Scots believed "the reduction of the diversity of institutions to some intelligible pattern" to be precisely "the hallmark of successful social science." This reduction serves an essential moral purpose in that it is not the particular but the universal that garners ethical significance.[101] As Poovey puts it, "the priority Newtonian philosophers assigned to universals and to the (invisible) laws of nature went hand in hand with a devaluation of the observed particular."[102] The Scots' "universal history" identifies those invisible laws, providing a moral and practical basis for guiding one's own society, particularly in its encounters with others. The rich diversity of "the ordinary" is repressed by the emphasis on the "exemplary," as Michael Shapiro puts it.[103] The "exemplary" is given the

---

98 See Wokler, "Anthropology," pp. 39–40.

99 Smith, *Theory of Moral Sentiments*, p. 316 [VII.iii.I.2]. That the Scots embrace an idea of spontaneous order is much noted. See especially Ronald Hamowy, *The Scottish Enlightenment and the Theory of Spontaneous Order*, Carbondale: Southern Illinois University, 1987; and Naeem Inayatullah, "Theories of Spontaneous Order," *Review of International Political Economy*, 1997, vol. 4, 319–48.

100 Ernst Cassirer, *The Philosophy of the Enlightenment*, Boston: Beacon, 1951, p. 197.

101 Berry, *Social Theory*, pp. 76, 88.

102 Mary Poovey, *A History of the Modern Fact: Problems of Knowledge in the Sciences of Wealth and Society*, Chicago: University of Chicago, 1998, p. 214.

103 Shapiro, *Reading "Adam Smith,"* p. 57.

power to drown out the examples and voices of the diverse particularities of human existence.

More precisely, Smith uses the "four-stages theory" to perform this repression, translating the diversity associated with a geocultural mapping of space into developmental time. Smith normally maps geocultural spaces onto what he calls "nations"—a term describing any social unit from tribes to empires.[104] Adjacent nations in Europe may exist in the same advanced temporal stage or may be separated in time by uneven processes of development. Nations far in physical distance from Europe might lay quite near to Europe temporally (e.g. China), though most of the rest of the world is seen as far-flung both spatially and temporally. The paradigmatic case, as seen above, opposes the social space of a developed, civilized Europe to savage or barbarous spaces in Africa, Asia, or the Americas. Smith's primary project in *The Wealth of Nations* is none other than to explain the differences in wealth associated with this temporal distance between savage and civilized nations (and secondarily those falling in between). What he does not explicitly allow is an overlap of temporal boundaries. The present is purified of the past. In this way, Smith also effects a compartmentalization of time into distinct national units; political economy forms as part and parcel of this Westphalianization of developmental time.[105]

Combining the previous two points, we can begin to understand how Smith barricades modern commercial society within a temporal/ethical fortress. Both time and space operate as a set of boundaries that demarcate "nations" by developmental level. Where a stage-theory of history informs moral judgment, the institutions and practices of the most-advanced serve as the basis for evaluating those of temporally backward nations. By implication, the civilized present is protected from the critical values and visions of "past" forms of society. As long as the boundary between the civilized and the savage remains clear, the values of a commercial society automatically take precedence: its values—wealth, social refinement—are the basis for assessing other (superseded) forms of society as well as for assessing its own successes and failures. A commercial society can only be evaluated as failing or succeeding *in its own terms*—by failing to provide wealth or refinement. Thus, even a critique from within the present validates that current societal forms occupy a superior temporal position.[106]

104 Though Onuf and Onuf, *Nations, Markets, and War*, pp. 14, 17, 49, suggest that Smith usually places his thinking within what is recognizably a society of states.

105 We have discussed the mutual constitution of international relations and modernization theory in Inayatullah and Blaney, *International Relations*, ch. 3. This points to R. B. J. Walker's characterization in *Inside/Outside: International Relations as Political Theory*, Cambridge: Cambridge University, 1993, of international relations as an effect of a separation of inside/outside. In this case, IPE is another effect of that separation.

106 Shapiro, *Reading "Adam Smith,"* p. 52; See also Oz-Salzberger, "Political Theory," pp. 169–70.

Like Lafitau, Smith "believed that traveling in space also meant traveling in time."[107] This equation of time and space makes sense where the "four-stages theory" rules the understanding of history. The social theorist moves through the ages of man as he consults contemporary narratives of far-away places and times. This is conceptual movement, since, as we have noted, Smith did not travel physically to the array of places he located along a temporal register. As Pagden evocatively puts it: the Enlightenment historians traveled from "text to text," searching for witnesses whose evidence might prove exemplary of the patterns of history.[108] Smith's temporal displacements are exemplary of the dominant patterns of Enlightenment modernity, a practice which infuses much of contemporary social theory and practice.[109] This suppression of the ethical "co-presence" of others serves to shield modern society from external criticism. It also purges all versions of global democracy that resist assimilation to a distinctly modern pattern.[110] Those who exemplify the pinnacle of human historical development comprise a chronocratic elite; their travels, whether real or conceptual, serve to confirm their status as scientists and purveyors of practical wisdom. This is only one aspect of the story, however. As we suggest in the next section, "co-presence" of the other is the "real"—something that the traveler both avoids and desires. Repression of the "co-presence" of self and other produces the double effect of the "symptomal mode": "co-presence" is what the traveler avoids in order to contain the other's potential criticism and it is what the traveler seeks so as to catalyze critical self-consciousness.[111]

III. The Savage Within the Walls of Political Economy

On the face of things, such critical consciousness hardly seems germane to Smith's purpose. In his hands history tends to assume a "providentialist" guise.[112] This is not to associate Smith with the Christian eschatology that shaped Lafitau's work but, following Becker, to see Smith as part of that movement that "demolished the Heavenly City of St. Augustine only to rebuild it with more up-to-date materials." Human life still appears as a "significant drama:" the "past, the present, and the future state of mankind"

107 Christopher Fox, "Introduction. How to Prepare a Noble Savage: The Spectacle of Human Science," in Christopher Fox, Roy Porter, and Robert Wokler (eds.) *Inventing Human Science: Eighteenth Century Domains*, Berkeley: University of California, 1995, p. 16.

108 Pagden, *European Encounters*, p. 86.

109 Our argument owes much to Johannes Fabian, *Time and the Other: How Anthropology Makes its Object*, New York: Columbia University, 1983.

110 See Inayatullah and Blaney, *International Relations*, pp. 116–23.

111 We discuss the "real" and the "symptomal mode" in the Introduction.

112 Skinner, "Economics and History," p. 22; Wokler, "Anthropology," pp. 34–5; Shapiro, *Reading 'Adam Smith,'* pp. xix–xxx, 50. But also see the contrary view of Fleischacker, *On Adam Smith's Wealth of Nations*, pp. 44–5. Poovey, *The Modern Fact*, p. 246, sees Smith's providentialism as only intermittent.

are reinterpreted as a theory of progress that replaces the classical cyclical theories or Christian eschatology.[113] Smith's optimism and political quietism are informed by his reading of the Stoics, who he describes approvingly:

> The ancient stoics were of opinion, that as the world was governed by the all-ruling providence of a wise, powerful, and good God, every single event ought to be regarded, as making a necessary part of the plan of the universe, and as tending to promote the general order and happiness of the whole: that the vices and follies of mankind, therefore, made as necessary a part of this plan as their wisdom or their virtue; and by that eternal art which educes good from ill, were made to tend equally to the prosperity and perfection of the great system of nature.[114]

As Smith moves from the events of the cosmos to those of society, the theological hue of this passage remains and the science of humankind takes on a mystical quality. Smith attests that we can see "[h]uman society" as that "immense machine," with its "harmonious movements" and "agreeable effects," when "we contemplate it in a certain abstract and philosophical light."[115] Despite this confidence in the beneficial effects of history, Smith's relative quietism is "haunted" by the "moral shortcomings in commercial society"[116]—what we have called the "wound of wealth."

Smith may indeed be haunted. But despite the substantial play he gives the moral failings of commercial society, pitting Enlightenment and counter-Enlightenment moments together at many points,[117] he works to restore the dominance of a salutary historical narrative after *every* critical discussion. Similarly, Smith cannot sustain the purity of the transition from savagery to civilization; it is neither a complete nor an absolute progression and, at numerous points, the repressed time of the other re-emerges to disturb the temporal confidence and security of commercial society. Even so, commercial society is consistently vindicated. While Smith recognizes that commercial society's impact on the great mass of workers is especially damaging, he nonetheless goes to great lengths to establish that a commercial society improves the lives of common people. Still, as we shall see, the suturing of the wound of wealth comes undone, as some of Smith's comparisons leave open

---

113 Becker, *Heavenly City*, pp. 31, 123–6.

114 Smith, *Theory of Moral Sentiments*, p. 36 [I.ii.3.4]. Smith's view has been described as a kind of Christian stoicism by Ingrid A. Merikoski, "The Challenge of Material Progress: The Scottish Enlightenment and Christian Stoicism," *The Journal of the Historical Society*, 2002, vol. II, pp. 60–5. Smith did not uncritically incorporate stoicism however. See Muller, *Adam Smith*, 96–8 and Fleischacker, *On Adam Smith's Wealth of Nations*, pp. 138–40.

115 Smith, *Theory of Moral Sentiments*, p. 316 [VII.iii.1.2].

116 Teichgraeber, "*Free Trade*," p. 128.

117 See Griswold, *Adam Smith and the Virtues*, pp. 7–21. He uses this language on p. 7.

greater space for a critical treatment of modern capitalism than he admits. The Enlightenment moment is not always dominant.

These rather serious cracks in the temporal fortress are necessarily present. If a benign God rules an orderly creation and human society runs like a beneficial machine, then even those who are sinful and unnatural are parts of a grand design. The difficulty associated with the Amerindians becomes not so much that they sin against God and conscience, as was the case for many prominent thinkers of earlier centuries, but how to account for their presence within the historical machine. Smith verges on tautology here. If even folly and vice produce prosperity, perfection, and agreeable effects, can there be anything that does not somehow produce order? Are there events or actions whose difference the machine cannot assimilate? Verging on tautology, as we shall see, is not the same as producing a tautological system; despite our intentions, something always escapes our desire and capacity to tame.[118] Indeed, Smith falls short of meeting the full expectations of his Stoic leanings; his time traveling depicts advantages held by the savages. He implies that the past and the future are under-specified and therefore more open-ended than suggested by his explicit historical narrative. As we shall see, he uneasily embraces projects of reform when nature does not automatically deliver.

Though Smith assumes that nations may be easily placed along a temporal hierarchy of development, spatial and temporal boundaries overlap disallowing any easily manageable and predictable moral cartography. The simplest example is that of the Scottish Highlanders who are spatially European but also can be equated with the Amerindians temporally.[119] Lacking in division of labor, wealth, and refinement, as Smith notes,[120] the Highlands appear as an "ethnological hinterland"[121] or a "sociological museum."[122] Though easily incorporated within the schema of "conjectural history," the Scottish Highlander's "backwardness" is more troubling because of its spatial and psychological closeness. Scottish universities had flourished for a century or

---

118 Carl Becker, *Heavenly City*, ch. 2, develops at length the paradox eighteenth-century thinkers create for themselves as they embrace nature. They insist on the mechanical and impersonal workings of nature but that threatens to undermine their claim that applying reason to nature allows us to discern good and evil. Good and evil not only have indistinguishable results, but reason does not give us access to truths about ultimate ends, as Hume warned. We might see this as an example of the "real" in a relatively abstract form.

119 Nick Onuf has warned us that, for Smith, the "Highlanders are reminders of the barbarian potential to reverse time." There is evidence, nonetheless, that the Highlanders are also equated to the Amerindians. See Margaret Connell Szasz, *Scottish Highlanders and Native Americans: Indigenous Education in the Eighteenth Century Atlantic World*, Norman: University of Oklahoma, 2007; and Arthur H. Williamson, "Scots, Indians and Empire: The Scottish Politics of Civilization 1519–1609," *Past and Present*, 1996, no. 150, 46–83.

120 Smith, "Report of 1762–3," *Lectures on Jurisprudence*, pp. 107, 146, 380; *Wealth of Nations*, pp. 21–2 [I, iii], 88–9 [I, viii].

121 Muller, *Adam Smith*, pp. 22–3.

122 Skinner, "Natural History," p. 37.

more and the union with England helped spur economic advancement in lowland cities to the extent that the figures of the Scottish Enlightenment would think of lowland Scotland as a commercial society. Most crucially, Scottish thought likely had surpassed that of England in its importance. Nevertheless, speaking an odd English and living amongst a less than refined populace, the Scots could not quite shake the sense of themselves as provincial.[123] Some distance might be created by associating the Highlanders with a backward state of mankind, but their otherness remained painfully near. These, perhaps internal others, also offered examples of the kind of generosity, martial spirit, and sense of honor that seemed eclipsed by commercial society, as Adam Ferguson is keen to stress.

The overlap of temporal boundaries is seen most forcefully when Smith blurs the analogy between infancy and adulthood that informs his universal history. Despite his tendency to oppose the savage and the civilized, Smith also suggests their commonality:

> A Child caresses the fruit that is agreeable to it, as it beats the stone that hurts it. The notions of a savage are not very different. The ancient Athenians, who solemnly punished the axe which had accidentally been the cause of the death of a man, erected altars, and offered sacrifices to the rainbow. Sentiments not unlike these, may sometimes, upon such occasions, begin to be felt *even* in the breasts of the most civilized, but are presently checked by the reflection, that the things are not their proper objects.[124]

Here Smith duplicates Lafitau's method of equating savages and the ancients, and reinforces the analogy to infancy. Simultaneously, however, Smith provides a moment where the sentiments of the child, the savage, and the ancient are seen by Smith to be co-present "*even* in the breasts of the most civilized." The irrational sentiments of children and savages—hurting stones, punishing axes, and offering sacrifices—exist within the manners of the most civilized of people. Overlaps between self and other, inside and outside space, developed and developing ages/stages erupt within Westphalianized developmental time. Here we have a problem that gets past Smith's stoic filters and spurs his energies. The wound is exposed and Smith seems worried that the social machine may not smooth such trespassing sentiments.

Despite this disclosure, Smith equivocates. He claims that a refinement of manners naturally accompanies the advance of human society. The normal operations of commercial society should promote a balance among the passions—the calm of one who possesses the virtues associated with

---

123 We draw on Berry, *Social Theory*, ch. 1; Muller, *Adam Smith*, ch. 1.
124 Smith, "History of Astronomy," pp. 48–9 [III.2]. Emphasis added.

self-command: moderation, generosity, humility, and frugality.[125] And yet, because he seems less than confident that the smoothing effect of the social machine will extend to all within society, Smith devotes considerable energy to assure us that the passions can in fact be restrained. Where the virtue of self-command fails, as it inevitably will, injuries to others must be punished by the rules of "justice."[126] Though justice is "but a negative virtue," in that it "only hinders us from hurting our neighbor," it is central to the tasks of civil government. Without justice, society breaks down into the atoms of inadequately self-commanded passions. Smith does not end here as might today's liberal economists. Even if a society based on justice alone is possible, other virtues should be cultivated. He charges the "civil magistrate" with "promoting the prosperity of the commonwealth, by establishing good discipline, and by discouraging every sort of vice and impropriety." Constraining injurious action is but one task; he "may also command mutual good offices to a certain degree."[127]

Smith returns to this point again in *Wealth of Nations*. The religious wars of the Reformation were not so far in the past that Smith could fail to register the fear of religious zeal and factionalism. But instead of seeing these as relics of the past, Smith locates them as a particular vulnerability of modern commercial society. In early stages of development, he notes, factions do not consolidate because people are divided into hundreds and thousands of sects. In modern societies, where the state has centralized religious practice, we must consider that

> [t]he interested and active zeal of religious teachers can be dangerous and troublesome only where there is, either but one sect tolerated in the society, or where the whole of a larger society is divided into two or three great sects; the teachers of each acting by concert, and under regular discipline and subordination.[128]

To ameliorate these modern problems of incivility—"faction and fanaticism" —which "have always been by far the greatest corrupters" of social order,[129] Smith turns, not to the smoothing effects of commerce, but to the *visible hand* of political intervention. In addition to the laws of "justice," he pins his hopes on public provision of education and entertainment. The most important intervention is the promotion of "the study of science and philosophy."

---

125   Emma Rothschild, *Economic Sentiments: Adam Smith, Condorcet, and the Enlightenment*, Cambridge: Harvard University, 2001, pp. 12–14, suggests that "fear" is constantly present in human society, but that commerce moderates those fears. See also Muller, *Adam Smith*, p. 95 and Teichgraeber, "*Free Trade*," pp. 13–14.

126   Smith, *Theory of Moral Sentiments*, pp. 80–1 [II.ii.I.6–8].

127   Ibid., pp. 81–2 [II.ii.I.8–9].

128   Smith, *Wealth of Nations*, p. 314 [V.I.iii].

129   Smith, *Theory of Moral Sentiments*, p. 156 [III.3.43].

For Smith, "[s]cience is the great antidote to the poison of enthusiasm and superstition." Where the cool and abstract light of philosophical reflection fails, which it will for many, Smith turns to a less demanding remedy: "the frequency and gaiety of the publick diversions." The state should encourage those, "who for their own interest would attempt, without scandal or indecency, to amuse and divert the people by painting and poetry, musick, dancing."[130]

Despite the tone of doubt, Smith is quick to restore civilized society to its position at the apex of human achievement. Though not without some redeeming traits, savages and barbarians seemingly lack much of what we associate with humanity:

> Barbarians . . . being obliged to smother and conceal the appearance of every passion, necessarily acquire the habits of falsehood and dissimulation. It is observed by all those who have been conversant with savage nations, whether in Asia, Africa, or America, that they are all equally impenetrable, and that, when they have a mind to conceal the truth, no examination is capable of drawing it from them. . . . The torture itself is incapable of making them confess. . . . The passions of the savage . . . are . . . mounted to the highest pitch of fury. Though he seldom shows any symptoms of anger, yet his vengeance, when he comes to give way to it, is always sanguinary and dreadful. The least affront drives him to despair. His countenance and discourse indeed are still sober and composed, and express nothing but the most perfect tranquility of mind: but his actions are often the most furious and violent.[131]

So "ignoble" does the savage appear that we cannot but appreciate the great changes history has wrought and a commercial society requires but minimal adjustment to sustain civility.

Two issues in particular—the corrupting effect of specialization and the problem of poverty—demonstrate how Smith's ambiguity may nevertheless be productive for contemporary debates in IPE. First in Smith's mind are the problems associated with specialization. In *Lectures on Jurisprudence*, we find a powerful set of passages concerning what Smith calls the "inconveniences" of the division of labor.[132] These concerns are largely replicated in Book V of *Wealth of Nations*:

> In the progress of the division of labor, the employment of the far greater part of those who live by labour, that is, of the great body of the people, comes to be confined to a few very simple operations, frequently to one

---

130 Smith, *Wealth of Nations*, p. 318 [V.I.iii].
131 Smith, *Theory of Moral Sentiments*, p. 208 [V.2.11].
132 Adam Smith, "Report Dated 1766," in *Lectures on Jurisprudence*, Indianapolis: Liberty Fund, 1982, pp. 539–41.

or two. But the understandings of the greater part of men are necessarily formed by their ordinary employments. The man whose whole life is spent in performing a few simple operations, the effects of which too are, always the same, or very nearly the same, has no occasion to exert his understanding, or to exercise his invention in finding out expedients for removing difficulties which never occur. He naturally loses, therefore, the habit of such exertion, and generally becomes as stupid and ignorant as it is possible for a human creature to become. The torpor of his mind renders him, not only incapable of relishing or bearing a part of any rational conversation, but of conceiving any generous, noble, or tender sentiment, and consequently of forming any just judgment concerning many even of the ordinary duties of private life. Of the great and extensive interests of his country, he is altogether incapable of judging; and unless very particular pains have been taken to render him otherwise, he is equally incapable of defending his country in war. The uniformity of his stationary life naturally corrupts the courage of his mind, and makes him regard with abhorrence the irregular, uncertain, and adventurous life of a soldier. It corrupts even the activity of his body, and renders him incapable of exerting his strength with vigor and perseverance, in any other employment than that to which he has been bred.[133]

Turning the common laborer into a specialist has a number of negative consequences: it makes him "stupid," incapable of "rational conversation," unable to "conceive any generous, noble, or tender sentiment," and therefore inept at forming judgments concerning the "duties of private life," as well as unqualified to ascertain the "interests of his country" and powerless in "defending his country in war." In direct contrast, the absence of a division of labor in savage and barbarous societies means that there exist "varied occupations" so that inventiveness is "kept alive;" "every man is a warrior" and a "statesman" so that each is able to "form a tolerable judgment concerning the interest of society." While specialization provides a material plenty unavailable to savage and barbarous societies, this advantage is "acquired at the expense of [the laborer's] intellectual, social, and martial virtues." The sober consequence is that, "in every improved and civilized society this is the state into which the laboring poor, that is, the great body of the people, must necessarily fall."[134]

It is difficult to tell from these passages if Smith believes, as he commonly asserts, that the working classes are better off than savages. So worried is Smith that he calls upon the state to provide public education. If the state does not provide such counter-measures, warns Smith, "all the nobler

133 Smith, *Wealth of Nations*, pp. 302–3 [V.iiii.i].
134 Ibid., pp. 303–4 [V.i.iii.ii].

parts of the human character may be, in a great measure, obliterated and extinguished in the great body of the people."[135]

In stark contrast to his quietist sensibilities, Smith advocates government intervention lest commercial society destroy the very thing it advances—ennobling and civilizing wealth.[136] Savage society here provides a mirror reflecting the moral failings of a commercial society but, in case we think Smith has become a romantic, he reasserts his dominant theme: a more limited division of labor is ethically irrelevant to the present. Savage and barbarous societies, though useful as a foil, are superseded temporally and cannot offer additional insight about how we might live today. Only a reformed commercial society combines wealth creation with a process of the refinement of character of human beings. The necessary degree of state reform of capitalism continues to spark debate, but this signals merely that Smith himself opens up and sustains a tension precisely where his name is often summoned to close debate—as with the claims of the Washington Consensus where free markets and free trade guarantee a path to a future Eden.[137]

Smith's treatment of poverty suggests a greater sensitivity to the wound of wealth and a more radical direction. He asserts again and again that a commercial society produces greater material well-being for common people than previous forms of society. Indeed, this is the key criterion by which to assess contemporary society:

> No society can surely be flourishing and happy, of which the far greater part of the members are poor and miserable. It is but equity, besides, that they who feed, cloath and lodge the whole body of the people, should have such a share of the produce of their own labour as to be themselves tolerably well fed, cloathed and lodged.[138]

Smith promises earlier in the text that, in a "well-governed society," the "universal opulence extends itself to the lowest ranks of the people."[139] In his discussion of wages, he explains that wages cannot fall below the level of subsistence (though, we should note, the mechanism involves higher infant mortality rates among the poor), and should rise above subsistence with vibrant growth.[140] However, such comparisons are not always entirely favorable to a commercial society where, Smith admits, we find "indigence:" "Wherever there is great property, there is great inequality. For one very rich

---

135 Smith, *Wealth of Nations*, p. 303 [V.i.ii.ii].
136 See Winch, *Riches and Poverty*, p. 119.
137 The recent revival of state regulation in the face of financial collapse may point us back to Smith's recessive moments of doubt and uncertainty.
138 Smith, *Wealth of Nations*, p. 88 [I.viii].
139 Ibid., p. 15 [I.i].
140 Ibid., I.viii, the chapter titled "Of the Wages of Labor." We take this up again in ch. 3.

man, there must be at least five hundred poor, and the affluence of the few supposes the indigence of the many."[141]

Smith in his stoic fashion unsurprisingly turns this gap into one of the major advantages of a commercial society. The relative well-being of the "ordinary day-labourer" is linked to the role of law in maintaining "the rich in the possession of their wealth against the violence and rapacity of the poor, and by that means preserve that usefull inequality in the fortunes of mankind which naturally and necessarily arises from the various degrees of capacity, industry, and diligence in the different individuals."[142] Similarly, in his parable of the "unfeeling landlord," Smith explains that the wealth of the landlord, though spent only on his selfish desires, employs vast numbers of people, spreading subsistence to many. The same "vain and insatiable desires" of the rich, lead them, as if "by an invisible hand," to "divide with the poor the produce of all their improvements" and "without intending it, without knowing it, advance the interest of the society."[143] Inequality, even where opulence and indigence stand in striking opposition, proves not the stark weakness that Smith seemed to indicate. Nonetheless, as our discussion of the damage done by relative poverty will indicate, Smith himself provides resources for challenging this sanguine conclusion.

A deeper tension may be read from the juxtaposition of rather puzzling comments about savage society. Smith suggests that "extremities of hunger" impose on the savage a kind of "Spartan discipline."[144] It is precisely this condition of scarcity that Smith believes a commercial society brings to an end. However, Smith also presents savages as possessed of the leisure to pursue music and dancing:

> It seems even to be amongst the most barbarous nations that the use and practice of them is both most frequent and most universal, as among the negroes of Africa and the savage tribes of America. In civilized nations, the inferior ranks of people have very little leisure. . . . Among savage nations, the great body of the people have frequently great intervals of leisure, and they have scarce any other amusement; they naturally, therefore, spend a great part of their time in almost the only one they have.[145]

This abundance of leisure for savages is quite damaging to Smith's claim

---

141 Smith, *Wealth of Nations*, p. 232 [V.i.b].
142 Smith, "Report of 1762–3," *Lectures on Jurisprudence*, p. 338 [vi.19].
143 Smith, *Theory of Moral Sentiments*, pp. 184–5 [IV.i.10–11]. This passage represents one of Smith's three uses of the language of the "invisible hand."
144 Ibid., p. 205 [V.2.9].
145 Adam Smith, "Of the Nature of that Imitation which Takes Place in What are Called the Imitative Arts," *Essays on Philosophical Subjects*, Indianapolis: Liberty Fund, 1980, p. 187 [II.i]. See a similar passage in *Wealth of Nations*, p. 219 [V.i.i], though Smith also suggests (p. 214 [V.i.i]) that the precarious subsistence of savages leaves them little time.

about the nature of their poverty. They cannot "spend a great part of their time" in music and dancing unless they can readily meet their minimum requirements as biological beings, a requirement that would seem to belie claims about their poverty.[146] And the lack of leisure of the masses of modern workers points in the opposite direction: it is modern men who live in a state of scarcity.

What might seem puzzling given Smith's historical narrative is perfectly consistent with Marshall Sahlins' account of the way of life of hunters and gatherers.[147] It is precisely the presence of abundant leisure that justifies treating hunters and gatherers as "affluent." Hunters and gatherers combine a low level of needs and wants with relatively plentiful means to meet those needs. Hence they are left with abundant free time. Turning the tables on the economist, Sahlins concludes that scarcity is instituted by "market-industrial society," not given by nature.[148] It is industrial society that shrinks leisure time by expanding needs and wants beyond the capacity of the society to readily produce them. Hegel, drawing perhaps on James Steuart, as we shall see in Chapters 3 and 5, notes similarly that the emergence of a modern market society itself promotes individual expression and self-seeking. And while that society generates wealth to support individualization and self-seeking, it also creates poverty and a subjugation of the least advantaged, such that the working classes suffer a loss of the "feeling of right, integrity and honor" that makes them part of society.[149]

Though we have perhaps tread into an area where Smith might claim that "absolute," not "relative," poverty is his concern, Smith's own language of "tolerably well" indicates that "necessities and conveniences" are both involved in understanding poverty. He recognizes quite well the social stigma and alienation accompanying relative poverty. "The poor man," Smith writes, "is ashamed of his poverty." This is hardly surprising, since indigence produces a kind of social invisibility: "The poor man goes out and comes in unheeded, and when in the midst of a crowd is in the same obscurity as if shut up in his own hovel."[150]

If this is so, even assuming Smith's most optimistic assumptions about a commercial society, we cannot sustain the claim that poverty is a condition

146 See Levine, *Economic Studies*, ch. 2, and Naeem Inayatullah, "Theories of Spontaneous Order."

147 Marshall Sahlins, *Stone Age Economics*, New York: Aldine, 1972. The relevant chapter is titled "The Original Affluent Society."

148 Sahlins, *Stone Age Economics*, p. 4.

149 G. W. F. Hegel, *Elements of the Philosophy of Right*, Cambridge: Cambridge University, 1991, pp. 182–3, 187, 241–4. Recent versions of this set of claims can be found in Majid Rahnema, "Poverty," in Wolfgang Sachs (ed.) *The Development Dictionary: A Guide to Knowledge as Power*, London: Zed Press, 1992, 158–76, and Serge Latouche, *In the Wake of the Affluent Society: An Exploration of Post-Development*, London: Zed Press, 1993, ch. 6.

150 Smith, *Theory of Moral Sentiments*, p. 51 [I.iii.2.2].

distinct to savage societies. Rather, poverty is strikingly associated with, perhaps even tied to the emergence of, commercial society. And, we might add, poverty cannot be assumed as an original condition for which commercial society is the antidote. Instead of the current bilateral and multilateral development efforts of the latest global war on poverty, mostly aimed at promoting economic growth to redress what is seen as a primordial backwardness, we might emulate the savages: create affluence by reducing our needs and wants. Our point is not so much that individuals in a capitalist society can simply decide their level and kind of neediness, though there may be some room for consciously shaping one's own consumer desires.[151] Rather, as we will see with Hegel, commercial society itself determines the shape of human neediness. If so, a much broader set of social transformations are required.

Like irrational sentiments and violent factionalism, poverty cannot be relegated to the past. Nor can our cognitive travels so readily ignore the moral resources offered by "superseded" forms of society. Nevertheless, as we have seen, Smith's dominant mode of relating to poverty (and other realities of commercial society) is either to reallocate them to the past or to dilute their potency by pointing to the advantages of the age of commerce. In effect he displaces these ills outside of the modern economy, into a sphere of past cultural forms that weigh on those so unlucky as to occupy a superseded time. But other elements in Smith's account seem to indicate that poverty and moral corruption are linked to and therefore not readily resolvable by a wealthy commercial society, serving as an (internal but repressed) other against which a commercial society is defined. Poverty and moral corruption appear, then, to return to Mitchell's terms, as a "constitutive outside"—that which modern society "depends on, even as it refuses to recognize, forebears and forces that escape its control."[152]

Despite Smith's dominant practice, there is part of him that engages this "constitutive other," the "real" of his travels in time and space. Perhaps inadvertently, he creates a horizon within which the other of commercial society ruptures the temporal walls of capitalism and becomes a living resource for political/ethical reflection. Eric Cheyfitz puts the point strikingly:

> Indian kinship economics, which, I . . . understand not as pre-capitalist but as anticapitalist, constitute a powerful *and continuing* critique of the waste of an expansive, acquisitive capitalism . . . that [Europe] could not *afford* to entertain. The loss in social vision was, and is, incalculable.[153]

---

151 For a call to "downsizing," see Juliet Schor, *The Overworked American: The Unexpected Decline of Leisure*, New York: Basic Books, 1992.

152 Timothy Mitchell, "The Stage of Modernity," in Timothy Mitchell (ed.) *Questions of Modernity*, Minneapolis: University of Minnesota, 2000, pp. 4–5, 12–13.

153 Eric Cheyfitz, "Savage Law," in Amy Kaplan and Donald E. Pease (eds.) *Cultures of United States Imperialism*, Durham: Duke University, 1993, p. 118.

Thus, Cheyfitz's *kinship economics*, Sahlin's *original affluent society* of hunters and gatherers, or Smith's *singing and dancing economy of savages* serve as a potential learning experience for a European commercial society and for those of us who remain immersed, in one way or another, in modern capitalism.

IV. Conclusion

Ashis Nandy notes that where we foreclose political and ethical recourse to various "pasts" (including those now being lived), we impair our capacity to imagine alternative "visions of the future."[154] We do not claim that Smith and the Scottish Enlightenment offer us nothing of value. On the contrary, Smith's engagement with the Amerindians is an important record of how we debate the merits and problems of a capitalist society. The significance of his cognitive travels, in Quentin Skinner's terms, is that they offer us a "repository of values we no longer endorse, of questions we no longer ask." The challenge is to recover this moment so that we might be able "to stand back from, and perhaps even to reappraise, some of our current assumptions and beliefs."[155] Seeing how Smith constructs a temporal fortress around commercial society alerts us, as Skinner might suggest, to a double legacy. On the one hand, the value of cultural histories and specific cultural practices are no defense against the charge of backwardness made by official development experts and non-governmental activists. Even past forms of modern capitalism are relegated to an ethically irretrievable past in order to justify the latest, restless phase of capital accumulation and social/political reform.[156] On the other hand, Smith's legacy also allows us, as Nandy recommends, to turn the tables—to consult the experiences of an outmoded past, including the savages he displaces from the present. Rereading Smith allows us to reflect on how other "pasts" can shape alternative futures.

Despite the temporal walls and spatial barriers Smith builds in order to protect liberal capitalism, his writings inspire us to retrieve alternative moments and recessive spaces that restore the co-presence of others as critical ethical resources. An encounter with the societies that the canonical Smith relegates to dead history might require contemporary IPE to hear and absorb the criticisms from beyond the temporal walls of capitalism. The chapters that follow are an effort to collect additional resources that might restore IPE's willingness to listen to the voices of others that lie both within and beyond.

---

154 Ashis Nandy, *Time Warps: Silent and Evasive Pasts in Indian Politics & Religion*, New Brunswick: Rutgers University, 2002, p. 5.

155 Quentin Skinner, *Liberty Before Liberalism*, Cambridge: Cambridge University, 1998, p. 112.

156 David Harvey, *The Condition of Postmodernity*, Oxford: Basil Blackwell, 1989, pp. 11–12.

3   Necro-economics and Steuart's geocultural political economy

James Steuart demonstrates less confidence in the great and harmonious machine than Smith. He explores and rejects the idea that a natural balance will reconcile the interests of all nations as they develop. Instead, commerce is fractured space: as countries' relative economic prospects rise and fall, neither the free market nor continued development can smooth out disturbances. Rather, states at different stages of industry must each pursue industrial policies adapted to their distinct developmental and cultural conditions. Further, unregulated markets fail to reconcile economic development with security and livelihood for the masses. Providence does not promise order, nor do our economic wounds necessarily serve a higher good. For Steuart, only skilled economic management can keep the forces of disorder in check.

We might say that Steuart's *An Inquiry into the Principles of Political Oeconomy* (1767) focuses our attention directly on the "real" of economic disorder that persists in civil society despite promises of natural harmony. Yet he betrays little of the anxiety that plagues Smith. Steuart's relative comfort with disorder is partly explained by his greater attention to difference; to a world of multiple and varied political economies. Perhaps his extended exile on the Continent sharpened his appreciation for the variety of economic circumstances offered by a commercial era,[1] and he presses us to see political economy as a theory and practice necessarily rooted in varying geocultural contexts. Or his sensitivity to Scottish dependence on England may have led him to see uneven development as part of a persistent wound of wealth that cannot be sutured by displacing the least advantaged into the past. Steuart's major themes—"defense of national difference, the sympathy with backward economies, the critique of English insularity"—"are all", as Davie notes,

---

1 Drawn to the cause of the restoration of the Scottish crown, the defeat of Prince Charles at Culloden left Steuart in exile. He was thus free to study the economic situation of France, Holland, and Germany. See the biographical essays by Andrew S. Skinner, "Biographical Sketch," in Sir James Steuart, *An Inquiry into the Principles of Political Oeconomy. Volume One*, Chicago: University of Chicago, 1966, xxi–lvii, and "Sir James Steuart: The Market and the State," *History of Economic Ideas*, 1993, vol. 1, 1–42.

"distillations of Scottish post-Union protest."[2] Thus, unlike Smith and Ferguson, he sees himself as a native of a colony, giving his work an anti-colonial (post-colonial?) vantage point perhaps. Most strikingly, Steuart repudiates what we call (see section IV below) Smith's necro-economics—the presentation of political economy as a set of natural laws to which states and peoples are utterly subject, even to the point of their very destruction. Indeed, he counters Smith's necro-economics with an endorsement of the state and the statesmen as agents of the common good. Though Steuart shares many of the Enlightenment sensibilities of his Scottish intellectual peers, he creates a distinctive international political economy (IPE) that is "un-English," and not simply because it is Scottish.[3]

Steuart's sensitivity to the embeddedness of economy in varying socio-cultural contexts moves us closer to an *intercultural* political economy.[4] But his appreciation of difference remains limited. Though skeptical of universal policy prescriptions, Steuart holds faithfully (much more so than Smith) to individual self-interest as the definitive motive for human action in a commercial age. Economic management that does not respect this motive, he warns, will fail to counter the instability of modern economic life. Thus, his understanding of difference is limited to modern European capitalisms; the socially embedded economies beyond European capitalisms remain closed to him. A rehabilitation of Steuart is compelling, nonetheless, since, as Deborah Redman has noted, both Steuart and Smith are asking the same question: "What kind of capitalism do we need?"[5] While this question limits our frame of reference, returning to their competing answers—to the intellectual battle-ground of their time[6]—may invigorate a similar debate in our own time. In this way, Steuart's work appears not as a superseded "precursor" of a properly liberal IPE, but as a distinctive view with "present significance."[7]

I. Difference and Science

Like Smith, Steuart sees himself as a man of science. His task, "reducing to principles, and forming into a regular science, the complicated interests of

---

2 G.E. Davie, "Anglophobe and Anglophil," *Scottish Journal of Political Economy*, 1967, vol. XIV, p. 291.

3 We paraphrase Joseph A. Schumpeter, *History of Economic Analysis*, New York: Oxford University, 1954, p. 176, note 9.

4 We tend to blur the notions of international and intercultural following our earlier work.

5 Deborah Redman, "Sir James Steuart's Statesman Revisited in Light of the Continental Influence," *Scottish Journal of Political Economy*, 1996, vol. 43, p. 66.

6 That Smith was responding to Steuart, though without mention of his name, is clear from Smith's own recorded comments. See E. G. West, *Adam Smith: The Man and his Works*, New Rochelle: Arlington House, 1969, pp. 167–8.

7 Robert Urquhart, "The Trade Wind, the Statesman and the System of Commerce: Sir James Steuart's Vision of Political Economy," *The European Journal of the History of Economic Thought*, 1996, vol. 3, p. 402.

domestic policy," bears more than a family resemblance to Smith's "science of the legislator." He aspires to a "general view of the domestic policy of the countries" he has seen; he aims for the "deduction of principles," instead of describing "a collection of institutions."[8] Nevertheless, he signals a break from the other Scots when he reminds readers that "no *general* rule can be laid down in political matters: every thing *there* must be considered according to the circumstances and spirit of the nations to which they relate."[9] As Urquhart suggests, "[o]f all political economists and economists, Steuart is the most insistent on the difficulty of the subject, on the need for caution and of avoiding overly general, absolute conclusions, especially those based on over-simplifications and reductive mechanisms."[10] Here the general is not necessarily exemplary and we find an openness to the "real" that is mostly absent in Smith.

The warning about "general" rules seems to parallel Smith's concerns about the "man of system," who "is often so enamoured with the supposed beauty of his own ideal plan of government, that he cannot suffer the smallest deviation from any part of it."[11] Nonetheless, we see Steuart's comments as a possible criticism of Smith's own practice and of those who have been inspired since that time to construct an economics stubbornly abstracted from the ubiquitous variations and contingencies of human social life.[12] As Steuart puts it, those that fall into "*Systèmes*" present "a chain of contingent consequences, drawn from a few fundamental maxims, adopted, perhaps rashly." "Such systems are mere conceits;" "they mislead the understanding."[13] Steuart acknowledges that his book "will not, in general, correspond to the meridian of national opinions anywhere." As if his readers would miss the point, he says just below: "If, from this work, I have any merit at all, it is by divesting myself of English notions, so far as to be able to expose in a fair light, the sentiments and policies of foreign nations, relatively to their own situation."[14] He calls the "scholar" to be "a citizen of the world," not a partisan of a particular national view.[15] We might imagine the Scottish and English literati bristling at the criticism.

Smith too gestures towards modifying policy according to circumstance. Free trade principles may be modified to account for issues of national

---

8 Sir James Steuart, *An Inquiry into the Principles of Political Oeconomy: Being an Essay on the Science of Domestic Policy in Free Nations*, Chicago: University of Chicago, 1966, pp. 6–7 [Preface].

9 Ibid., pp. 3–5 [Preface].

10 Urquhart, "The Trade Wind," p. 384.

11 Smith, *Theory of Moral Sentiments*, pp. 233–4 [VI.ii.2.17]. The pleasures of a system that pretends to master the world has been noted in the Preface, where we glossed Lacanian thinking.

12 We discuss Smith's commitment to the general over the particular in ch. 2.

13 Steuart, *Political Oeconomy*, p. 8 [Preface].

14 Ibid., pp. 4–5 [Preface].

15 Ibid., p. 17 [I. Introduction].

defense, the need for national revenue, and as a response to protection elsewhere. In his "Digression on the Corn Trade," Smith acknowledges that government may have to respect the irrational belief of citizens that access to subsistence goods should be secured even if he also believes that good policies and the force of history will erase this view gradually.[16] The main thread of Smith's chapters on trade policy suggests that outcomes dictated by the operation of universal economic laws cannot really be modified by public action.[17]

Steuart's emphasis is notably different:

> If one considers the variety which is found in different countries, in the distribution of property, subordination of classes, genius of the people, proceeding from the variety of forms of government, laws, climate, and manners, one may conclude, that the political oeconomy in each must necessarily be different, and that principles, however universally true, may become quite ineffectual in practice, without a sufficient preparation of the spirit of a people.[18]

Political economy appears as a "great art," adapted to circumstances, although aiming also "to be able to introduce a set of new and more useful institutions."[19] Steuart hints that policies are not simply dictated by economic laws or passive reflections of the national spirit. And changes in national spirit, rather than being the result of natural forces, require public discussion; popular knowledge of political economy must undergo transformation and new structures and institutions become popularly legitimated in a free nation. Starkly put, the operations of political economy are not best when they go on, like an invisible hand, behind the backs of people: "while people remain blind they are always distrustful."[20] Steuart's political economy appears less as mechanical and more a form of knowledgeable practice and political decision,[21] as contemporary constructivists would have it.[22]

Why the greater emphasis on difference? Many point to Steuart's first-hand knowledge of the varying developmental experiences of the countries of Europe[23] or, as we stressed above, his is also sensitivity to the issue of Scottish difference. We should not miss, however, that Steuart is intervening in an intellectual debate, featuring principally Hume and Montesquieu, on the

---

16 Adam Smith, *An Inquiry into the Nature and Causes of the Wealth of Nations*, edited by Edwin Cannan, Chicago: University of Chicago, 1976, pp. 48–9, 52 [IV.v].

17 Ibid., Book IV, ch. 2.

18 Steuart, *Political Oeconomy*, p. 17 [I.Introduction], though we might be skeptical of the idea of a "national spirit."

19 Ibid., p. 16 [I. Introduction].

20 Steuart develops this argument in Ibid., pp. 17–18 [I. Introduction]. The quotation is on p. 18.

21 See Urquhart, "The Trade Wind," p. 385.

22 See Mark Blyth, *Great Transformations: Economic Ideas and Institutional Change in the Twentieth Century*, Cambridge: Cambridge University, 2002.

23 Redman, "Sir James Steuart's Statesman," p. 51.

relativity of manners, customs, and institutions.[24] Montesquieu tends towards a "geographical determinism"—most (in)famously in his claim that the temperate zones are uniquely compatible with moral development. We noted in Chapter 2 that the Scots resisted Montesquieu's relativism, emphasizing instead common moral causes of development that support a "universal history." Hume insisted that "the character of a people is formed by custom" and that custom is formed by processes of sympathy and "imitation" across classes and, importantly, between peoples across time. The consequence is that "no natural determinism hinders the peaceful diffusion of the principles of good government." For Hume, there is no blockage or limit to the natural laws of the economy unfolding across all of global social space.[25]

Steuart stakes out a middle ground between Montesquieu's relativism and Hume's universal history. He rejects a climatic determinism that confines industry or the spirit of liberty to certain regions. But he is not thereby Humean. However much he shares Hume's notion that differences are due most importantly to moral causes (i.e., that they are cultural in more contemporary terms), he rejects that differences in national spirit can simply be overcome by foreign contact. Steuart thereby resists the suspicion that difference is suspect and must inevitably be superseded by uniformity.

Steuart lays out his argument in several steps. Like the other Scots, he accepts a certain uniformity of human nature: "Man we find acting uniformly in all ages, in all countries, and in all climates, from the principles of self-interest, duty or passion." But he immediately qualifies the point: "In this he is alike, in nothing else." Indeed, these common motives "produce such a variety of circumstances, that if we consider the species of animals in the creation, we shall find the individuals of no class so unlike to one another, as man to man." Varying circumstances generate differences "in opinion with regard to every thing almost which relates to our species." Varying modes of human sociability, "in all ages, climates and countries," produce "a certain modification of government and subordination established among them. Here again we are presented with as great a variety as there are different societies."[26]

Challenging our faith in the workings of impersonal laws, Steuart turns us to the unavoidable contingencies of politics: "government must be continually in action." But we are not left completely adrift; government policies must be "relative . . . to the spirit which prevails among" a people.[27]

24 We rely here on Paul E. Chamley, "The Conflict between Montesquieu and Hume: A Study of the Origins of Adam Smith's Universalism," in Andrew S. Skinner and Thomas Wilson (eds.) *Essays on Adam Smith*, Oxford: Clarendon, 1975, 274–305. See also Albert O. Hirschman, *The Passions and the Interests: Political Arguments for Capitalism before its Triumph*, Princeton: Princeton University, 1977, pp. 81–8.
25 Chamley, "Montesquieu and Hume," pp. 274, 279–80.
26 Steuart, *Political Oeconomy*, p. 20 [I.1].
27 Ibid., pp. 20–1 [I.1].

National differences in manners or form of government carry a sociological and ethical weight that Hume refuses them. Time has more duration for Steuart; it is sticky and persisting, but neither are differences eternally fixed: "the spirit of a nation changes according to circumstances."[28] It is precisely the task of leaders to generate positive change in the face of resistance. While Smith's emphasis on natural history displaces political intentions from political economy, Steuart, as Urquhart puts it, "rejects natural history in order to save human intention." He thereby rescues politics for political economy.[29]

This complex picture of stability and change might remind us of today's understanding of culture as possessing "structural" features, as at once settled and stable but also always changing and contestable. For Steuart, the implication is that particular national differences, though not eternal, should be respected by policymakers. Differences across space are neither necessarily nor appropriately erased by the workings of a uniformity-producing history. Thus, in an aside that apparently draws on his experience as a colonized Scot, he denies conquest its humanitarian impulse and justification:

> From these considerations, we may find the reason, why nothing is more difficult to bear than the government of conquerors, in spite of all their endeavours to render themselves agreeable to the conquered. Of this, experience has ever proved the truth, and princes are so much persuaded of it, that when a country is subdued in our days . . ., there is seldom any question of altering, but by very slow degrees and length of time, the established laws and customs of the inhabitants. I might safely say, there is no form of government upon earth so excellent in itself, as, necessarily, to make the people happy under it. Freedom itself, *imposed* upon a people groaning under the greatest slavery, will not make them happy, unless it is made to undergo certain modifications, relative to their established habits.[30]

Despite the power of this proposition, we doubt Steuart's judgment that princes (or presidents, or economists, or activists) have learned this lesson.

II. Difference, Development, and the Failure of Self-Regulation

In *Political Oeconomy*, Steuart continously draws our attention to a particular form of difference between countries: differing levels of economic development. Like Smith's *Wealth of Nations*, Steuart's work might be read as a

---

28 Steuart, *Political Oeconomy*, pp. 302–3 [II.25].

29 Robert Urquhart, "Reciprocating Monads: Individuals, *The Wealth of Nations*, and the Dream of Economic Science," *Scottish Journal of Political Science*, 1994, vol. 41, pp. 400–1.

30 Steuart, *Political Oeconomy*, p. 23 [I.2] and Book IV, chs. 7–8.

theory of development.[31] The savage figures prominently in defining the early or initial stages of human existence. Steuart associates savagery with an economy of self-subsistent beings, "living on the fruits of the earth." Lacking surplus, there can be no trade and little social division of labor.[32] And without substantial industry and exchange, there is no basis for talking about price. Steuart strongly suggests that the "laws" of economy that we elevate to such heights are restricted in their temporal and cultural application; they apply only to societies with more developed trade and industry.[33]

The key to national development, Steuart stresses, is a mutually reinforcing relationship between the growth of needs and the growth in trade and industry,[34] or what we might call, following Hegel, a system of mutual dependence. But it is only with the introduction of money as a *"universal measure of what is called value, and an adequate equivalent for any thing alienable,"* that needs are truly unleashed, since money itself becomes "a new object of want." As a consequence, "mankind become industrious, in turning their labour towards every object which may engage the rich to part with it."[35] Along with the growth of needs and wants goes greater industry and "time becomes precious."[36] We have now moved from a state of leisurely self-subsistence, hinted at by Smith and Sahlins, to the industry and scarcity of modern economy.

Indeed, the cultivation of scarcity is built into the very fibers of a commercial society. Steuart explains that merchants and manufacturers naturally do the work of creating a new "standard of taste."[37] Manufacturers create new goods that fulfill needs "which mankind seldom perceive to be such, till the way of removing them be contrived." Merchants buy the produce of the "pin-maker," for example, and move it where it will be demanded. The main task of the merchant is to create spaces for goods to be viewed and needs to be created; it is "nowhere so quickly" as in a "shop" that an individual discovers his wants; it is there that he is transformed into what we would recognize as a "consumer," a term Steuart uses:[38]

---

31 In this respect his theories are recognizably Scottish. Though S. R. Sen, *The Economics of Sir James Steuart*, Cambridge: Harvard University, 1957, pp. 19–20, claims that "Steuart is among the first authors to introduce an evolutionist approach in economics studies," including appearing "as a pioneer writer on the theory of economic growth," Ronald L. Meek, "The Rehabilitation of Sir James Steuart," in *Economics and Ideology and Other Essays: Studies in the Development of Economic Thought*, London: Chapman and Hall, 1967, p. 13, notes that this places him right at the center of the Scottish Enlightenment. See also Andrew Skinner, "Sir James Steuart: Economics and Politics," *Scottish Journal of Political Economy*, 1962, vol. 9, 17–22; and Redman, "Sir James Steuart's Statesman," pp. 52–3.

32 Steuart, *Political Oeconomy*, pp. 34–6 [I.4].

33 Ibid., pp. 340–1 [II.28].

34 Ibid., pp. 150–1 [II.1]. This aspect of Steuart's work is stressed by Robert V. Eagly, "Sir James Steuart and the 'Aspiration Effect'," *Economica* (new series), 1961, vol. 28, 53–61.

35 Steuart, *Political Oeconomy*, pp. 44–5 [I.6].

36 Ibid., p. 150 [II.1].

37 Ibid., p. 46 [I.6].

38 Ibid., pp. 156–8 [II.3].

Everything he sees appears either necessary, or at least convenient; and he begins to wonder (especially if he be rich) how he could have been so long without that which the ingenuity of the workman alone had invented, in order that from the novelty it might excite his desire; for when it is bought, he will never once think more of it perhaps, nor ever apply it to the use for which it first appeared so necessary.[39]

"Physical necessities" are superseded by what he calls "political necessities." These point at once to their conventional or social character, being acquired by "habit and education," but also to their role in informing social "ranks."[40] In an analysis that may well have influenced Hegel's characterization of poverty, Steuart establishes neediness as a social condition and points, thereby, to the distinctive quality of needs and deprivation in a commercial society—what we have called the wound of wealth.

In all of this, Steuart assumes what we might call a closed economy, but soon he introduces foreign trade. With trade, countries of very different levels of economic development and conflicting interests come into contact:

While there are different states, there must be separate interests; and when no one statesman is found at the head of these interests, there can be no such thing as a common good; and when there is no common good, every interest must be considered separately.[41]

Trade inevitably involves countries in a competition among nations and their traders. Steuart is one of the first to discuss the "balance of trade" and how shifting balances affect the health of a country's economy in the short and long run. But there is no natural harmony: a balance can be maintained only where there is a relative equality among nations.[42]

Trade does have advantages, however. It augments wealth, promotes continuing industry and ingenuity, and helps maintain a decent standard of living for virtually the entire population. At the same time, livelihood is linked to the volatility of international exchanges. Trade, as Steuart puts it, is a system of "universal emulation" where "the most industrious, the most ingenious, and the most frugal will constantly carry off the prize." Even the "richest men in a trading system have no security against poverty," by which he means a sharp decline in social status. The consequences for masses of workers are more severe so that the term "poverty" is more telling.[43]

---

39 Steuart, *Political Oeconomy*, p. 157 [II.3].
40 Ibid., Book II, ch. 11.
41 Ibid., p. 365 [II. 29].
42 Ibid., Book II, ch. 29. Jacob Viner, *Studies in the Theory of International Trade*, New York: Harper, 1937, p. 10, argues that Steuart is one of the first to deploy the notion of a "favourable balance of trade."
43 Steuart, *Political Oeconomy*, Book II, ch. 9.

Steuart thus positions himself in opposition to other Scots in the so-called "rich country-poor country debate" in which the orderliness of international trade and the prospects for sustaining or acquiring wealth were heatedly discussed.[44]

Hume's 1752 essays are exemplary of the dominant position. He argues that natural mechanisms work to disperse wealth across countries such that state intervention to reduce imports (to defend the position of the rich country) or artificially stimulate economic progress (to augment the position of the poor country) are unnecessary and undesirable. On the one side, poor countries are not permanently disadvantaged because "the advantages initially gained" by some "are compensated . . . by the low price of labor." "Manufactures" will, then, "gradually shift their places, leaving these countries and provinces which they have already enriched, and flying to others." The key equilibrating mechanism involves the flow of specie into the successful trading nation that, by "a maxim almost self-evident," raises the prices of commodities and shifts trade in another state's direction.[45] On the other side, Hume insists that rich countries will not suffer substantially. As in later theories of product life-cycles or the new international division of labor,[46] "the finest arts" will remain in the centers of production, with "coarser" arts alone moving to "remote countries."[47] The process of specie outflow, which signals some industries to move, will also shift resources to domestic production or to upgrade exports.[48] Hume resorts to a powerful image in equating this harmonizing mechanism with "the course of nature:" "All water, wherever it communicates, remains always at a level. Ask naturalists the reason: they tell you, that, were it to be raised in one place, the superior gravity of that part not being balanced, must depress it, till it meet a counterpoise."[49]

Steuart does not share Hume's faith; the "course of nature" is too unruly to trust in the unbridled operation of providence. He responds directly to Hume in Book II, Chapters 28 and 29, where he suggests that we can expect no simple relation between shifts in the quantum of specie and changes in the quantum of money in circulation or of the general level of prices. The money

---

44 We draw on Istvan Hont, "The 'Rich Country-Poor Country' Debate in Scottish Political Economy," in Istvan Hont and Michael Ignatieff (eds.) *Wealth and Virtue: The Shaping of Political Economy in the Scottish Enlightenment*, Cambridge: Cambridge University, 1985, 271–316, for our treatment of Hume.

45 David Hume, "Of Money," in *Essays: Moral, Political, and Literary*, Indianapolis: Liberty Fund, 1985, pp. 283–4, 290.

46 See Raymond Vernon, "International Investment and International Trade in the Product Life Cycle," *Quarterly Journal of Economics*, 1966, vol. 80, 190–207; Folker Froebel, Jurgen Heinrich, and Otto Kreye, *The New International Division of Labor*, Cambridge: Cambridge University, 1980.

47 Quoted in Hont, "The 'Rich Country-Poor Country' Debate," p. 276.

48 See Michael I. Duke, "David Hume and Monetary Adjustment," *History of Political Economy*, 1979, vol. 11, 572–87.

49 David Hume, "Of the Balance of Trade," in *Essays*, p. 312.

supply also is affected by the velocity of money and government policy, and it is wrong to reason in terms of general shifts in price levels; price changes will occur only as mediated by the competitive conditions for each commodity.[50] As Andrew Skinner notes, Hayek himself dismisses theories like Hume's that simply "postulate ... relationships between magnitudes" as "*theoretically unsound*" because it is not clear how these magnitudes operate through the actual decisions of individuals.[51] Steuart justifiably argues that we cannot be certain that shifts in specie will be self-correcting; they are as likely to be self-reinforcing, as perhaps evidenced by financial crises in East Asia, Latin America, and Russia in the 1990s and the US and the world generally as we write.

Steuart is therefore less sanguine than Hume about the prospects of the rich country necessarily being able to secure its well-being in such a fluid situation or about the capacity of many poor countries to make large advances in a world in which they are weak competitors, without, that is, government strategies to compensate. Most importantly, he argues that an unchecked adjustment process is very costly, reducing demand for local products, deflating the economy, and starving or dislocating parts of the population.[52] To return to Hume's analogy: water levels may gradually rise above people's heads. Or extending Hume's image, water reaching its level might flow violently across the countryside, smashing structures and carrying away families. Where the flows of specie and adjustments of prices are abrupt, of the instantaneous kind that contemporary economics assumes and perhaps illustrated by various financial panics and crises, the repercussions will include "annihilating both industry and the industrious."[53]

International inequality is not an issue to be dodged via equilibrating metaphors. Steuart makes clear that unequal relationships of trade subordinate the weaker to the stronger, since, as in feudal relationships, some control other's "means of procuring subsistence." Modern exchange economies obviate this subordination to some degree; there is a more reciprocal dependence where each must come to the market with an "adequate equivalent" to exchange.[54] However, a country with a "passive" stance towards international commerce—importing what it wants in exchange for an accidental surplus—will find itself "at the mercy of those who are active," unless, like today's producers of high-value natural resources, they are "greatly favored, indeed,

50 Andew S. Skinner, "Money and Prices: A Critique of the Quantity Theory," *Scottish Journal of Political Economy*, 1967, vol. 14, pp. 287–8.

51 Ibid., p. 289. Skinner is referring to Friedrich Hayek's *Prices and Production*, New York: Augustus M. Kelley, 1967.

52 See Walter Eltis, "Sir James Steuart's Corporate State," in. R. D. Collison Black (ed.) *Ideas in Economics*, Totawa: Barnes and Noble, 1986, pp. 49–52.

53 Steuart, *Political Oeconomy*, Book II, ch. 29.

54 Ibid., Book II, ch. 13. Steuart uses the notion of an "adequate equivalent" at various points. See also p. 310 [II. 26]. Steuart's theory of dependence is discussed by Skinner, "Economics and Politics," pp. 23–4.

by natural advantages, or by a constant flux of gold and silver."[55] Or to update Steuart, absent such resources, international obligations accumulate, loans pile up, international institutions intervene, and the country is structurally adjusted to the immediate and, probably, long-term disadvantage of "industry and the industrious."

Lest we are charged with anachronism, Steuart recognizes these relations of dependence as colonial in character.[56] Early in *Political Oeconomy*, he describes the competitive strategies used by traders from the advanced economies as they face relatively undeveloped areas. The story is familiar. Traders, serving the function of merchants above, study "the taste of the strangers," hoping "to captivate their desires by every possible means." Once the tastes of the local people are changed so that the goods from the more advanced countries appear as needs, they are, as Steuart puts it, "fit for the slaughter." In general, as his illustrations make clear, the backward society provides various natural products in exchange for manufactured goods or, over time, they may improve agriculture to increase the amount of goods they have to exchange. Though this process does induce some "refinement" in backward areas, Steuart understands that many impacts of trade are what we might call "path dependent," reinforcing the advantages of the early innovators and the disadvantages of the late-developers. Spatial difference resists uniformity and, unless these "unpolished nations in the world" quickly learn the ways of industry and commerce, they may remain "perpetually [at] a disadvantage," placing national independence at risk. Where the natives fail to develop agriculture and natural trade goods are exhausted or lose their value, the stronger trading nation may take it upon itself to force labor (hut or labor taxes were common) as a way of instigating agricultural change. There will be little inclination to promote, or even allow, the development of local traders, because this would shift the competitive conditions between the advanced and the backward. Steuart's account suffers little in comparison with more contemporary work on colonial enclave economies and the impact of the expansion of neediness on the trade relations and development of Third World countries.[57]

---

55 Steuart, *Political Oeconomy*, p. 180. Steuart may have had Spain and Portugal in mind as countries able to live beyond their means to produce because of imports of precious metals from the New World. Today we might think of oil exporters. This general principle of unequal dependence was laid out for modern readers by A. O. Hirschman, *National Power and the Structure of International Trade*, Berkeley: University of California, 1945. For an application of Hirschman to the conditions of contemporary Third World states, see James A. Caporaso, "Dependence, Dependency, and Power in the Global System: A Structural and Behavioral Analysis," *International Organization*, 1978, vol. 32, 13–44.

56 We draw here on Steuart, *Political Oeconomy*, Book II, chs. 5 and 6.

57 On the colonial enclave, see Eric Wolf, *Europe and the People without History*, Berkeley: University of California, 1982, and E. A. Brett, *Colonialism and Underdevelopment in East Africa: The Politics of Economic Change, 1919–39*, Farnham: Ashgate, 1992. Ragnar Nurkse, *Problems of Capital Formation in Underdeveloped Countries and Patterns of Trade and Development*, New York: Oxford, 1967, pp. 57–81, suggests that adopting modern consumer aspirations may stunt local capital formation by depriving the country of savings.

Steuart recognizes that the advantage is not always permanent, but neither does he promote Hume's hydrological equilibrium. The world economy is constantly in flux; economies rise and fall.[58] Steuart organizes and fixes this flux with a set of general categories into which all trading states fall, more or less, at any one point in chronological time.[59] "[T]he whole region of trade" can be "divided into its different districts: infant, foreign, and inland." "Infant trade" exists where a country's industry focuses on supplying most of its own wants, not yet moving into an emphasis on exporting to foreign markets. "Foreign trade" describes the circumstances of a thriving trading nation that must constantly guard its competitive position, since that might be undermined by high profits and a growing taste for luxury or some other shift in circumstance. "Inland trade" describes a situation where a country turns inward as a response to a decline occasioned by loss of its industries' competitive position. Steuart believes these heuristic devices might be applied as easily to regions within countries or to particular industries.[60] Though he uses a spatial metaphor, "district," it is clear that these are also temporal categories—different times in the *cycles*, not stages, of commercial nations. He gives volumes of advice to statesman, tailored to these three different spatio-temporal circumstances, qualified by numerous contingencies and spread throughout the text, making summary difficult. We will restrict ourselves to his advice to those states (regions or industries) at the infant stage, that is, what we now call late-developers.

Steuart assumes that the global division of labor is not natural, but contrived—a product of moral causes alterable over time.[61] In a program reminding one of Japan's MITI or the mechanisms of industrial coordination in South Korea, the statesman devises policies appropriate to the "developmental state:"[62]

> The statesman who resolves to improve this infant trade into foreign commerce, must examine the wants of other nations, and consider the productions of his own country. He must then determine, what kinds of manufactures are best adapted for supplying the first, and for consuming the latter. He must introduce the use of such manufactures among his subjects; and endeavour to extend his population and agriculture. . . .

58 Steuart, *Political Oeconomy*, p. 203 [II.12]. See also Book II, chs. 17, and 18.
59 On Steuart's account of trade, see Sen, *The Economics of James Steuart*, ch. VI; Skinner, "Market and State," pp. 23–8.
60 Ibid., Book II, ch. 19.
61 Ibid., pp. 238–9 [II.16].
62 The classic work is Chalmers Johnson, *MITI and the Japanese Miracle: The Growth of Industrial Policy, 1925–1975*, Stanford: Stanford University, 1982. On the NICS and industrialization policies more generally, see Peter Evans, *Embedded Autonomy: States and Industrial Transformation*, Princeton: Princeton University, 1995; and Meredith Woo-Cumings (ed.) *The Developmental State*, Ithaca: Cornell University, 1999.

He must provide his people with the best masters; he must supply them with every useful machine; . . .

A considerable time must of necessity be required to bring a people to a dexterity in manufactures. The branches of these are many; and every one requires a particular slight of hand, which cannot be acquired but under the eye of a skilful master, able to point out the rudiments of the art. People do not perceive this inconvenience, in countries where the arts are already introduced; and many a projector has been ruined for want of attention to it.[63]

In contemporary terms, late-development entails a healthy agricultural sector, technology transfer, and enhanced human capital.

Still in parallel to the "development state," the statesman should leverage the one advantage countries in the "infancy of industry" usually possess, that is, "cheap labour," warning leaders to guard against labor shortages that raise costs as industry (and specialization) develops.[64] The new industrializer's advantage may depend on sustaining a spirit of industriousness and frugality relative to other countries' "luxurious consumers."[65] Frugality may be secured temporarily by protecting the domestic market from foreign luxury goods.[66] In particular, he recommends identifying imports that might be replaced over time by domestic production (i.e., import substitution),[67] but this trading state also should strive to produce higher value-added goods for export.[68] Soon the limited domestic market begins to appear as a break on industry (particularly if foreign markets are saturated or dry up) and, at that point, Steuart recommends a gradual "introduction of luxury, or superfluous consumption."[69] The key to late-industrialization is that the statesman should maintain an active competition policy, assuring enough competition among both suppliers and demanders so that prices remain relatively low and only fluctuate in a narrow band. In this way, goods remain competitive in foreign markets for a longer time period.[70] The long-term danger of creating or allowing monopolies is clear to Steuart.[71]

With effective policies and favorable international conditions, success in trade may become self-perpetuating but, where such policies fail, the statesman might consider reducing dependence on trade, a turn to self-reliance, as

---

63 Steuart, *Political Oeconomy*, p. 262 [II.19].
64 Ibid., p. 199 [II.11]. He also warns (pp. 275–6 [II.21]) of possible abuses of workers as their necessity for free time is taxed for the sake of international competitiveness.
65 Ibid., pp. 228–9 [II.15].
66 Ibid., pp. 263–4 [II.19]. See also II.150.
67 Ibid., pp. 292–3 [II.24].
68 We are extrapolating from Ibid., p. 295 [II.24].
69 Ibid., p. 229 [II.15].
70 Ibid., p. 200 [II.11].
71 Ibid., pp. 273–4 [II.21] and II.169–70.

we might call it. Though the costs in loss of wealth are high, it is important that those costs are shared. It may also be the case that "happiness, security, and ease" may come without great wealth[72] and frugality may be re-learned as a virtue.[73] Steuart's advice to the failed competitor may seem to entail reversion to an earlier, pre-commercial stage, but we read the point differently; he seems to be identifying a cyclical pattern *within* modernity itself. Though he translates the spatial heterogeneity of capitalism as differences in temporality (as IPE continues to do: uneven development; backward or advanced), these stages are not simply successive; developmental time runs in both directions and states cannot escape the flux of the global economy. At best they manage it to their advantage. At worst, it crushes them. The "real" must be faced; it cannot be wished away with fanciful notions of self-equilibrating mechanisms.

III. The Statesman and the Ambiguous Laws of the Market

Steuart, like all the Scots, makes his argument partly against the backdrop of the language of Renaissance humanism and its concern with processes not only of growth, but also of corruption and decay.[74] For Smith, a natural order smoothes out irregularities, which only the political economist, who posits such order as the basis of his science, can identify. Steuart, like Ferguson as we shall see, places *Fortuna*, the goddess of fortune, at the center of civil society: domestic and international markets alike may bring both gain and destruction to individuals and polities. Market failures, as we might put it today, abound. This potential disorder or disharmony may be managed, but it cannot be completely erased. Strikingly, though, Steuart's confidence in economic management is buttressed by a faith in the uniformity of economic laws.

He shows his faith in such laws through an image that Enlightenment thinkers found compelling—the watch. Steuart asks the reader to think of the economy like a watch, but not the watch of the divine author, exemplifying perfect craftsmanship. His watch is of human construction:

> watches . . . are continually going wrong; sometimes the spring is found too weak, at other times too strong for the machine: and when the wheels are not made according to a determined proportion, . . . they do not tally well with one another; then the machine stops, and if it be forced, some part gives way; and the workman's hand becomes necessary to set it right.[75]

72 Steuart, *Political Oeconomy*, p. 213 [II.13].
73 Ibid., p. 244 [II.17]. See Steuart's advice for declining powers (Book II, chs. 22, 23, and 24).
74 Ruhdan Doujon, "Steuart's Position on Economic Progress," *The European Journal of the History of Economic Thought*, 1994, vol. 1, 495–518, makes this central to his interpretation of Steuart.
75 Steuart, *Political Oeconomy*, p. 217 [II.13].

If human social life is more like Steuart's watch, then the automatic harmony of Smith's political economy trades in illusions. The economy requires not just Smith's night watchman but also a watch repairman. Worse, Smith's *laissez-faire* imaginary serves the dominance of early-developers like England. Late-developers, like Scotland, are deprived of the very economic strategies they require to produce economic growth and political independence.[76]

The success of the statesman depends, nonetheless, on the operation of economic laws. The predictability of self-interested action allows statesmen to calculate the effects of their actions. Steuart repeats again and again that "the principle of self-interest" is the "ruling principle" of economics; it serves as the "main spring, the only motive which a statesman should make use of, to engage a free people to concur in the plans which he lays down."[77] In introducing the image of the statesman as a ship's captain,[78] Steuart says:

> the abilities of a statesman are discovered, in directing and conducting what I call the delicacy of national competition. We shall then observe him imitating the mariners, who do not take in their sails when the wind falls calm, but keep them trimmed and ready to profit of the least breath of a favourable gale. Let me follow my comparison: the trading nations of Europe represent a fleet of ships, every one striving who shall get first to a certain port. The statesman of each is the master. The same wind blows upon all; and this wind is the principle of self-interest, which engages every consumer to seek the cheapest and the best market. No trade wind can be more general, or more constant than this; the natural advantage of each country represent this degree of goodness of each vessel; but the master who sails with the greatest dexterity, and he who can lay his rivals under the lee of his sails, will, caeteris paribus, undoubtedly get before them, and maintain his advantage.[79]

Able mariners can achieve much as long as they can read the signs that nature provides. That is, statesmen can achieve macroeconomic management as long as they respect the microeconomic forces at play.

Statesmen have a large role, but Steuart's political economy is not authoritarian. He prefers republican forms, opposing any sort of arbitrary power. Nor is he a precursor of central planning; he recommends acting with "the

---

76 Davie, "Anglophobe and Anglophil," pp. 295–6, 299. Eric Helleiner, "Economic Nationalism as a Challenge to Economic Liberalism? Lessons from the 19th Century," *International Studies Quarterly*, 2002, vol. 46, 307–29, argues it is difficult not to see liberal economic prescriptions as a nationalist tool.

77 Ibid., pp. 142–3 [II.Introduction].

78 Urquhart, "the Trade Wind," p. 79, stresses this image as "animating" Steuart's vision of political economy.

79 Steuart, *Political Oeconomy*, p. 203 [II.12].

gentlest hand."[80] Statesmen exercise what Steuart calls "an artful hand," as if in contrast with the idea of the "invisible hand."[81] He believes that economic management is consistent with the liberal spirit of a commercial age. Certainly statesmen are constrained by the laws of self-interest operating in the economy—"the most effective bridle ever was invented against the folly of despotism."[82] Further, common causes can garner support among the population only if presented openly and clearly by able statesmen. The restrictions on freedom entailed will not be resisted if the population can see the good ends that result. As Steuart notes, the growing role of government in everyday social life has come to be accepted as normal and as consistent with liberty.[83]

The main motive for the use of regulatory tools is a common cause: to guarantee adequate subsistence production to support the large class of "free hands" who do the work. This explains why Steuart is so attentive to the dangers of excessive competition among buyers when subsistence is in short supply.[84] Competition among free hands may reduce their wages to starvation levels: "From this results the principal cause of decay in modern states: it results from liberty, and is inseparably connected with it." After all, it is "[u]pon the proper employment of the free hands" that "the prosperity of every state must depend." Statesmen should make sure that mutual dependence is maintained; individuals should not be allowed to become so vulnerable that they fall into the subordination characteristic of societies prior to an era of liberty.[85]

Where demand collapses, statesmen must act to compensate for the loss of employment "by making soldiers of them; by employing them in public works; or by sending them out of the country to become useful in its colonies."[86] In an analysis that may prefigure Keynes, as many have noted,[87] Steuart explains that one especially useful tool is to monitor and adjust

---

80 Steuart, *Political Oeconomy*, p. 210 [II.13], pp. 278–9 [II.22]. An assertion to the contrary, by Gary M. Anderson and Robert D. Tolliver, "Sir James Steuart as the Apotheosis of Mercantilism and his Relation to Adam Smith," *Southern Economic Journal*, 1984, vol. 51, 456–68, seems unwarranted. It makes more sense to claim, as does Redman, "Sir James Steuart's Statesman," pp. 55–6, that Steuart's notion of freedom contains elements of classical ideas of discipline. In this, he is much like Smith.

81 Steuart, *Political Oeconomy*, p. 201 [II.11]. Steuart writes well before *The Wealth of Nations*, though he would have been familiar with Smith's use of the term in *Theory of Moral Sentiments*.

82 Ibid., pp. 278–9 [II.22].

83 Ibid., Book I, ch. 2.

84 Ibid., p. 187 [II.9].

85 Ibid., pp. 76–7 [I.12] and pp. 228–30 [II.15].

86 Ibid., pp. 202–3 [II.12]. Steuart may be the source of Hegel's view of colonies as a solution for poverty. See Gabriel Paquette, "Hegel's Analysis of Colonialism and Its Roots in Scottish Political Economy," *CLIO*, 2003, vol. 32, pp. 420, 430–2.

87 See Sen, *The Economics of James Steuart*, ch. 9; Redman, "Sir James Steuart's Statesman," p. 50.

the money supply so as to avoid stagnation.[88] Or just below, he suggests the importance of promoting the development of new industries to replace those on the decline, and of increasing and cheapening the supply of skilled labor (via training programs or by encouraging immigration). Additionally, statesmen might temporarily subsidize exports that are losing out to foreign competition or subsidize basic goods that affect the cost or production of exports. He does warn that all this must be done gently in order to avoid the "jealousy" of "rival nations;" he is attentive to the possibility of reprisals and trade wars.[89] The key in all of this is to stop self-perpetuating decline; there is none of Hume's faith that international mechanisms will simply restore balances without substantial human loss. Steuart's statesmen intervene to correct for market failures.

Similarly, when Steuart comments on the impact of machines, he stresses that the introduction of even "the smallest innovation," no matter how "reasonable" and "profitable," also brings "inconveniences" for some laborers, "throwing many people into idleness." Where innovation threatens "systematical ruin" for any group, the task of the "statesman" is clear: not to inhibit innovation, which is the lifeblood of modern society, but to protect the welfare of those affected adversely. Specifically, public action must feed or employ those displaced. These "inconveniences" of technological innovation are usually "temporary" while the "advantage is permanent" (unless the innovations are being made by competitors), such that policy must necessarily support the introduction of methods "of abridging labour and expense."[90]

Markets may be sources of disorder, but the imperative is to correct for market failure or use economic forces to produce certain public purposes. Steuart's more judicious assessment (than Smith's) of domestic and international markets is not, then, a frontal challenge to the market logic of society. Rather, he takes market society for granted but also insists on managing the flux and the wounds that modern markets produce. The resemblance to Keynesian industrial policy is clear and might serve as inspiration for elements of a post-neoliberal vision of capitalist economics.[91] A more radical response would challenge a belief in the primacy of laws of economic behavior. Steuart cannot take us there.

IV. Reversing Smith's Necro-Economics

Steuart condemns "as Machiavellian principles, every sentiment, approving the sacrifice of private concerns in favor of a general plan," even the plan of

88 Steuart, *Political Oeconomy*, Book II, ch. 23.
89 Ibid. pp. 202–5 [II.12], 232–4 [II.15], and 251, 257–8 [II.18].
90 Steuart, *Political Oeconomy*, Book I, ch. 19.
91 This impulse is common. See, for example, John Gerard Ruggie, "At Home Abroad, Abroad at Home: International Liberalisation and Domestic Stability in the New World Economy," *International Studies Quarterly*, 1994, vol. 24, 507–26; Jonathan Kirshner, "Keynes, Capital

laissez-faire economics.[92] He claims that the "Principal object" of political economy "is to secure a certain fund of subsistence for *all* the inhabitants, to obviate *every circumstance* which may render it precarious; to provide *every thing necessary* for supplying the wants of society."[93] Though he refers to the magistrate's "humanity" as a motive for action,[94] Steuart also grounds his concern in the nature of modern social life itself.

Relations of mutual dependence constitute modern society. This material and social dependence gives social life a tightly woven structure; a strong social bond interconnects all citizens:[95]

> The political oeconomy of government is brought to perfection, when every class in general, and every individual in particular, is made to be aiding and assisting to the community, in proportion to the assistance he receives from it. This conveys my idea of a free and perfect society, which is, *a general tacit contract, from which reciprocal and proportional services result universally between all those who compose it.*
>
> Whenever therefore any one is found, upon whom nobody depends, and who depends upon every one, as is the case with him who is willing to work for his bread, but who can find no employment, this is a breach of the contract, and an abuse. For the same reason, if we can suppose any person entirely taken up in feeding himself, depending upon no one, and having nobody depending on him, we lose the idea of society, because there are no reciprocal obligations between such a person and the other members of the society.[96]

Steuart regards the unemployment of human resources and the attendant poverty that results as a source of corruption and decay. By weakening the reciprocal ties of a free society, unemployment and poverty undercut the tacit contract, weakening social bonds.[97] Steuart's political economy cannot

---

Mobility and the Crisis of Embedded Liberalism," *Review of International Political Economy*, 1999, vol. 6, 315–37; and Jacqueline Best, "Hollowing Out Keynesian Norms: How the Search for a Technical Fix Undermined the Bretton Woods Regime," *Review of International Studies*, 2004, vol. 30, 383–404.

92 Ibid., pp. 10–1 [Preface]. We gloss Karl Polanyi, *The Great Transformation: The Political and Economic Origins of Our Time*, Boston: Beacon, 2001.

93 Steuart, *Political Oeconomy* p. 17 [I. Introduction]; emphasis added.

94 Ibid., p. 177 [II.7].

95 Redman, "Sir James Steuart's Statesman," p. 58, comments that his more "organic" notion of society may derive from German Cameralists.

96 Ibid., p. 88 [I.14].

97 Steuart sees a similar bond of interdependence being created by international trade, but he doesn't draw out the same ethical implication; he only notes, or perhaps bemoans, the loss of internal social integration concomitant on the strengthening of foreign linkages and the tentative establishment of a "new kind of society among nations." Ibid., pp. 231–2 [II.15]. Many claim that we have reached the point when drawing out this ethical implication is an imperative.

accept that many will be sacrificed for the good of the whole, nor accept such iniquity as a lubricant to the economic machine. The contrast with Smith is illustrative.

Smith is aware of the interdependencies of a commercial society. If we only "[o]bserve the accommodation of the most common artificer or day-labourer in a civilized and thriving country," we are unable to count the number who contribute to meeting his needs: it "is the produce of the joint labour of a great multitude of workman."[98] And, as Smith famously notes, the workman who "has almost constant occasion for the help of his brethren" cannot expect that help "from benevolence alone." Rather, he achieves the steady assistance of others via a set of bargains, where he offers an equivalent in exchange.[99] Smith's understanding of our mutual obligations remains minimalist. We are enjoined only to honor contracts and avoid damaging others; society is organized principally around a "negative virtue" of justice through which individuals can be compelled to fulfill their legal obligations. Society owes us nothing else (though individual charity might moderate some suffering).

These two visions of society—one based principally on minimal legal obligations; the other on a stronger sense of social obligation—inform the thinkers' ethical assessments of one of the most basic operations of the economy, the price mechanism. Smith's account of the setting of wages in Book I, Chapter 8 of *Wealth of Nations* is especially instructive. In Chapter 1, he promises that a "general plenty diffuses itself through all the different ranks of society,"[100] but by Chapter 8 he seems less confident of this bold conclusion. The move from Chapter 1 to Chapter 8 involves traveling some historical distance, from a rude state of society, "in which the labourer enjoyed the whole produce of his own labour," to a civilized society, in which "the greater part of the workmen stand in need of a master to advance them the material of their work, and their wages." "The consequence," as Marx also emphasized, "is that the master now shares in the produce of their labour."[101] The amount that the master shares "depends every where upon the contract made between those two parties, whose interests are by no means the same."[102] And as Smith makes clear, this is a bargain usually struck to the disadvantage of the laborers:

> It is not, however, difficult to foresee which of the two parties must, upon all ordinary occasions, have the advantage in the dispute, and force the other into a compliance with their terms. The masters, being fewer in number, can combine much more easily; and the law, besides, authorises,

98 Smith, *Wealth of Nations*, p. 15 [I.i].
99 Ibid., p. 18 [I.ii].
100 Ibid., p. 15 [I.i].
101 Ibid., pp. 73–4 [I.viii].
102 Ibid., p. 74 [I.viii].

or at least does not prohibit their combinations, while it prohibits those of the workmen. . . . In all such disputes the masters can hold out much longer. . . . Many workmen could not subsist a week, few could subsist a month, and scarce any a year without employment. In the long-run the workman may be as necessary to his master as his master is to him, but the necessity is not so immediate.[103]

Smith assures us that in this "ordinary" condition, masters combine to keep wages at their minimum level—the cost of labor or subsistence—or even "to sink the wages of labour below this rate." That workmen and their families are threatened by starvation is not lost on them; they act, as Smith says, "with the folly and extravagance of desperate men, who must either starve, or frighten their masters into an immediate compliance with their demands." Fortunately, this "most shocking violence and outrage" is put to rest by the "civil magistrate."[104] Smith is not simply an apologist for the masters, though we sense his relief. Lest we become anxious that the society might fall into disorder, he assuages us: the great machine of nature offers an automatic solution, assuring that wages stay at roughly their natural level.

Smith's account of wages includes population dynamics, the growth or decline in the supply of workmen. Vibrant economic growth seems to keep the demand for labor high, pushing wages above subsistence for some time, until the higher wages encourage higher fertility and the increase in the supply of workmen.[105] But where the economy is stagnant, the wages of labor are "sunk" below the level of subsistence, below a level that is required to support a family. Where wages fall, fewer children survive until adulthood, thereby decreasing the supply of labor and forcing wages back to subsistence. As Smith puts it, "poverty . . . does not always prevent marriage. It seems even to be favorable to generation." However, "poverty . . . is extremely unfavorable to the rearing of children. The tender plant is produced, but in so cold a soil, and so severe a climate, soon withers and dies."[106] For the market, people are no different than other commodities: "the demand for men, like that for any other commodity, necessarily regulates the production of men; quickens it when it goes too slowly, and stops it when it advances too fast."[107]

Smith's treatment of people as like any commodity at once highlights and hides the way the market, as Warren Montag bluntly puts it, "rations . . . life itself:"[108]

103 Adam Smith, *An Inquiry into the Nature and Causes of the Wealth of Nations*, pp. 74–5 [I.viii].
104 Ibid., p. 75 [I.viii].
105 Ibid., pp. 76–80 [I.viii].
106 Ibid., p. 88 [I.viii].
107 Ibid., p. 89 [I.viii].
108 Warren Montag, "Necro-Economics: Adam Smith and Death in the Life of the Universal," *Radical Philosophy*, 2005, no. 134, p. 15.

Smith postulates an equilibrium or harmony productive of life that is paradoxically created and maintained by the power of the negative, of death: that the allowing of death is necessary to the production of the life of the universal. Smith's economics is a necro-economics. The market reduces and rations life; it not only allows death, it demands that death be allowed by the sovereign power, as well as by those who suffer it. In other words, it demands and requires that the latter allow themselves to die. From this we must conclude that underneath the appearance of a system whose intricate harmony might be appreciated as a kind of austere and awful beauty, a self-regulating system, not the ideal perhaps, but the best of all possible systems, is the demand that some must allow themselves to die. This of course raises the possibility that those so called upon will refuse this demand—that is, they will refuse to allow themselves to die. It is at this point that the state, which might appear to have no other relation to the market than one of a contemplative acquiescence, is called into action: those who refuse to allow themselves to die must be compelled by force to do so.[109]

Smith's account of the regulation of wages via the price mechanism does not offer the instantaneous adjustments promised by the differential calculus of neoclassical economists. Rather, adjustments occur at the pace of human suffering and death. Here is the wound of wealth in its starkest form.

What does this mean for the workman? We doubt that the workers' recognition that intergenerational patterns of infant mortality are part of a natural mechanism will mitigate their sense of being violated. They will resist this violence and the state, as Smith knows, will be called upon to end the violence and secure market rationing. In this way, the workings of the supposedly self-regulating mechanism rely on masters' cold calculations and magistrates' suppression of worker organization and resistance. Equilibrium depends on class power, state violence, and the eventual submission of the worker and his/her family to their fate. Only then can the self-regulation of population dynamics and labor markets play themselves out.

Though Smith, like Steuart, sees the "first" object of "political oeconomy" as providing "a plentiful revenue or subsistent for the people," he quickly amends that statement to read: "or more properly to enable them to provide such a revenue or subsistence for themselves."[110] Steuart would not disagree with the amendment. However, he would judge both irresponsible and immoral any political economy that ties human subsistence absolutely to market fluctuations.

Smith also relies on this "necro-economics" in his discussion of corn duties, though here he resorts more fully to "a gesture of theoretical/historical

109 *Radical Philosophy*, p. 16.
110 Smith, *Wealth of Nations*, p. 449 [IV.Introduction].

denial."[111] Smith's discussion emphasizes conditions of relative "dearth," since increases in the price of grains generate the greatest calls for government intervention in subsidizing grain prices, or restricting exports of grain.[112] He assures us that the grain trader in a free market is, in fact, the friend of the consumer. Both share the same interest: "that the daily, weekly, and monthly consumption, should be proportioned as exactly as possible to the supply of the season." If he raises prices too high, consumption will drop, leaving him with excess supplies of a commodity, driving prices down further when the new crop arrives. If he sets prices too low, hungry people will consume at a higher level, exhausting supplies before the next crop comes in.[113] The market effectuates a "disciplining of the hungry"[114] that, Smith asserts, will preserve their lives through a very lean season.

Smith uses his own analogy of a ship's captain, in this case one who rations provisions when they run short, in order to invoke the harmonious workings of the market:

> Without intending the interest of the people, [the trader] is necessarily led, by a regard to his own interest, to treat them, even in years of scarcity, pretty much in the same manner as the prudent master of a vessel is sometimes obliged to treat his crew. When he foresees that provisions are likely to run short, he puts them upon short allowance. Though from excess of caution he should sometimes do this without any real necessity, yet all the inconveniences of which his crew can thereby suffer are inconsiderable, in comparison of the danger, misery, and ruin, to which they might sometimes be exposed by a less provident conduct. Though from excess of avarice, in the same manner, the inland corn merchant should sometimes raise the price of his corn somewhat higher than the scarcity of the season requires, yet all the inconveniences which the people can suffer from this conduct, which effectually secures them from a famine in the end of the season, are inconsiderable, in comparison of what they might have been exposed to by a more liberal way of dealing in the beginning of it.[115]

But what this analogy misses is buying power. The ship's captain rations to each seaman equally (or perhaps according to rank; ordinary seamen do not eat at the officers' table), but in either case seamen do not depend for their provisions on their effective demand. The market, by contrast, rations provisions according to ability to pay; some can afford the higher prices and will

---

111 Montag, "Necro-Economics," p. 15.
112 As some Asian nations did recently, limiting exports of rice.
113 Smith, *Wealth of Nations*, p. 30 [IV.v].
114 Montag, "Necro-Economics," p. 15.
115 Smith, *Wealth of Nations*, p. 31 [IV.v].

maintain something like their normal level of consumption. Others will be forced to consume less and less, or even be forced out of the market itself. The price mechanism of a free market may well assure that grain supplies last a season, but not that the masses of grain consumers survive the season. We might see this as a form of the ecological fallacy: the false assumption that what holds true for the whole also holds true for each of the parts that make up the whole.

Studies of famine also suggest that Smith's analogy misleads him. People starve not because improper price signals have emptied the local or international markets of grain, but because they are poor and priced out of the market.[116] The most likely scenario is this: famine results where public officials fail to secure the buying power of the poor. The failure of such officials might be due to their incapacity, their incompetence, their venality, or their faith in free market principles. In the latter case, the integrity of the market is preserved, but at the cost of sacrificing individuals to the "austere and awful beauty," to use Montag's phrasing, of the free market.

Steuart refuses the vampire aesthetics of a market order. For him, to draw again on Montag, "society or community is not simply necessary for humanity's development and progress, it is necessary from the point of view of human life itself."[117] The market, though central to civilized community, cannot be allowed to ration life as part of its natural (unrestrained) operations.[118] Market sovereignty is appropriately limited when the government secures reasonable prices by maintaining reserve stocks.[119] Steuart demands, as noted earlier, that statesmen intervene in the market to assure that competition among buyers of subsistence does not lead to misery and death.

It is not that Steuart ignores the price mechanism; his analysis of supply and demand is acute.[120] Steuart believes that the state should aim to maintain a stable "balance," where "prices are found in the adequate proportion of the real expense of making the goods, with a small addition for profit to the manufacturer and merchant."[121] When working properly, the cost of

---

116 See, for example, Amartya Sen, *Poverty and Famine: An Essay on Entitlement and Deprivation*, Oxford: Oxford University, 1981; Mike Davis, *Late-Victorian Holocausts: El Nino Famines and the Making of the Third World*, London: Verso, 2002; and, Jenny Edkins, *Whose Hunger? Concepts of Famine, Practices of Aid*, Minneapolis: University of Minnesota, 2000.

117 Montag, "Necro-Economics," p. 8.

118 Steuart does hope that a functioning (and regulated) market will reduce the likelihood of famine. Steuart, *Political Oeconomy*, pp. 342–3 [II.28]. Smith, in "Digression concerning the Corn Trade and Corn Laws," in *Wealth of Nations*, Book IV, ch. V, believes this happens without regulation.

119 Steuart, *Political Oeconomy*, p. 403 [II. 30].

120 See Skinner, "Money and Prices," p. 279 and Sen, *Economics of Sir James Steuart*, ch. 6. What Steuart does miss, as Meek, "Rehabilitation," pp. 7–8, makes clear, is the central role of capital and the capitalist.

121 Steuart, *Political Oeconomy*, p. 189 [II.10].

production sets a floor under which prices cannot fall for any length of time, since that would put manufacturers out of business, thereby reducing competition among sellers. He also sees that the "faculties" (effective demand) of descending income classes set some ceiling on the extent to which prices can rise, since each quantum of increased price will reduce by similar quantum the extent to which income groups can compete for those goods.[122]

Despite these forces that promote "balance," Steuart finds no guarantees that the market will automatically serve social goals, including securing subsistence. He recognizes that an unrestrained market becomes a tool for rationing life and death. He emphasizes the human costs of changes in competitive conditions. At times, he uses a quite contemporary term, "shock," to indicate the consequences of abrupt adjustments.[123] Such shocks lead to a "natural restitution" of prices and demand for goods that may threaten "workman, with unemployment and the loss of subsistence." This "state of perpetual convulsion," not the gentler "vibrations" of prices, supply and demand (to use one of Steuart's favorite images), is of central concern to the magistrate. And as Steuart notes, these transitions in competitiveness "never can be sudden or easy."[124] Thus, it is the role of public authority to smooth these shocks, securing, directly or indirectly, subsistence for the needy.

All of this depends on good policymaking. Steuart notes that successful political economy requires relative justice and skill in those who govern[125] and he acknowledges that statesman may make mistakes requiring correction.[126] Smith would likely see Steuart's position as naïve; Smith notes that government is rarely good and is often influenced by conspiracies among business people. He recommends that we take the operations of the economy out of the hands of the magistrate.[127] This perhaps incipiently Marxist point about the political dominance of the business class would seem to undercut our confidence in Steuart's statesmen. His interventionism, much like Keynes' later vision of economic management, depends on a state bureaucracy that is simultaneously disinterested and technically skilled.[128] Smith thinks finding this combination is difficult, if not impossible.

But Smith's position seems to require a similar naïveté. He treats economics

---

122 Steuart, *Political Oeconomy*, Book II, chs. 2, 4, 6, 7, and 10, are good examples of Steuart's account of the price mechanism in a commercial society. See also Book II, ch. 30, where he discusses income classes and the maximum level of prices.

123 See Naomi Klein, *The Shock Doctrine: The Rise of Disaster Capitalism*, New York: Metropolitan, 2007.

124 Steuart, *Political Oeconomy*, pp. 192–6 [II.10].

125 Ibid., pp. 10–2 [I. Preface].

126 Ibid., pp. 197–8 [II.11].

127 Smith, *Wealth of Nations*, Book I, ch. X, Part II.

128 James A. Caporaso and David Levine, *Theories of Political Economy*, Cambridge: Cambridge University, 1992, ch. 5.

as separable from the state. He implies that a society run on market principles and mostly free from governmental interference is sufficient for human well-being. Nowhere has this strict separation achieved its goal, whatever the dominant rhetoric. And, as Karl Polanyi notes, efforts to establish this separation threaten to annihilate "the human and natural substance of society" and result in a counter-movement of societal self-protection. In this respect, Smith's "idea of a self-adjusting market" is not just utopian but, in Polanyi's terms, "a stark utopia."[129] When Polanyi turns his eye to the issue of famine, he delivers a similar indictment of necro-economics. In India, he suggests,

> [t]he actual source of famines in the last years was the free marketing of grain combined with local failure of incomes. Failure of crops was, of course, part of the picture, but dispatch of grain by rail made it possible to send relief to the threatened areas; the trouble was that the people were unable to buy the corn at rocketing prices, which on a free but incompletely organized market were bound to be the reaction to shortage. In former times small local stores had been held against harvest failure, but had been now discontinued or swept away into the big market. . . . While under the regime of feudalism and of the village community, *noblesse oblige*, clan solidarity, and regulation of the corn market checked famines, under the rule of the market the people could not be prevented from starving according to the rules of the game.[130]

Steuart would recognize the central point, but would be less likely to affirm the institutions of a pre-modern India. In this judgment, he shares much with Marx, as we shall see, though Marx suggests the need to look beyond the institutions of a market society for resources to address a necro-economic world.

V. Conclusions

Steuart defends the value of national independence, rejecting imperialism outright. Since international economic relations may threaten national independence, he devotes large parts of his *Political Oeconomy* to policies that support national integrity and the well-being of the nation's citizens. Steuart, like later dependency theorists, differentiates two domains of value. He recognizes that participation in international markets, if managed properly, can enhance national wealth and social refinement. But this value must also be weighed against national independence or, as we might put it,

---

129 Polanyi, *The Great Transformation*, p. 3.
130 Ibid., p. 167.

sovereignty.[131] Steuart is loathe to sacrifice a society's capacity to direct its own future, even if such a sacrifice, like the Union of Scotland and England, might bring economic growth and gains in efficiency.

This anti-imperial strain in Steuart highlights his greater concern with the issue of "difference." Robert Urquhart suggests that Steuart "is the last major political economist to have a true theoretical commitment to complexity."[132] As we noted in the first chapter, attention to cultural complexity threatens the elegance of a nomothetically inclined science. Steuart reminds us, however, that policymakers cannot afford to fall victim to the abstract assertions of economists; they face a messy world in which lives (and forms of life) are at stake. Thus, he warns that the dogmatic application of free trade policies may bring ruin to many people in both rich and poor countries. He implies that the doctrine of free trade is simply a tool of powerful trading nations. In response to this doctrine, he sees political economy is an "art" of recognizing national difference.

At the same time, Steuart's understanding of difference is still quite restricted. Urquhart proposes three possible readings of Steuart:

1. There is one political economy dictated by the logic of modern commerce, and gradually all nations will come to conform to it, through the organizing power of commercial activity. It will assert itself especially through the unitary form that the pursuit of self-interest takes in modern commerce.
2. There is one political economy in principle, but national differences will always make the practice of political economy variable. In particular, the subjective power of the spirit of a people will, on occasion, suspend what, in principle, seem to be objective laws of political economy.
3. There are many different political economies, owing to the varieties of national spirit, and of the choices of statesmen.[133]

Urquhart's tentative judgment, that Steuart generally moves us beyond the first position, one occupied more clearly by Hume and Smith, is helpful. But he misses a key point: Steuart, just like these thinkers, takes for granted a temporal scheme that displaces from political economy any but the "laws" and motivations of commercial societies. A commercial era itself may be fractured spatially and temporally, so that it is not possible to speak of a great and harmonious machine, but Steuart believes it is the *only* operative machine and we are compelled to adapt to its constraints. Thus, we find it difficult to share Urquhart's view that Steuart "often speaks as though the

131 Naeem Inayatullah and David L. Blaney, "Realizing Sovereignty," *Review of International Studies*, 1995, vol. 21, 3–20.
132 Urquhart, "The Trade Wind," p. 403.
133 Ibid., p. 394.

third interpretation," that there are multiple political economies, "is the correct one," even if it is clear that "his argument does not really support it."[134]

Steuart actually seems to embrace some combination of points one and two in Urquhart's schema. He acknowledges and examines the "real," but attempts then to re-suture the wound. As in the first step, that there is only "one political economy dictated by the logic of commerce," he accepts that "gradually all nations will come to conform to it." He only contests that they will be equally successful as competitors or that their interests naturally coincide. He strongly suggests that, as policymakers pursue their varied interests, they must respect "the unitary form that self-interest takes in modern commerce." None of this is inconsistent with the second point: "national difference will always make the practice of political economy variable," but this is a variation within modern commercial practice and always constrained by uniform laws of economic behavior.

Steuart's insights may well support a growing body of literature on the diversity of forms of capitalism, capitalist states, and policy strategies and to extend a point, diverse forms of social protection,[135] but they do not offer a fully imagined cultural political economy. However helpful he may be to us in countering the standardized and homogenizing neoliberal accounts of development prospects that achieved a kind of hegemony in the 1980s, Steuart does not offer an alternative to modern commerce or the modern economic man. He confines our vision to defining problems in modern terms and offering solutions that proceed from a modern understanding of human behavior, liberal rights, a uniform polity, and state action. We are constrained to the limited question that Smith and Steuart share: "what kind of capitalism do we need?"

Steuart thereby excludes the very elements that Karl Polanyi points to in his understanding of an embedded economy: visions of the human that differ from modern egoistic individualism; the village as a source of social security and social action; the role of centralized redistributional structures in securing livelihood.[136] Though Steuart remains trapped within the temporal displacements of the Scottish Enlightenment, there is a hint of more. Steuart is more clear, perhaps more honest, in exploring the fracturing of a modern

---

134 Urquhart, "The Trade Wind," pp. 394–5.

135 See, for example, Suzanne Berger and Ronald Dore, *National Diversity and Global Capitalism*, Ithaca: Cornell University, 1996; Peter A. Hall and David Soskice (eds.) *Varieties of Capitalism: The Institutional Foundations of Comparative Advantage*, New York: Oxford University, 2001; and Robert N. Gwynne, Thomas Klak, and Denis J. B. Shaw, *Alternative Capitalisms: Geographies of Emerging Regions*, London: Arnold, 2003. The variety of developmental states is suggested by Woo-Cumings, *The Developmental State*. Eric Ringmar, *Surviving Capitalism: How we Learned to Live with the Market and Remained Almost Human*, London: Anthem, 2005, explores the variety of forms of social protection in some depth.

136 See Polanyi, *Great Transformation*; and Inayatullah and Blaney, *International Relations*, ch. 5.

commercial era. He understands that political economy constructs universal policy prescriptions only by suppressing differences across European capitalisms and across stages of capitalism itself. This political economy of natural laws promises affluence but, Steuart insists, only at the cost of a necro-economics veiled as the operations of a self-correcting mechanism.

Beneath, beyond, and within a vision that takes capitalism as the norm, Gibson-Graham suggest that we might "create or reveal landscapes of economic difference." To reject the temporal displacements of political economy is, in their words, "to enlarge the economic imaginary" and "perform alternative economies." More specifically, they call us to develop "new, richer local languages of economy and economic possibility;" to cultivate "ourselves and others as subjects of noncapitalist development;" and to work "collaboratively to produce alternative economic organizations and spaces in place."[137]

These "organizations and spaces" push us beyond an exclusively "intra-modern discussion," claims Escobar, revealing an " 'exteriority' to the modern world system." But this is not a "pure outside, untouched by the modern." Rather, it is an "outside that is constituted as difference by a hegemonic discourse."[138] Boaventura de Sousa Santos likewise warns that an emphasis on localization alone may be counterproductive: "localization," as he puts it, "is the globalization of the losers." The local intersects with the global and we must think not only of "separation" but also of a "union" that reshapes global space.[139] We might see this, as does Ringmar, as the articulation of a "right to continue to be different from the global."[140] If we add, as Polanyi emphasized, that every effort to institutionalize the free market calls forth a counter-movement, drawing on various models (including from the past) of embedded economies, we begin to uncover a political economy of difference. We may still ask, "what kind of capitalism do we need?" But we can refuse to let this question repress all other questions about economy. Recognizing these repressed others draws us into the kind of "dialogue" among alternative visions or utopias that Ashis Nandy would recommend.[141]

137 J. K. Gibson-Graham, *The End of Capitalism (as we knew it)*, Minneapolis: University of Minnesota, 2006, pp. ix–x.

138 Arturo Escobar, "Worlds and Knowledges Otherwise: The Latin American Modernity/ Coloniality Research Program," *Cultural Studies*, 2007, vol. 21, pp. 181, 186.

139 Boaventura de Sousa Santos, "*Nuestra America*: Reinventing a Subaltern Paradigm of Recognition and Redistribution," *Theory, Culture and Society*, 2001, vol. 18, pp. 189–93.

140 Ringmar, *Surviving Capitalism*, pp. 141–2.

141 Ashis Nandy, *Traditions, Tyranny, and Utopias: Essays on the Politics of Awareness*, Delhi, Oxford University, 1987.

4 Capitalism's wounds

Ferguson's international political economy

If Smith appears torn internally in his assessments of civil society, Adam Ferguson's work reveals a still more divided self.[1] He seems to speak at once for modern commerce and in the voice of the "backward" Highlander who is immersed in an order of manly virtues, strong social connections, and active citizenship. Ferguson was born on the fringes of the Highlands and grew up among Highlanders. His command of Gaelic and loyalty to the Union earned him a post in 1745 as a chaplain to the Black Watch, a Highland military unit serving mostly in Europe. For Ferguson, Highlanders are more than an abstraction fitted into the "four-stages theory." They are not simply a nearby other against which he, as an Enlightenment intellectual, constructs his self. Rather, the Highlands appear as a living presence in Ferguson's thinking, especially in *An Essay on the History of Civil Society* (1767). Reflecting "[h]is birthplace . . . on the frontier between primitive and advanced societies," Fania Oz-Salzberger suggests that "Scotland was the *Essay*'s hidden source of insight and urgency."[2] Or, as Duncan Forbes argues, the absence of any mention of the Highland clans should not obscure the *Essay*'s "Highland provenance" that "throws into relief the fundamental question which . . . was the real inspiration of the book: what happens to *man* in the progress of society?"[3]

Though a relatively positive assessment of "rude nations" informs his "historico-moral cost-benefit analysis of the transition to modernity,"[4] Ferguson's retrieval of the past is not simpleminded. His analysis of the wound opened up by a commercial age is powerful, as Marx himself later noted.[5]

1 We follow David Kettler, *The Social and Political Thought of Adam Ferguson*, Columbus: Ohio State, 1965.
2 Fania Oz-Salzberger, *Translating the Enlightenment: Scottish Civic Discourse in Eighteenth-Century Germany*, New York: Oxford, 1995, p. 99.
3 Duncan Forbes, "Adam Ferguson and the Idea of Community," in Douglas Young, et al. (eds.) *Edinburgh in the Age of Reason: A Commemoration*, Edinburgh: Edinburgh University, 1967, p. 41.
4 Roy Porter, *The Creation of the Modern World: The Untold Story of the British Enlightenment*, New York: W.W. Norton, 2001, pp. 246–7.
5 Karl Marx, *Capital. A Critique of Political Economy, Volume 1*, New York: Vintage, 1977, pp. 474, 482–4.

Indeed, Ferguson's vision is darker than Marx's in some respects. Not unlike Steuart, Ferguson's trepidations about the modern heighten his perception of the contingencies in *all* polities. *Fortuna* stands in place of the "real;" the goddess deals out prosperity and refinement as well as disorder, conflict, and domination.[6] For Ferguson, modern civil societies emerge from the historical tensions and conflicts of international (or is it intercultural?) relations, and are beset by persistent dangers magnified by the concentration of power in modern states. Despite Hume's and Smith's assurances that the rise of an interest-driven way of life will calm the passions, Ferguson believes that civil society remains vulnerable to a combination of external geo-economic competition fueled by greed and vanity, the complacency of a citizenry dominated by commercial concerns, and an ostensibly liberal but highly militarized polity that threatens liberty. Doubts about civil society are *not* displaced behind the temporal walls of the past (as for Smith) or the future (as for Marx, as we shall see). Ferguson sees corruption and decay as present and persistent realities that must be faced rather than displaced; he more tightly encircles the "real."

Consistent with this less optimistic picture of a commercial era, Ferguson reveals a more complicated temporal understanding—one that undercuts the privilege of the modern and thereby recognizes that the time of the modern overlaps with that of the past. On the one hand, this critical move is quite powerful, reminding us of Karl Polanyi's analysis of the self-defeating quality of those efforts to disembed the economy from society. Like Polanyi, Ferguson seems to suggest that extending the logic of the market is destructive of human well-being and of the health of societies. On the other hand, Ferguson does not follow this powerful diagnosis of the wound of wealth with a compelling recommendation. Where Polanyi draws on the experience of non-modern societies to indicate the social responses and institutional reforms necessary to protect human society, Ferguson's appeal to the manly virtues he associates with both rude and classical societies appears as a relatively empty form of moralizing. He pits moral vigilance, not social or institutional transformations, against the corruption intrinsic to capitalism. His turn to past virtues as an ethical resource might inspire in us the kind of time-travel that Ashis Nandy recommends, but it also seems to expose the limits of today's communitarian recourse to "civic liberalism" or other traditionalist or revivalist moralizing appeals as a response to the wound of wealth.

I. The Complexities of History

Distinguishing Ferguson from his contemporaries does not belie how closely he aligns himself with Smith and his fellow Scots. He explains historical

---

6 By contrast, Richard Boyd extols the Scots' "liberal" notion of civil society in "Reappraising the Scottish Moralists and Civil Society," *Polity*, 2000, vol. 33, 101–25.

advance as they do, with an account of the human being as "susceptible of improvement," having "in himself a principle of improvement."[7] More strongly, Ferguson writes:

> Destined to cultivate his own nature, or to mend his own situation, man finds a continued subject of attention, ingenuity, and labour. Even where he does not propose any personal improvement, his faculties are strengthened by those very exercises in which he seems to forget himself: his reason and his affections are thus profitably engaged in the affairs of society; his invention and his skill are exercised in procuring his accommodation and his food; his particular pursuits are prescribed to him by circumstances of the age and of the country in which he lives; .... He suits his means to the ends he has in view; and by multiplying contrivances, proceeds, by degrees, to the perfection of his arts.[8]

Ferguson emphasizes that humans are active, creative beings, who, in phrases similar to Hegel and Marx, work on their own being while they simultaneously work as parts of society.

Thus, "progress" is central to human existence, as development of the species recapitulates the developmental life of individuals: "Not only the individual advances from infancy to manhood, but the species itself from rudeness to civilization."[9] Ferguson elaborates:

> the species has a progress as well as the individual; they build in every subsequent age on foundations formerly laid, and, in a succession of years, tend to a perfection in the application of their faculties, to which the aid of long experience is required, and to which many generations must have combined their endeavors.[10]

This perfection, he stresses, is a long process, taking human beings through several stages.

In hunting and gathering societies, "the means of subsistence are procured with ... much difficulty" and the want of subsistence proves a great check on the population in most times and in many parts of the world.[11] This condition of scarcity is contrasted with the plenty available in commercial society. No doubt drawing on Smith,[12] Ferguson argues that "a people can make no great progress in cultivating the arts of life, until they have separated, and

---

7 Adam Ferguson, *An Essay on the History of Civil Society*, Cambridge: Cambridge University, 1995, p. 7.
8 Ibid., p. 161.
9 Ibid., p. 7.
10 Ibid., p. 10.
11 Ibid., pp. 91 and 137.
12 Smith accused Ferguson of plagiarism on this point. See Kettler, *Adam Ferguson*, pp. 74–5, n. 50.

committed to different persons, the several tasks, which require a peculiar skill and attention." The savage or barbarian is checked by the fatigue and lack of skill accompanying the effort of providing by himself "the diversity of his wants."[13] Once begun, this process of dividing labor seems irresistible:

> [T]he prospect of being able to exchange one commodity for another, turns, by degrees the hunter and the warrior into a tradesman and a merchant. The accidents which distribute the means of subsistence unequally, inclination, and favourable opportunities, assign the different occupations of men; and a sense of utility leads them, without end, to subdivide their professions.[14]

As each "individual is distinguished by his calling, and has a place to which he is fitted . . . the sources of wealth are laid open; every species of material is wrought up to the greatest perfection, and every commodity is produced in the greatest abundance." This "progress of arts" finally bestows on "polished nations" the very "ends that were pursued by the savage in his forest, knowledge, order and wealth."[15]

Consistent with the dominant theme of Scottish Enlightenment historiography, Ferguson locates a smooth and beneficial congruence between basic human motivations and historical progress. In fact, his discussion of the law of unintended consequences, often taken as definitive of the Scottish view, is duly famous:[16]

> Mankind, in following the present sense of their minds, in striving to remove inconveniences, or to gain apparent and contiguous advantages, arrive at ends which even their imagination could not anticipate. . . .
>
> Every step and every movement of the multitude, even in what are termed enlightened ages, are made with equal blindness to the future; and nations stumble upon establishments, which are indeed the result of human action, but not the execution of any human design.[17]

Spontaneous order and development, the workings of that harmonious machine upon which Smith depends, appear crucial for Ferguson as well.[18]

---

13 Ferguson, *Essay*, p. 172.
14 Ibid.
15 Ibid., pp. 173 and 175.
16 See Christopher S. Berry, *Social Theory of the Scottish Enlightenment*, Edinburgh: Edinburgh University, pp. 40–8.
17 Ferguson, *Essay*, p. 119.
18 Ferguson's providentialist teleology is well documented. See Kettler, *Adam Ferguson*, pp. 122–35, and Lisa Hill, "Adam Ferguson and the Paradox of Progress and Decline," *History of Political Thought*, 1997, vol. XVIII, 677–706. On the idea of spontaneous order, see Naeem Inayatullah, "Theories of Spontaneous Disorder," *Review of International Political Economy*, 1997, vol. 4, 319–48.

Ferguson departs from Smith in a key respect, however, with important implications for his understanding of the role of passions and virtue in social life. He is expressly skeptical about the use of "conjectures and different opinions of what man must have been in the first age of his being." The search for a "state of nature," he stresses, has "led to many fruitless inquiries, and given rise to many wild suppositions," especially the tactic of selecting "one or a few particulars" among "various qualities" humankind possesses in order to construct some theory of the present.[19] Modern scholars tend to

> impute every advantage of our nature to those arts which we ourselves possess; and to imagine, that a mere negation of all our virtues is a sufficient description of man in his original state. We are ourselves the supposed standard of politeness and civilization; and where our own features do not appear, we apprehend, that there is nothing which deserves to be known.[20]

Contra Smith, who privileges his present as the standard of civilization, Ferguson is explicitly critical of that move, despite the confident universal history he embraces at other points.

Ferguson suggests a less polarized picture of human origins. He begins with what he takes as a simple fact: that human beings everywhere are found in society—that they have "wandered or settled, agreed or quarrelled, in troops and companies," in his clear military imagery.[21] This "fact" of human sociality seems consistent with the general picture of Scottish Enlightenment thinking we presented earlier. Amidst the great diversity offered by history— the "multiplicity of particulars" and "apparent inconsistencies" that we find in the historical record—Ferguson believes he can locate a key common element in sociability.[22] Though he searches in vain for a single principle to explain the human propensity to group together,[23] he turns, still not surprisingly, to "men who live in the simplest condition" for the best evidence. In the American societies, "acquaintance and habitude nourish affection" and enliven the human passions of courage and friendship and all this apart from whether or not the form of society offers substantial "external conveniences."[24] Like Smith, Ferguson turns attention away from claims (by Hobbes, Mandeville, Hume, etc.) that sociability rests wholly on a utilitarian calculus.

---

19 Ferguson, *Essay*, pp. 7–8, 10.
20 Ibid., p. 75.
21 Ibid., pp. 9, 20–1.
22 Ibid., p. 21.
23 He works (Ibid., pp. 21–2) through a number of possibilities—mutual attraction, the compulsion of a common enemy (othering!), and mutual interest—without ever settling on a fully satisfactory explanation. The interplay of attraction and animosity plays a key role in explaining war and dissension in Part I, Section IV of the *Essay*. We will return to this issue.
24 Ibid., pp. 20–3. Ferguson, like Smith, consistently draws on Lafitau.

Human motives are irreducibly complex and cannot be compressed to those highlighted by the rise of commerce.

Building on this less polarized picture of savage and modern, Ferguson partly inverts his peers' historical theories. It is precisely where human progress is at its zenith that "man is sometimes found a detached and a solitary being: he has found an object that sets him in competition with his fellow-creatures, and he deals with them as he does with his cattle and his soil, for the sake of the profits they bring." The usual mistake, he argues, is to read the modern social condition as the epitome of human nature and human society. What close observation suggests, instead, is that the "mighty engine which we suppose to have formed society, only tends to set its members at variance. . . ."[25] The very commercial practices that bring progress also set humans at "variance," creating what Marx called alienation. The sociality of a commercial society is distinctly anti-social. We are tempted to see Ferguson's dissatisfaction with the emerging commercial society in parallel to Karl Polanyi's, where the effort to create a society on the basis of free markets undercuts the very *social* basis of human social relations, a theme we return to below.[26] Ferguson regards as dangerous the tendency of a commercial society to isolate individuals and pit them into competitive relationships. This danger threatens the very social fabric on which a good polity depends.

If Ferguson is not shy about casting past peoples in a story about the origins and progress of humankind, still this is not Smith's conjectural history. By refusing to allow the commercial society to define human sociability *per se*, he opens up the present to a more complex means of critical reflection. He suggests that the Amerindians present "a mirrour" that allows us access to "the features of our progenitors."[27] Though this might sound like Smith's method (learned from Lafitau and others), Ferguson does not use his knowledge of the Amerindians to fully polarize the savage and the civilized. Unlike Smith, he works to reduce the distance by carefully avoiding claims that exaggerate the differences between humans in the earliest ages and those today. "[I]nstead of supposing that the beginning of our story was nearly of a piece with the sequel," thinkers tend either to reject the present conditions of humans as wholly unnatural or, as he especially decries, to picture humans in earlier ages as no more than animals.[28] In Tzvetan Todorov's terms, Ferguson is avoiding the "double movement." He resists translating others' differences into cultural or temporal inferiority. Instead, he presents a more cautious set of comparisons that suggests both commonalities and differences and

25 Ferguson, *Essay*, pp. 23–4.
26 Karl Polanyi, *The Great Transformation: The Political and Economic Origins of Our Time*, Boston: Beacon, 2001.
27 Ferguson, *Essay*, p. 80.
28 Ibid., p. 11.

relative strengths and weaknesses.[29] Society, reason, the arts, invention, holding to tradition, and forging change are features of humanity throughout its many ages; the "savage" as well as the "citizen" show "proofs of human invention" and the state of human beings in all times and places is "equally natural."[30] In some respects—"in forces of imagination, and elocution, an ardour of mind, an affection and courage"—contemporary nations could do well to learn from the savage.[31]

Reducing this temporal gap gives the manners and customs of supposed past ages a more explicitly prominent position in Ferguson's reasoning about the current state of human existence. First, it suggests that society cannot (or should not) be imagined principally in market terms; social life is deeper and richer than that—and the very institutions of a commercial society, including market and state, depend on a vital, even passionate, social life that Smith relegates to the past. Second, we should not experience this eruption of the past into the commercial present as simply danger and disorder as Smith is wont to do. The overlapping of past and present may hint of disorder and danger, but it also offers opportunities by expanding our political imagination beyond the narrow confines that Smith allows.

II. War and Civilized Society

The Scottish Enlightenment's understanding of civilization contains a distinctly "militaristic strand," as Bruce Buchan puts it.[32] For Smith and Hume, the account of international relations is mostly optimistic. Civil societies appear capable of restraint in international relations, constructing stable balances of power unheard of in the relations of polities in earlier eras. And when modern states face off against barbarous or savage others, commercial societies invariably have the upper hand. Ferguson is less sanguine. He doubts that modern virtues of calculation and self-command will temper behavior, since commerce itself draws countries into unwise and internally corrupting expansionary adventures.[33] Simply extending civil society across space cannot erase these dangers. The automatic mechanisms of historical progress cannot be counted upon to subdue a world of contingency and danger. Why this difference? We have already noted Ferguson's departures from the

---

29 Tzvetan Todorov, *The Conquest of America: The Question of the Other*, New York: Harper and Row, 1984.

30 Ferguson, *Essay*, p. 14.

31 Ibid., p. 76.

32 Bruce Buchan, "Civilisation, Sovereignty and War: The Scottish Enlightenment and International Relations," *International Relations*, 2006, vol. 20, p. 178. See also Robert A. Manzer, "The Promise of Peace? Hume and Smith on the Effects of Commerce on War and Peace," *Hume Studies*, 1996, vol. XXII, 369–82.

33 His account reminds us of Thucydides' diagnosis of Athenian decline and we would stress Ferguson's debt to a study of Greece and Rome.

confident secular providentialism of Smith, but something deeper is at work: Ferguson introduces the logic of identity/difference from which he finds no clear exit. We see this discussion as key to understanding Ferguson's urgency about the deficiencies of commercial society, which we take up below.

Smith and Hume express less urgency over the results of history. Hume waxes at length about the civilizing consequences of human progress. Growing commerce and extension of manufacturing arts by necessity bring "[l]aws, order, police, discipline" to a new "degree of perfection." This advance in "knowledge of the arts of government naturally begets mildness and moderation, by instructing men in the advantages of humane maxims above rigour and severity." By comparison with "times of barbarity and ignorance," with their infestations of "superstition, which throws government off its bias," "[f]actions are then less inveterate, revolutions less tragical, authority less severe, and seditions less frequent." This pacification of internal affairs is accompanied by a parallel civilizing of external affairs. "Even foreign wars abate of their cruelty," but if wars must be fought, Hume assures us that this loss of "ferocity" will not be accompanied by a decline in citizens' "martial spirit" or the willingness to be "vigorous in defense of their country."[34]

Smith too is famed for suggesting that the primary motive of commerce, that is, self love, may serve to keep human behavior within the bounds of justice and prudence, supporting a relative harmony among people.[35] Though harmony should extend into the domain of international relations, Smith strongly defends the idea that a commercial society represents the pinnacle of war-fighting capabilities. The relatively meager martial capabilities of previous societies were the result of limited application of the division of labor and the consequent lack of advance in the mechanical arts.[36] Smith did worry that social advance might dilute the martial fervor and skillfulness of the general population, but this disadvantage is easily corrected by a properly trained and equipped standing army—a group of highly disciplined and technologically advanced specialists in warfare. In the end, Smith assures us

---

34 David Hume, "Of Refinement in the Arts," in *Essays: Moral, Political, and Literary*, Indianapolis: Liberty Fund, 1985, pp. 273–4.

35 Adam Smith, *The Theory of Moral Sentiments*, Indianapolis: Liberty Fund, 1976, pp. 171–8, 212–17 [IV.i; VI.i]. See Albert Hirschman's classic account, *The Passions and the Interests: Political Arguments for Capitalism before its Triumph*, Princeton: Princeton University, 1977.

36 Adam Smith, *An Inquiry into the Nature and Causes of the Wealth of Nations*, Chicago, IL: University of Chicago, 1976, 213–9 [V.i.i]. Andrew Wyatt-Walter, "Adam Smith and the Liberal Tradition in International Relations," *Review of International Studies*, 1996, vol. 22, 5–28, reads Smith as a realist, but this misreads the recent provenance of realism. See Daniel H. Deudney, *Bounding Power: Republican Security Theory from the Polis to the Global Village*, Princeton: Princeton University, 2007.

that we can defend ourselves from savages.[37] We hear similar promises in today's "war on terror."

Indeed, the creation of a standing army—as opposed to militias or irregular forces—is a marker of a civilized state. For Smith, only the modern (imperial) state is capable of exercising "sovereignty, with an irresistible force" over even "the remotest provinces of the empire." Since the sovereignty of civilized nations includes maintaining "some degree of regular government in countries which could not otherwise admit of any," it appears that the modern world order is itself a function of empire. In case we do not get the point about the historical role of modern empire, Smith notes that the "invention of firearms" might be thought "pernicious," but "is certainly favourable both to the permanency and to the extension of civilization."[38] In his *History of England*, Hume similarly suggests that the flourishing of trade, the polishing of arts, and the better organization of central government reduce the excesses of royal ambition. These developments also create more effective use of military force by a modern sovereign state, as in the extension of rule and trade via the creation of colonies.[39] And, he adds, with advances in modern military technology (here, artillery), even these foreign adventures of civilized states appear less dangerous:

> Though it seems contrived for the destruction of mankind, and the overthrow of empires, has in the issue rendered battles less bloody, and has given greater stability to civil societies. Nations by its means have been brought more to a level: Conquests have become less frequent and rapid: Success in war has been reduced nearly to a matter of calculation: And any nation overmatched by its enemies, either yields to their demands or secures itself by alliances against their violence and invasion.[40]

Apparently Hume means that competing empires are less likely to engage in damaging warfare, not that the uncivilized will check the spread of civilization by force. Such a balance of power checks military adventures across the sovereign spaces of modern civilization but *not across temporal difference*, as we will see below.

Ferguson would likely see this talk about civilized "reason" or "prudence" as wishful thinking. He remained unconvinced that calculative rationality would automatically pacify international affairs. Though civil societies may be more moderate and just in war,[41] Ferguson feared that "civilisation also

---

37 Smith, *Wealth of Nations.*, pp. 219–23 [V.i.i].
38 Ibid., pp. 228–9, 231 [V.i.i].
39 We rely on Buchan, "Civilisation, Sovereignty and War," pp. 177–8.
40 David Hume, *The History of England from the Invasion of Julius Caesar to the Revolution of 1688. Volume II*, London: J. Mcreery, 1807, p. 432, quoted in Buchan, "Civilisation, Sovereignty and War," p. 178.
41 Ferguson, *Essay*, pp. 188–90.

created the military strength that may become a menace to civil society and to peaceful coexistence among sovereign states."[42] Like Smith, he attributes increased military capabilities to the impact of technological advance,[43] but the relationship also runs in the other direction: war itself calls mankind (and he does mean men) to a true state of "excellence." It is "competition among rival states" that brings to the fore the greatest virtues of self-sacrifice and solidarity and prods invention and national advance:[44]

> Without the rivalship of nations, and the practice of war, civil society could scarcely have found an object, or a form. Mankind might have traded without any formal convention, but they cannot be safe without a national concert. The necessity of a public defense, has given rise to many departments of state, and the intellectual talents of men have found their busiest scene in wielding their national forces. To overawe or intimidate, or, when we cannot persuade with reason, to resist with fortitude, are the occupations which give its most animating exercise, and its greatest triumphs, to a vigorous mind; and he who has never struggled with his fellow creatures, is a stranger to half the sentiments of mankind.[45]

Civil society—that nexus of modern state and market society—was born and thrives, says Ferguson, in the crucible of international competition and war. It is also clear that the emergence of civil society transforms international competition and war, so that it is possible now to see understandings of international relations as subsumed by IPE.[46]

Reason does not persuade, nor does it check the ambitions and vanity of the civilized. The prudence or calculated rationality for which Hume and Smith hope (Ferguson speaks in terms of "interests") are often counterbalanced "by sloth or intemperance; by personal attachments, or personal animosities." Calculated rationality fails to pacify international affairs because the legitimate concern of securing the independence of the political community gives way to "claims to precedence or profit,"[47] fostering belligerence and expansion:

---

42 Buchan, "Civilisation, Sovereignty and War," p. 183.

43 Ferguson, *Essay*, p. 180.

44 Ibid., pp. 47, 29.

45 Ibid., p. 28. Others have made a similar claim about war and state competition as spur to innovation. See Paul Kennedy, *The Rise and Fall of the Great Powers: Economic Change and Military Conflict from 1500–2000*, New York: Random House, 1987; and E. L. Jones, *The European Economic Miracle: Environments, Economies, and Geopolitics in the History of Europe and Asia*, Cambridge: Cambridge University, 1987. We find this tone in Hegel as well.

46 See Susan Strange, "Wake up Krasner! The World *has* Changed." *Review of International Political Economy*, 1994, vol. 1, p. 218. Benjamin J. Cohen highlights Strange's views in "The Transatlantic Divide: Why are American and British IPE so Different?" *Review of International Political Economy*, 2007, vol. 14, pp. 208–9.

47 Ferguson, *Essay*, pp. 121–2. See also pp. 200–1.

The love of safety, and the desire of dominion, equally lead mankind to wish for accessions of strength. Whether as victors or as vanquished, they tend to a coalition; and powerful nations considering a province or a fortress acquired on their frontier, as so much grained, are perpetually intent on extending their limits.[48]

However much "we pretend to found our opinions on reason," Ferguson warns,

we frequently bestow our esteem on circumstances which do not relate to national character, and which have little tendency to promote the welfare of mankind. Conquest, or great extent of territory, however peopled, and great wealth, however distributed or employed, are titles upon which we indulge our own, and the vanity of other nations, as we do that of private men on the score of their fortunes and honours.[49]

Interests do not displace the passions but are joined with them. Thus, dangers that for Smith and Hume are barely visible doubts and that they readily sweep into the past via the great and harmonious machine are seen by Ferguson as eruptions of the "real" in civil society.

Combine animosity, vanity, and self-interest with the superior military capacities of civilized states and you get predation of the temporally backward by the temporally advanced. At some points, this predation appears to Ferguson simply as part of historical progress: "For want of these advantages, rude nations in general . . . always yield to the superior arts, and the discipline of more civilized nations . . . and hence the Europeans have a growing ascendancy over the nations of Africa and America." Despite the language of yielding, he declares that only through force can the "savage . . . be made to quit that manner of life in which he is trained," since there is a "remarkable . . . mutual contempt and aversion, which nations, under a different state of commercial arts, bestow on each other."[50] This mutual contempt has the rather bloody consequences that Ferguson elucidates when he compares the Crusades, the religious warfare of early modern Europe, and contemporary European expansion:

The subsequent ages of enterprise in Europe, were those in which the alarm of enthusiasm was rung, and the followers of the cross invaded the East, to plunder a country, and to recover a sepulcher; those in which the people in different states contended for freedom, and assaulted the fabric of civil or religious usurpation; that in which having found means

48 Ferguson, *Essay*, p. 146.
49 Ibid., p. 195.
50 Ibid., p. 94.

to cross the Atlantic, and to double the Cape of Good Hope, the inhabitants of one half the world were let loose on the other, and the parties from every quarter, *wading in blood*, and at the expense of every crime, and of every danger, traversed the earth in search of gold.[51]

His note of disapproval seems accompanied by historical acceptance of European colonialism. However, a fuller reading implies that something deeper may be at work in Ferguson.

He takes the antipathy of one group for another not simply as a problem, but as foundational for group identity itself. Earlier in the *Essay*, he links the natural social urges—of "mutual need" and "mutual compassion"—with the existence of "war and dissension." At one point, he seems to indicate that "variance and dissension" are embraced by humankind "with alacrity and pleasure," that "animosity" towards others is a disposition of the species itself. And he suggests that humans "are fond of distinctions; we place ourselves in opposition, and quarrel under the denominations of faction and party, without any material subject of controversy." Ferguson's claims become increasingly strong, suggesting that difference/identity are logically and socially necessary oppositions: "The titles of *fellow-citizen* and *countryman*, [if] unopposed to those of *alien* and *foreigner*, to which they refer, would fall into disuse." Nations would have no basis for existence without a "sense of common danger" and, as he notes, "the assaults of an enemy, have been frequently useful to nations, by uniting their members more firmly together, and by preventing the secessions and actual separations in which their civil discord might otherwise terminate."[52] Or as David Campbell puts it in our times: "The constant articulation of danger through foreign policy is thus not a threat to a state's identity or existence: it is its condition of possibility."[53] Whatever the case, Ferguson sees the world as "for ever separated into bands, and form[ing] a plurality of nations."[54]

Ferguson's view seems to build on Smith's understanding of the role of "sympathy" in constructing human sociality and sentiments. Smith understood that human sympathies change or weaken as they extend across social and physical space.[55] Smith begins with the inner circle of the individual who, appropriately, "is more deeply interested in whatever immediately concerns himself."[56] But he insists that our concerns extend outward in circles beyond ourselves. Those we know best (family and neighbors) fall within a circle of

---

51 Ferguson, *Essay*, p. 201, emphasis added.
52 Ibid., pp. 24–6.
53 David Campbell, *Writing Security: United States Foreign Policy and the Politics of Identity*, Minneapolis: University of Minnesota, 1998, p. 13.
54 Ferguson, *Essay*, p. 26.
55 See Jack Russell Weinstein, "Sympathy, Difference, and Education: Social Unity in the Work of Adam Smith," *Economics and Philosophy*, 2006, vol. 221, pp. 82–91.
56 Smith, *Moral Sentiments*, pp. 82–3 [II.ii.2.1–2].

strong moral concern.[57] Even the much larger and more impersonal unit, the state, has a strong moral hold on us:

> The state or sovereignty in which we have been born and educated, and under the protection of which we continue to live, is, in ordinary cases, the greatest society upon whose happiness or misery, our good or bad conduct can have much influence. It is accordingly, by nature, most strongly recommended to us. . . . Upon account of our own connection with it, its prosperity and glory seem to reflect some sort of honour upon ourselves. When we compare it with other societies of the same kind, we are proud of its superiority, and mortified in some degree, if it appears in any respect below them.[58]

Our sympathies are much weakened as we move beyond the state. Indeed, without a greater society, Smith concludes that each state faces all others as an individual, which can expect only "little justice" from others and "is disposed to treat them with as little as he expects."[59]

We would expect many in the community of IR scholars to make immediate appeal to the structure of anarchy and the defensive poise that each state must adopt. Smith's references to the balance of power and his refusal to accept that "[n]ational prejudices and hatreds" are the key factors motivating leaders to take hostile actions against other states[60] lend support to that interpretation. Unlike many in contemporary IR, however, Smith does not presume anarchy. He believes that social institutions are products of human interactions across history. The lack of a greater global or transnational society and the limits of the operation of conscience are moral facts associated with the current state of human social development, not eternal verities. Distance does dilute the intensity of our concern; therefore, state boundaries in our era demarcate a sphere of identification beyond which the strongest of sympathies are weakened, though, he would stress, *not* eliminated.[61] However contingent, state boundaries are crucial to the rise of civilization. They demarcate spaces of national development that are juxtaposed to an international system of states. Some force, perhaps technological change or imperial advance, may restructure these separated spaces into a world society or a world of uneven development ruled by the most advanced civil societies.

---

57 Smith, *Moral Sentiments*, p. 224 [VI.ii.I.16]. Charles Griswold, *Adam Smith and the Virtues of Enlightenment*, Cambridge: Cambridge University, 1999, pp. 119, 141–2, uses the language of "circles of sympathy."
58 Smith, *Moral Sentiments*, p. 228 [VI.ii.2.2].
59 Ibid., p. 228 [VI.II.2.3].
60 Ibid., pp. 229–30 [VI.ii.2.5–6].
61 The similarity to Alex Wendt's understanding of interaction and the extent of human sociality is notable and startling. See Alexander Wendt, "Why a World State is Inevitable," *European Journal of International Relations*, 2003, vol. 9, 491–542.

But for the present, Smith accepts and ethically validates the demarcation of separate states.

Ferguson draws out this implication of Smith's moral psychology. Membership in a nation draws one into a dynamic of identity/difference—a process of comparison that invariably favors your own kind. He begins with a claim about the biases of any nation's view, one that reproduces his condemnation of the partiality of conjectural histories discussed above:

> No nation is so unfortunate to think itself inferior to the rest of mankind: few are even willing to put up with the claim of equality. The greater part having chosen themselves, as at once, judges and the models of what is excellent in their kind, are first in their own opinion, and give to others consideration or eminence, so far only as they approach to their own condition.[62]

Where conjectural history translates difference into backwardness and creates a temporal prejudice, the identities constructing and constructed by an international society of states perpetuate a spatial prejudice.

Perhaps these spatial and temporal elements play into each other. Once again, Ferguson's diagnosis is similar to Todorov's. Intercultural relations are often governed, Todorov tells us, by the tendency to translate the difference of others into an assessment of inferiority and to translate their similarities into an assimilative identification that purges all difference.[63] In a startling move, Ferguson himself turns this criticism on the very categories of the Scottish Enlightenment:

> The term *polished*, if we may judge from its etymology, originally referred to the state of nations in respect to their laws and government. In its later applications, it refers no less to their proficiency in the liberal and mechanical arts, in literature, and in commerce. But whatever its application, it appears, that if there were a name still more respectable than this, every nation, even the most barbarous, or the most corrupted, would assume it; and bestow its reverse where they conceived a dislike, or apprehended a difference. The names of *alien*, or *foreigner*, are seldom pronounced without some degree of intended reproach. That of *barbarian*, in use with one arrogant people, and that of *gentil*, with another, only served to distinguish the stranger, whose language and pedigree differed from theirs.[64]

Here even the categories "civilized" and "barbarian" are (mostly) unfastened from their historical and moral certainty, revealing no more than the user's condescending point of view.

---

62 Ferguson, *Essay*, p. 194.
63 Todorov, *The Conquest of America*, pp. 42, 146.
64 Ferguson, *Essay*, p. 195.

At this point, Ferguson delivers his judgment that "we pretend to found our opinions on reason" we quoted earlier. Reason's fallibility appears systematic, central to modern identity itself. Modern reason is infected by a repression or subordination of difference that makes possible the identity of the reasoning being. Extending the realm of civil society across space merely extends the ills along with the advances and Enlightenment's light dims. Despite Hume's and Smith's promise of harmony, it is Feguson's observation (quoted earlier) that this is a colonial era—that the world is "wading in blood"—which resonates. (We will see this again in Hegel's refreshingly open embrace of colonialism.) Ferguson's vision cuts through the providentialist mist that envelops and ignores such blood. To put the point in contemporary terms, he envisions not a liberal peace, but an unleashing of simultaneously greedy, vain, and righteous, albeit liberal, warriors on a world of "failed states" and "evildoers."

III. The Corruption of Civil Society

As Kettler notes, Ferguson is no radical; he commits to stability and, at most, gradual, measured change.[65] Indeed, Ferguson appears an orthodox Smithian on economic policy. The "great object of policy," he says, is to "secure to the family its means of subsistence and settlement."[66] But this is no activist government. He argues that the "motives of interest" are the major spur to "labour" and the "lucrative arts." The public task is thereby quite limited:

> Secure to the workman the fruit of his labour, give him the prospects of independence or freedom, the public has found a faithful minister in the acquisition of wealth, and a faithful steward in hoarding what he has gained. The statesman in this . . . can do little more than avoid doing mischief.[67]

Since "private interest is a better patron of commerce and plenty," the "refinements of state" must be limited: "If a protection is required, it must be granted; if crimes and frauds be committed, they must be repressed; and government can pretend no more."[68] Even in the face of the creation of serious social divisions, Ferguson seems to maintain this position. People

> must be suffered to enjoy their wealth, in order that they may take the trouble of becoming rich. Property, in the common course of human affairs, is unequally divided: we are therefore obliged to suffer the wealthy to squander, that the poor may subsist; we are obliged to tolerate

---

65 Kettler, *Adam Ferguson*, ch. IV.
66 Ferguson, *Essay*, p. 139.
67 Ibid., p. 138.
68 Ibid., p. 139.

certain orders of men, who are above the necessity of labour, in order
that, in their condition, there may be an object of ambition, and a rank
to which the busy aspire.[69]

The "invisible hand" logic of a commercial society is accepted as an historical
necessity, if not an unambiguous moral achievement. In this, Ferguson
departs little from Smith.

Ferguson is not complacent, however. His acceptance of the invisible hand
is paired with an acute appreciation of the deficiencies of a commercial
society. Though he narrates the weaknesses of commercial society using the
same categories, Ferguson's critique takes a different tone than Smith's. It
reverberates with the concern that commerce corrupts civic life and threatens
both domestic political liberty and national security.

The primary danger facing commercial society lies in how commerce dims
civic spirit.[70] Ferguson strives for a balanced account. On the one side, he
embraces the idea, comparable to Smith and Hume, that commerce polishes
the manners of human beings. Commerce takes the "short-sighted, fraudu-
lent, and mercenary" individual of a more barbarous time and transforms
him so that "his views are enlarged, his maxims are established" and "he
becomes punctual, liberal, faithful and enterprising."[71] On the basis of
expanded wealth, society comes to "erect a superstructure suitable to their
views," including the refinements of law, the development of professional
skills and codes, the luxury of time to speculate, converse, and study.[72] Along
with wealth and the cultivation of the arts, commercial society gives birth
to the bourgeois gentleman.

On the other side, the division of labor is a source of grave concern, since
its consequences threaten to undermine completely this salutary vision. Here
Ferguson displays what is taken to be his distinguishing "pessimistic mood."[73]
He doubts that the division of labor really enhances the mechanical capacities of a nation *as a whole*:

> Many mechanical arts, indeed, require no capacity; they succeed best
> under a total suppression of sentiment and reason; and ignorance is the
> mother of industry as well as of superstition. Reflection and fancy are

69 Ferguson, *Essay*, p. 225.
70 Kettler, *Adam Ferguson*, ch. VII, gives a thorough account. See also Hill, "Paradox of
Progress and Decline," and Anthony Brewer, "Adam Ferguson, Adam Smith, and the
Concept of Economic Growth," *History of Political Economy*, 1999, vol. 31, 237–54.
71 Ferguson, *Essay*, p. 138.
72 Ibid., p. 180. Ferguson traces the term's etymology from meaning polish in government to
its current application to "the liberal and mechanical arts, in literature, and in commerce"
(p. 195).
73 Hill, "Paradox of Progress and Decline," p. 677. As Hill puts it, Ferguson's work is normally
seen to juxtapose the idea of spontaneous order and "impending doom."

subject to err; but a habit of moving the hand, or the foot, is independent of either. Manufactures, accordingly, prosper most, where the mind is least consulted, and where the workshop may, without any great effort of imagination, be considered as an engine, the parts of which are men.[74]

In this case the individual and the social do not harmonize to produce the greater good; social gain comes at the expense of individuals.

We can understand how Ferguson's evocative account appeals to Marx.[75] Engagement in this detailed work tends "to contract and to limit the views of the mind." Masters are separated from the average "workman" whose mind "lies waste." "[T]hinking itself, in this age of separation, may become a peculiar craft." And markedly, those who possess greater knowledge and skill than the large majority are placed in a "superior class." Such a division was common in the classical era, as Ferguson suggests, but this division is more of an affront to the sensibilities of a "commercial state" in which, "notwithstanding any pretension to equal rights, the exaltation of the few must depress the many." Refinement is not a general condition; it is a matter of class—of the division between masters and workmen. The promise of liberal equality is seriously undercut.

Ferguson recognizes that many "refer to such classes, as an image of what our species must have been in its rude and uncultivated state" but, following his critique of conjectural history, he rejects this comparison. It is in a commercial era that the masses congregate in the cities and are corrupted by "circumstances." "Ignorance" is compounded by a distinctly commercial ethos: an "admiration of wealth unpossessed, becoming a principle of envy, or of servility; a habit of acting perpetually with a view to profit and under a sense of subjection." The savage, by contrast, is "unacquainted with our vices."[76] The institutions of the modern era do spur industry; they overcome "sloth" and promote "enjoyment" as individuals employ a temporal sensibility that defers gain into the future, calculating returns "with a view to distant objects." But this transition also produces a distinct pattern of "subordination." The savage state is characterized by shared tasks and shared returns, a consciousness of equality and a "tenacious" defense of freedom and independence. In an era of property, by contrast, humans begin to "know what it is to be poor and rich. They know the relations of patron and client, of servant and master, and suffer themselves to be classed according to their measures of wealth."[77] The emergence of this pattern of subordination (or class structure) may help explain why the savage is so resistant to "quit

---

74 Ferguson, *Essay*, p. 174.
75 This paragraph draws on ibid., pp. 174–80. Kettler, *Adam Ferguson*, p. 9, notes that Ferguson's thinking presages later Marxist themes of "over-rationalization, dehumanization, atomization, alienation, and bureaucratization."
76 Ferguson, *Essay*, pp. 177–8.
77 Ibid., pp. 81–3.

the manner of life in which he is trained."[78] By exposing what was implicit and suppressed in Smith, Ferguson draws on the judgment of the "savage" to reveal the wound of wealth.

Ferguson extends the image of the savage to cast a general shadow over the pursuit of luxury and the accumulation of wealth. Donald Winch notes that the so-called "luxury debate" had just about run its course by the middle of the eighteenth century; Hume and Smith are seen as key figures in setting concerns about the corrupting influences of luxury to the side.[79] In this respect Ferguson might appear as a throwback to an earlier age, a view perhaps harbored by his own friends.[80] Contra Winch, it is possible to find the "luxury" debate arising again and again throughout the following two and more centuries, most recently in the form of an obsession with the sources of human happiness. Economist Richard Layard and political scientist Robert Lane draw on the findings of sociologists, psychologists and behavioral economists to suggest that escalating consumption, instead of producing happiness, seems to crowd out aspects of social life, including family relations and political connections, that contribute more to well-being.[81] In our own times, where wealth is nearly universally an expectation or, at least, an aspiration, the merits of wealth continually remain in doubt. Reading Ferguson reminds us, then, that political economy did not resolve the "luxury" debate. It persists as a symptom of the "real" of political economy.

Indeed, Ferguson's account seems contemporary. He argues that the desire for "property and fortune" became disconnected from subsistence long ago. In a view that parallels Smith's, he contends that there would be little stimulus to human creativity if our desires were freed from the pull of "vanity"—from the lures of social comparison:

> . . . if our solicitude on this subject were removed, not only the toils of the mechanic, but the studies of the learned, would cease; every department of public business would become unnecessary; every senate-house would be shut up, and every palace deserted.[82]

Where social comparison shapes our experience of well-being, a point Hegel develops, a sense of deprivation becomes pervasive. In Ferguson's terms, the idea of a *"necessary of life* is a vague and a relative term; it is one thing in

---

78 Ferguson, *Essay*, p. 94.
79 Donald Winch, *Riches and Poverty: An Intellectual History of Political Economy in Britain, 1750–1834*, Cambridge: Cambridge University, 1996, pp. 58–9. For a longer discussion, see Christopher Berry, *The Idea of Luxury: A Conceptual and Historical Investigation*, Cambridge: Cambridge University, 1994, ch. 6.
80 Hume's appraisal of Ferguson's *Essay* is a case in point. See Kettler, *Ferguson*, pp. 57–60.
81 Richard Layard, *Happiness: Lessons from a New Science*, New York: Penguin, 2005; Robert Lane, *The Loss of Happiness in Market Democracies*, New Haven: Yale University, 2001.
82 Ferguson, *Essay*, p. 35.

the opinion of the savage; another in that of the polished citizen: it has a reference to the fancy, and to the habits of living." Thus, the individual in commercial society may assess "a scene overflowing with plenty" as inadequate to his "supposed rank" or "his wishes." And "[n]o remedy is applied to this evil, by merely accumulating wealth;" "For it is the continual increase of riches, not any measure attained, that keeps the craving imagination at ease."[83] Ferguson senses that the accumulation of wealth by a commercial society institutionalizes scarcity and social deprivation.

By contrast with Smith, he seems unsure that market society can offer a plausible remedy for the wound of wealth. For Ferguson, it is an active connection to society—to social purposes—that provides the real wellspring of human flourishing. Happiness revolves around a well-rounded existence, acquitting oneself well with family, neighbors, in the marketplace, and, not to be minimized, in political life.[84] Ferguson argues that a modern commercialized society, with its attendant division of labor, renders this image of a well-rounded person obsolete and disables any active politics. "Nations of tradesman," he says, "come to consist of members who, beyond their own particular trade, are ignorant of all human affairs."[85] And, in addition to isolating men from each other, a commercial society of "polished" times and citizens cultivates a sense of complacency about public affairs. Commerce becomes the "great object of nations" and "personal fortune . . . the sole object of care;" public duties are neglected at the very moment when the prosperous search for some diversion "to fill up the blanks of a listless life."[86] The dangers intensify when one adds that a society based on property tends also to "favour its unequal division." He calls for restrictions that "weaken the desire of riches, and . . . preserve in the breast of the citizen, that moderation and equity which ought to regulate his conduct." But he warns that these restrictions must be consistent with the continued flourishing of commerce.[87] It is not clear, then, what restrictions or reforms he would countenance. In the end, Ferguson is pessimistic that commercial society, with its intrinsically "unequal division of property" that allows "fortune . . . to bestow distinction and rank," can at all "shut up this source of corruption."[88]

Indeed, the personal pursuit of wealth central to commerce threatens to become fully destructive of human virtues:

> The subjects of property, considered with a view to subsistence, or even to enjoyment, have little effect in corrupting mankind, or in awakening the spirit of competition and of jealousy; but considered with a view to

83   Ferguson, *Essay*, pp. 137–8.
84   Ibid., p. 244.
85   Ibid., p. 173.
86   Ibid., p. 58.
87   Ibid., pp. 151–2.
88   Ibid.

distinction and honour, where fortune constitutes rank, they excite the most vehement passions, and absorb all the sentiments of the human soul: they reconcile avarice and meanness with ambition and vanity; and lead men through the practice of sordid and mercenary arts to the possession of a supposed elevation and dignity.[89]

Ferguson doubts that those beset by avarice can be counted on to live freely with others as self-governing citizens.[90] Like Smith, he recommends an extensive system of public justice in order to restrain the vices and corruption that beset a commercial society.[91] As Marx would later warn, bourgeois justice does little to redress the alienation of capitalism. Ferguson anticipates this assessment, exhibiting what Oz-Salzberger refers to as his "civic distrust" of "legalism."[92] He emphasizes that where people rely solely on justice, they come to ignore the "virtues," mistaking "for an improvement of human nature, a mere accession of accommodation, or of riches."[93] Unchecked by something beyond legalities that enforce contracts and prohibit injury, the logic of a market society unleashes a passion for pleasure that produces not happiness, but misery; not the sentiments that foster affection and fair-dealing but a rapaciousness and disregard of others. The consequence is that "the public is poor, while its members are rich"[94] and that the "cravings for luxury" may "silence" the spirit necessary for political life—a silence that cannot be compensated by laws alone.[95] As Alisdair MacIntyre explains, Ferguson's central point is that modern institutions endanger the "traditional virtues" that are central to the maintenance of those very modern institutions.[96] Thus, the more we extend the logic of the market, the more we lose important human values on which our collective life depends. And the promise that capitalism will heal the wound of wealth, of which market society itself is the cause, is revealed as an illusion.

Polanyi's dissection of market society again comes to mind. Polanyi argues that "man's economy, as a rule, is submerged in his social relationships;"[97] that human productive relationships are "an instituted process" that gives economic life its "definite function" by embedding it in wider social and

---

89 Ferguson, *Essay*, p. 154.
90 Ibid., pp. 154–5.
91 Ibid., p. 155.
92 Oz-Salzberger, *Translating the Enlightenment*, p. 121.
93 Ferguson, *Essay*, p. 212.
94 Ibid., p. 221.
95 Ibid., pp. 248–9. Richard F. Teichgraeber, III, *"Free Trade" and Moral Philosophy: Rethinking the Sources of Adam Smith's Wealth of Nations*, Durham: Duke University, 1986, p. 18, notes that Ferguson, like Rousseau "saw (and denounced)" the "sharply and consciously circumscribed view of the place of politics in human life" advocated by his fellow Scots.
96 Alasdair MacIntyre, *After Virtue*, Notre Dame: Notre Dame University, 1981, p. 182.
97 Polanyi, *Great Transformation*, p. 46.

political purposes.[98] Along with Ferguson, Polanyi sees the consequences of the attempt to replace more complex and varied social and political relations with the logic of the market as "stark," as we noted in the previous chapter. In a phrase Ferguson might have uttered, Polanyi suggests that subjecting human beings to unrestrained market relations "would incidentally dispose of the physical, psychological, and moral entity 'man'."[99] In Ferguson, as in Polanyi, it is not property or markets or commercial activity *per se* that produces the damage, but the effort to create a society founded on commercial relationships alone.

Ferguson's powerful diagnosis of the ills of market society places him among the most acute critics of capitalism. The power of his diagnosis turns, in part, on how he deploys the savage as an ethical resource. Ferguson draws on the evidence and example of what he sees as the past in order to formulate his understanding of the present. As his civically minded Highland side informs him, the modern era's institutions cannot rest on self-interest and the institution of justice alone. Where an active civic sense is undercut by the imperatives of commerce, individuals fail to give the concerns of the community due ethical weight and fail to defend the community's interests with courage. The strong virtues of past societies appear not outmoded, but as necessary conditions of the survival of a commercial society. In drawing a parallel between the view the Romans held of their own ancestors and the contemporary view of the savage past, Ferguson points approvingly to the "system of virtues, which all simple nations perhaps equally possess; a contempt of riches, love of their country, patience of hardship, danger, and fatigue."[100] His solution to the wound of wealth involves, then, reviving this sense of public spirit: the cultivation of "vigorous, public-spirited, and resolute men," who take on the character of the "statesman and warrior," instead of the "clerk and accountant."[101]

We find Ferguson's juxtaposition of social solidarity against a market vision of abstract individuals useful. We drew on Polanyi to make this same point in the last chapter. Ferguson, like Polanyi, uses the ethical resources of the past to critique modernity's pretensions. In both, the triumphal story of modern progress is left in tatters, but something important divides the two. Polanyi draws on the wide variety of ways in which humans have organized productive activity to suggest the kinds of institutional responses and social reforms necessary to embed a modern economy in

---

98   Karl Polanyi, "The Economy as Instituted Process," in George Dalton (ed.) *Primitive, Archaic, and Modern Economies: Essays of Karl Polanyi*, Garden City: Anchor, 1968, pp. 146–8.

99   Polanyi, *Great Transformation*, p. 73.

100   Ferguson, *Essay*, p. 78.

101   Ferguson, *Essay*, pp. 213–14. As Laurence Dickey, *Hegel: Religion, Economics, and the Politics of Spirit, 1770–1807*, Cambridge: Cambridge University, 1987, pp. 187–93, points out, Ferguson hoped that these civic virtues would balance the passions for gain.

wider social and political purpose.[102] Ferguson gives scant attention to institutional reform while proscribing any major alterations to the operation of the unregulated market. He deploys the warrior-statesman of an earlier era to defeat the clerk and accountant of his own era. But this is not a fair fight. Given his strong claim that market logic produces a potentially calamitous situation of inequality and alienation, it seems highly unlikely that the individual cultivation of virtues will alter the *social* logic of a commercial society.[103] There is simply little place for the sociability of the warrior-statesmen in a market society and Ferguson overlooks how reviving the ethos of community might require substantial social and institutional changes.

Given the incisiveness of Ferguson's critique, his thin response seems puzzling. Market society is intolerable but also inevitable and inviolable. It seems that he left himself with little recourse but to moralize.[104] The part of his self that identifies with the modern cannot be denied, but it also provides little solace. There appears to be no escape but into the past—the intimate other and ethical mirror that motivates his critique. Ferguson offers us the alternative of a golden age of civic virtue, but he does not allow this side of himself to alter the modern other. He holds onto both images and we are left with a standoff: a golden age of manly virtues perpetually poised against the inviolable logic of the market. Thus, we doubt Lisa Hill's claim that Ferguson "mourns no lost paradise."[105] We doubt further that Ferguson's recourse to civic virtue offers us much beyond the contemporary (liberal) communitarian's perpetual and often ineffectual counterpoising of markets and civic life. We will return to this issue in the conclusion.

IV. The Empire of Civil Society[106]

Ferguson uses the image of the "statesman and warrior" to further indict the political corruption of the "empire of civil society." It is not just that liberty fosters inequality or that avarice weakens manly virtues; Smith shared these doubts though he submerged them within providentialist claims of harmony or modest reform. Ferguson's central concern in the *Essay* is that commercial

---

102 Polanyi, *Great Transformation*, Part Two, section II. See the characterization of Polanyi's view in Marguerite Mendell, "Karl Polanyi and Feasible Socialism," in Kari Polanyi-Levitt (ed.) *The Life and Work of Karl Polanyi: A Celebration*, Montreal: Black Rose, 1990, 66–77.

103 We walk only so far with constructivists. See Naeem Inayatullah and David L. Blaney, "Knowing Encounters: Beyond Parochialism in IR Theory," in Yosef Lapid and Friedrich Kratochwil (eds.) *The Return of Culture and Identity in IR Theory*, Boulder: Lynne Rienner, 1996, 65–84.

104 See Wendy Brown, *Politics out of History*, Princeton: Princeton University, 2001, chs. 1 and 2.

105 Hill, "Paradox of Progress and Decline," pp. 687–8.

106 The term is Justin Rosenberg's: *The Empire of Civil Society: A Critique of the Realist Theory of International Relations*, London: Verso, 1994.

liberty may undermine the capacity for self-governance both internally and in relation to the dangers posed by other political communities. Smith too perceived these problems but, as we have seen, he proffered relatively simple solutions. Public education would cultivate an adequate capacity for self-command among the masses (and little else was necessary, since politics is highly circumscribed), and a professional army provides a more than adequate defense of the realm. By contrast, Ferguson's account leaves little comfort; the bloody destruction of empire is now turned inward to demolish the civility of commercial society itself.

In Ferguson's account (as in Polanyi's),[107] the threat to domestic liberty and the challenges of international affairs are intimately connected. For Ferguson, the connection turns mostly on the consequences of a modern division of labor. Though an extension of the division of labor continues to promote the "commercial and lucrative arts,"

> the separation of professions . . . in its termination, and ultimate effects, serves, in some measure, to break the bands of society, to substitute form in place of ingenuity, and to withdraw individuals from the common scene of occupation, on which the sentiments of the heart, and the mind, are most happily employed.[108]

More precisely, individuals are at risk of losing "the sense of every connection, but that of kindred or neighborhood; and have not common affairs to transact, but those of trade."[109] In this situation, the people may find their property secure, but their political life impoverished: "the constitution may indeed be free, but its members may likewise become unworthy of the freedom they possess, and unfit to preserve it."[110]

These dangers are compounded when Ferguson turns to military affairs. The key to a sound military force is a body of (male) citizens "inured to equality; and where the meanest citizen may consider himself on occasion, as destined to command as well as obey."[111] Thus, we see again that the level of inequality in society is of concern: "he who has forgotten that men were originally equal, easily degenerates into a slave; or in the capacity of a master, is not to be trusted with the rights of his fellow-creatures."[112]

But the division of labor between civilian and military affairs is a more direct threat to political liberty. We quote Ferguson's impassioned prose at length:

107 Polanyi, *Great Transformation*, Part One.
108 Ferguson, *Essay*, pp. 206–7.
109 Ibid., p. 298.
110 Ibid., p. 210.
111 Ibid., p. 144.
112 Ibid., p. 87. See also p. 153.

In the progress of arts and policy, the members of every state are divided into classes; and in the commencement of this distribution, there is no distinction more serious than that of the warrior and the pacific habitant; no more is required to place men in the relation of master and slave. Even when the rigours of an established slavery abate, as they have done in modern Europe, ... this distinction serves still to separate the noble from the base, and to point out that class of men who are destined to reign and to domineer in their country.

It was certainly never foreseen by mankind, that in the pursuit of refinement, they were to reverse this order; or even that they were to place the government, and the military force of nations, in different hands. But is it equally unforeseen, that the former order may again take place? and that the pacific citizen, however distinguished by privilege and rank, must one day bow to the person with whom he has entrusted his sword. If such revolutions should actually follow, will this new master revive in his own order the spirit of the noble and the free? Will he restore to his country the civil and military virtues? I am afraid to reply.[113]

Ferguson does reply. He argues that standing armies may become the enemy that a people must resist to secure their independence.[114] If his descriptions of the domination of military affairs seem a precursor to accounts of the national security state, then his discussion of the dangers of empire might well remind us of the integration of military and commercial interests so important to modern forms of imperialism. We have already noted that he believes foreign expansion may emerge from narrow commercial interests, but the greater danger is that empire becomes an end in itself:

It is vain to affirm, that the genius of any nation is adverse to conquest. Its real interests indeed most commonly are so; but every state which is prepared to defend itself, and to obtain victories, is likewise in hazard of being tempted to conquer.

In Europe, where mercenary and disciplined armies are every where formed, and ready to traverse the earth, where like a flood pent up by slender banks, they are only restrained by political forms, or a temporary balance of power; if the sluices should break, what inundations may we not expect to behold.[115]

The separation of the citizen and statesman impairs not only the capacities of the citizen, but also the judgment of leaders: "self-interested functionaries

---

113 Ferguson, *Essay*, p. 145.
114 Ibid., p. 215.
115 Ibid., p. 148.

and men of narrow vision," who are seduced by glory or gain disconnected from the good of the country.[116] And the turn to empire may be almost imperceptible, emerging by "slow degrees" only to be rapidly extended.[117] Ferguson forces us to behold a world where Europeans are "let loose on the other," producing a world that is "wading in blood."

There are also internal dangers. As empires expand, they drain national resources and states turn to "credit" in order "to disguise the hazards they ran." The cost is shifted thereby to the future:

> They have seemed, by their manner of erecting transferable funds, to leave the capital for purposes of trade, in the hands of the subject, while it is actually expended by the government. They have, by these means, proceeded to the execution of great national projects, without suspending private industry, and have left future ages to answer. . . .[118]

In addition to long-term financial decline, empire breeds resistance among far-flung populations, requiring persistent "subjection by military force." This need for eternal military vigilance breeds "usurpation" of the liberties of citizens. Dictatorial powers turn inward; leaders begin to see any opposition as a threat from an enemy. And where the population has been bred to a happy and affluent servility, they may readily acquiesce to a "usurpation" of their freedoms.[119]

Once established, this external/internal empire is difficult to overturn. Fragmented by commercial life, the political community is incapable of acting as a "free people." Those who feel the weight of oppression will find their protests mostly unheard, "for his fellow subject is comforted, that the hand of oppression has not seized on himself: he studies his interest, or snatches his pleasure, under that degree of safety which obscurity and concealment bestow."[120]

Ferguson himself ends the *Essay* with a warning to all who take refuge in the promises of a law of historical progress (or some religiously inflected claim of destiny): "The institutions of men, if not calculated for the preservation of virtue, are indeed, likely to have an end as well as a beginning."[121]

Lest the realities of an uncivil world of civil societies overwhelm those of

---

116 Ted Benton, "Adam Ferguson and the Enterprise Culture," in Peter Hulme and Ludmilla Jordanova (eds.) *The Enlightenment and Its Shadows*, London: Routledge, 1990, p. 114. This follows Ferguson's own description of the commercialized citizenry. Buchan, "Civilisation, Sovereignty, and War," pp. 184–5, argues that Ferguson is more explicit about the defects of leadership in other writings.

117 Ferguson, *Essay*, p. 128.

118 Ibid., p. 222.

119 Ibid., pp. 258–9.

120 Ibid., pp. 262–3.

121 We are quoting from the 1768 edition (see Ibid., p. 264, dd.).

us still reeling from Bush's "Freedom Agenda," Ferguson is quick to note that the actual situation is "mixed"—that commercial society benefits from that mixture of good and evil sentiments "instinctive" to humans. Despite the "frequent neglect of virtue as a political object," modern citizens, as Smith had also stressed, will still exhibit in some measure "a love of integrity and candour," "an esteem for what is honourable and praise-worthy," "a zeal for their own community, and courage to maintain its rights."[122] But Ferguson is not willing to leave the natural machine alone, as was Smith. Doing nothing risks the dangers of instability and decline; doubts *cannot* be laid to rest with the incantation of the invisible hand. His point is not to reject commercial society, as we have stressed; we needn't begrudge its advantages. But neither can we ignore its wounds. The deficiencies of a commercial society "inhere in" and are intrinsic to the very process of human progress.[123] Thus, progress has a complex temporal structure for Ferguson; we don't have to treat the past as separated from us by a temporal wall. This is a key insight, even as we remain unimpressed by his claim that individually cultivating virtues exemplary of earlier stages of society will redress the venality of a market society or avoid the kinds of imperial projects that lead its citizens to financial, moral, and political ruin.

Ferguson provides lessons for those who continue to live in militarized liberal democracies. He suggests that the ills of the empire of civil society will not be easily cured. He forces us to recognize that our anxious impulse to fix the defects of the empire through its extension is massively destructive and self-defeating. And he inadvertently reveals that pious calls to virtue do not constitute an alternative vision of social life.

V. Conclusions

Ferguson stresses that commercial society has something to teach "rude nations" where "manners . . . require to be reformed." Commercial societies create "a state of greater tranquility" which brings "many happy effects," by comparison with the "foreign quarrels" and "domestic dissensions" he attributes to other forms of life.[124] In this, Ferguson sounds like Smith though he does not police the temporal distance between the savage and the civilized; learning is not a one-way journey that privileges the civilized as teachers. From other, often past or technologically lesser, societies, the civilized may learn to appreciate the importance of social connection and civil commitment. He can make this move because he explicitly repudiates the

---

122 Ferguson, *Essay*, p. 156.
123 Hill, "Paradox of Progress and Decline," p. 683. Hill (pp. 687–91) argues against other views that Ferguson nests cyclical elements within a theory of progress. See also Oz-Salzberger, *Translating the Enlightenment*, p. 117.
124 Ferguson, *Essay*, p. 208.

conceptual polarity of "polished" and "barbarous" as a form of prejudice. He complicates developmental theory by combining commonality and difference in a manner that challenges conjectural history's polarization of the civilized and the savage. Finally, his general account of a commercial society blurs the opposition of the modern and the rude by highlighting the domestic and international barbarities of modernity. It is Ferguson who unflinchingly faces the wound of wealth. He sees most clearly that no great machine smoothes out war and domination in the empire of civil society.

Though Smith and Hume might regard Ferguson as wrong-headed and nostalgic, he returns us to an easily forgotten point: that the social ties making modernity possible extend beyond those of contract and exchange. This deeper social and ethical connection also is obscured by many contemporary accounts of interdependence in IPE. Returning to Ferguson allows us to highlight that these social and ethical connections are central to the market and the discipline of political economy. And we are given a vision of a political economy that avoids the unsatisfactory choices suggested in Chapter 1: either a "science" of economy that ignores the ethical foundations of economic life or a cultural critique of economy that places the economy beyond culture.

Another, still rather unpromising, option is open to us. Ferguson's legacy is reflected in today's (liberal) communitarian thinkers.[125] For example, Amitai Etzioni points to an "anarchic drift" besetting a modern society, where commitment to public responsibility has been displaced by "a strong sense of entitlement." As a solution to our current malaise (a generalized corruption of political life), we are called to cultivate the virtues of public spiritedness that Ferguson had stressed.[126] Similarly, Robert Bellah argues that we must restore a sense of moral purpose to our individual and public lives in order to combat the "destructive side of individualism." Indeed, the language of individualism itself impoverishes our capacity to envision our lives as anything but "isolated and arbitrary." What we require is a strong dose of the idea of "civic responsibility."[127] Or, perhaps more strongly, Benjamin Barber suggests that the liberal emphasis on individual liberty produces only the thinnest kind of democracy—a democracy without a well developed notion of "citizenship, participation, public goods, or civic virtue."[128]

Two centuries after Ferguson, the concern that market society weakens

---

125 Including some non-liberals from beyond the West. See Roxanne L. Euben, *The Enemy in the Mirror*, Princeton: Princeton University, 1999, on the parallels between contemporary communitarians and Islamist thinkers.

126 Amitai Etzioni, *The Spirit of Community: The Reinvention of American Life*, New York: Touchstone, 1993, pp. 3, 11, 89–90, 209–17.

127 Robert Bellah, et al., *Habits of the Heart: Individualism and Commitment in American Life*, New York: Harper and Row, 1985, pp. vi–vii, 20–1, 26.

128 Benjamin Barber, *Strong Democracy: Participatory Politics for a New Age*, Berkeley: University of California, 1984, p. 4.

effective citizen rule has not diminished.[129] Nor, we would add, has the appeal to civic virtue as an antidote to the wound of wealth improved with age. Recognizing that the pressures of modern society leave us bowling alone does not mean that joining associations alters the character of work, modifies the processes of social comparison that feed consumption and relative deprivation, or significantly changes the relative powers of social actors. Gareth Steadman Jones might share much of the communitarians' diagnosis of the ills of a market society, but he cautions that we should "not become the guileless consumers" of "simple-minded reconstructions" that pit "periodic homilies about communitarian sentiment" against an unregulated market.[130]

"Periodic homilies" will not do. Some contemporary thinkers in IPE understand this. The idea that markets or the economy must be institutionally embedded in wider social and political purposes may be seen as a response to empty homilies. Such work draws much inspiration from Karl Polanyi.[131] One interesting application of the idea of an embedded economy in twentieth- and now twenty-first-century writings is to question the same kinds of stadial theories resisted by Ferguson. Despite the popularity of claims that "globalization" is somehow inevitable and inexorable and that "neoliberalism" has now put Keynesian management eternally to rest, much of the work on the embeddedness of modern capitalism hints that the lessons of the postwar domestic and international regimes remain alive. The liberalization of trade and financial markets is read as a second great transformation,[132] and the efforts to resist liberalization, re-regulate financial markets, and establish sub-national and supra-national regional economic schemes are seen as

129 Defense of commercial virtues, though more aligned with Smith, also has seen a revival. The target is not only communtarian nay-sayers, but also economists who continue to embrace a simplistic notion of human behavior. See Francis Fukuyama, *Trust: The Social Virtues and the Creation of Prosperity*, New York: Free Press, 1995; John Mueller, *Capitalism, Democracy, and Ralph's Pretty Good Grocery*, Princeton: Princeton University, 1999; and Deidre N. McCloskey, *The Bourgeois Virtues: Ethics for an Age of Commerce*, Chicago: University of Chicago, 2006.

130 Gareth Stedman Jones, *An End to Poverty: A Historical Debate*, London: Profile Books, 2004, p. 2. The recent US election suggests how "guileless" citizens may be in this regard. A call to public service is nicely juxtaposed to an economic team, composed of Lawrence Summers and Timothy Geithner, whose task is to restore the financial system.

131 Though deriving from Polanyi, the work of sociologist Mark Granovetter, "Economic Action and Social Structure: The Problem of Embeddedness," *American Journal of Sociology*, 1985, vol. 91, 481–510, is treated as a touchstone itself. Many make the case that the economy is always embedded, even in its so-called disembedded form as a (relatively) free market. See Andrew Sayer, "For a Critical Cultural Political Economy," *Antipode*, 2001, vol. 33, 687–708; and Bob Jessop, "Critical Semiotic Analysis and Cultural Political Economy," *Critical Discourse Studies*, 2004, vol. 1, 159–74.

132 We gloss the title of Mitchell Bernard, "Ecology, Political Economy and the Counter-Movement: Karl Polanyi and the Second Great Transformation," in Stephen Gill and James H. Mittelman (eds.) *Innovation and Transformation in International Studies*, Cambridge: Cambridge University, 1997, 75–89.

efforts to subordinate markets once again to wider social and political purposes.[133]

This temporal point can be pushed further—beyond a return to a reputedly "golden age" of western capitalism.[134] Re-embedding the economy in Polanyi's vision may draw on resources from social forms that are treated as temporally superseded by capitalism itself. Various forms of postdevelopment thinking highlight the alternative practices of small-scale communities across the globe as social and institutional responses to attempts to subordinate local social life to the forces of the capitalist market.[135] Similarly, Gibson-Graham invokes the diverse practices of a "community economy" that necessarily exist within, beyond, and beside the formal market economy. These practices inspire a wider reimagination of our selves, our ways of life, and wider movements for social and institutional change.[136] To draw on Ashis Nandy's framing, perhaps these time-travels, like Ferguson's, may inspire our own.

---

133 See, for instance, Robert Latham, "Globalisation and Democratic Provisionism: Re-reading Polanyi," *New Political Economy*, 1997, vol. 2, 53–62; Vicki Birchfield, "Contesting the Hegemony of Market Ideology: Gramsci's 'Good Sense' and Polanyi's 'Double Movement,' " *Review of International Political Economy*, 1999, vol. 6, 27–54; and Björn Hettne, "The Double Movement: Global Market Versus Regionalism," in Robert W. Cox (ed.) *The New Realism: Perspectives on Multilateralism and World Order*, Tokyo: UN University, 1997, 223–42.

134 Most strikingly, see Stephen Marglin and Juliet Schor (eds.) *The Golden Age of Capitalism: Reinterpreting the Postwar Experience*, Oxford: Clarendon Press, 1990.

135 See Gustavo Esteva, "Development," in Wolfgang Sachs (ed.) *The Development Dictionary: A Guide to Knowledge as Power*, London, Zed, 1993, 6–25; Arturo Escobar, *Encountering Development: The Making and Unmaking of the Third World*, Princeton: Princeton University, 1995.

136 See J. K. Gibson-Graham, *The End of Capitalism (as we knew it): A Feminist Critique of Political Economy*, Minneapolis: University of Minnesota, 2006.

5   Shed no tears

Hegel's necro-philosophy

For Smith, "nations" and the mostly interchangeable terms, such as "people," "tribe," and "race," refer to patterns of cultural difference that can be placed on a ladder of development.[1] The Scots' understanding of what we can think of as cultural differences supports the optimism of the eighteenth century that peoples everywhere might receive a "cultural makeover," inspired if not directly managed by civilized Europeans.[2] However, this civilizational analysis gradually came to assume, as George Stocking suggests, at least a "quasi-racial aspect."[3] Civilization and race become intertwined, producing a distinctive racism that flourished in the nineteenth century. The defects exhibited by the lower races are no longer seen as malleable. Instead their tribal violence and indolence seem permanent. Accordingly, the negative effects that emerge from such defects must either be checked by civilized peoples, or swept aside by the forces of history.[4] Kant might wonder, then, as he did in his *Philosophy of the History of Mankind* (1785), what purpose Tahitians serve in human history: "why they bothered to exist at all, and whether it would not have been just as well that this island should have been occupied by

---

1 Prior to the development of this stadial scheme, the major markers of difference and, thereby valuation, centered on "Christianity, civility, and rank," as Roxann Wheeler, *The Complexion of Race: Categories of Difference in Eighteenth Century British Culture*, Philadelphia: University of Pennsylvania, 2000, p. 7, puts it. James Muldoon, *Popes, Lawyers, and Infidels: The Church and the Non-Christian World 1250–1550*, Philadelphia: University of Pennsylvania, 1979, pp. 159–60, argues that this is largely consistent with medieval patterns of ethnocentrism, rooted as they are in religious and cultural practices instead of biology. See also Ivan Hannaford, *Race: The History of an Idea in the West*, Baltimore: Johns Hopkins, 1996; and Helen Scott, "Was There a Time Before Race? Capitalist Modernity and the Origins of Racism," in Crystal Bartolovich and Neil Lazarus (eds.) *Marxism, Modernity, and Postcolonial Studies*, Cambridge: Cambridge University, 2002, pp. 174–5.
2 Wheeler, *Complexion of Race*, p. 289.
3 George W. Stocking, Jr., *Victorian Anthropology*, New York: Free Press, 1987, p. 18.
4 Nicholas Hudson, "From 'Nation' to 'Race': The Origin of Racial Classification in Eighteenth-Century Thought," *Eighteenth-Century Studies*, 1996, vol. 29, pp. 248, 253, 256–8. See also his " 'Hottentots' and the Evolution of European Racism," *Journal of European Studies*, 2004, vol. 34, 308–33.

happy sheep and cattle as by happy men engaged in mere pleasure?"[5] This formulation is crucial to Hegel's own historical understanding.

Commentators rarely foreground Hegel's racial constructions; they are loathe even to acknowledge them. By contrast, we highlight the way Hegel makes such racializing moves central to the modern project of political economy. Hegel's *Philosophy of Right* (1821) is at once a "philosophical reconstruction of modern ethical life" and an historical account, seeking to demonstrate that "modern European culture was a product of a long historical evolution."[6] Hegel's linkage of the modern with the European is not incidental. It is Western Europeans who embody modernity's possibilities, particularly the realization of freedom. As Hegel suggests in *Philosophy of Right*, and clarifies in his *Lectures on the Philosophy of World History* (1822, 1828, 1830), non-Europeans remain outside of the modern world. In pronouncing this judgment, Hegel maps racial categories on to continents such that (now racialized) non-European peoples are deemed irrelevant to the tasks of "world history" and accordingly condemned to extinction, enslavement, or colonization. As in Smith, the machine of history often achieves its nobler ends through death and destruction. We emphasize colonialism's crucial role in Hegel's account of the problem of poverty in modern civil society: colonial expansion "solves" the problem of the internal disintegration of civil society and it extends modern civilization to undeveloped areas.

This racialized picture in which some are condemned to physical or social death stands in some tension with Hegel's vision of modernity as the universal actualization of freedom. Our goal is not merely to show that Hegel's racialized historical theory justifies colonialism, but also to argue that Hegel's analysis of the problem of poverty in civil society leads him to offer a racialized colonialism as the only solution to the wound of wealth. Hegel's denigration of non-Europeans is not, therefore, incidental. It is a crucial and necessary part of his attempt to preserve the harmony and universality of the modern symbolic order. Hegel shifts the wound onto others and then carefully veils this displacement with his theory of history. His historical theory produces unity by repressing the spatial and cultural differences remaining within the modern era.

---

5 Quoted in Tsenay Serequeberhan, "Eurocentrism in Philosophy: The Case of Immanuel Kant," *The Philosophical Forum*, 1996, vol. 27, p. 341. See also the excellent essay by Andreas Behnke, " 'Eternal Peace' as the Graveyard of the Political: A Critique of Kant's *Zum Ewigen Frieden*," *Millennium*, 2008, vol. 36, 513–31.

6 Z. A. Pelczynski, "Introduction: The Significance of Hegel's Separation of the State and Civil Society," in Z. A. Pelczynski (ed.) *The State and Civil Society: Studies in Hegel's Political Philosophy*, Cambridge: Cambridge University, 1984, p. 7.

I. Civil Society and the Actualization of Freedom

In *Philosophy of Right*, Hegel places civil society at the center of his account of the modern world and freedom at the center of his understanding of civil society.[7] By his own account, he grounds his thinking in the "science" of "political economy."[8] Though Hegel mentions Smith, Ricardo, and Say by name, there is no evidence that Hegel ever read the latter two. We know, however, from both the content of Hegel's writings and evidence from his biography, that he was quite familiar with Smith, Steuart, and perhaps Ferguson.[9]

Hegel, like the Scots, begins with the idea that humans are social beings. The ground and first dimension of modern sociality is the family. In the family's relations of love, the human being exists not so much as an individual, but as a "member." Nonetheless, the family also nurtures each of its members so that they are prepared to act as independent individuals in the wider society.[10] And where the unity and self-sufficiency of the family gives way, we find civil society.[11]

---

7 In thinking through Hegel's notion of civil society, we draw on Peter G. Stillman, "Partiality and Wholeness: Economic Freedom, Individual Development, and Ethical Institutions in Hegel's Political Thought," in William Maker (ed.) *Hegel on Economics and Freedom*, Macon: Mercer University, 1987, 65–93 and "Hegel's Civil Society: A Locus of Freedom," *Polity*, 1980, vol. XII, 622–46; K.-H. Ilting, "The Dialectic of Civil Society," in Z. A. Pelczynski (ed.) *The State and Civil Society: Studies in Hegel's Political Philosophy*, Cambridge: Cambridge University, 1984, 211–26, and "The Structure of Hegel's 'Philosophy of Right' " in Z. A. Pelzcynski (ed.) *Hegel's Political Philosophy: Problems and Perspectives*, Cambridge: Cambridge University, 1971, 90–110; and Raymond Plant, "Hegel and the Political Economy," in Maker (ed.) *Hegel on Economics and Freedom*, Macon: Mercer University, 1987, 95–126.

8 G. W. F. Hegel, *Elements of the Philosophy of Right*, Cambridge: Cambridge University, 1991, section 187. This edition contains the translation by H. B. Nisbet and we rely on it almost exclusively. The translation by T. M. Knox, *Hegel's Philosophy of Right*, London: Oxford, 1967, is widely cited and we quote it at one point.

9 Norbert Waszek, *The Scottish Enlightenment and Hegel's Account of "Civil Society,"* Dordrecht: Kluwer Academic, 1988, especially chs. 3, 4 and 5, provides an exhaustive account of this topic. As a corrective, Keith Tribe, *Governing Economy: The Reformation of German Economic Discourse 1750–1840*, Cambridge: Cambridge University, 1988, p. 15, suggests that it is easy to exaggerate the influence of the Scots on Hegel and ignore the influence of varieties of Cameralist notions of statecraft. As if in response, Mark Neocleous, "Policing the System of Needs: Hegel, Political Economy, and the Police of the Market," *History of European Ideas*, 1998, vol. 24, pp. 49–52, argues that Cameralist ideas may have come to Hegel mostly via Steuart. These subtleties may not be important for our purposes.

10 Hegel, *Philosophy of Right*, sections 158, 174–5. For accounts and serious criticisms of Hegel's understanding of the family, see Susan Armstrong, "A Feminist Reading of Hegel and Kierkegaard," in Shaun Gallagher (ed.) *Hegel, History, and Interpretation*, Albany: State University of New York, 1997, 227–41; Joan B. Landes, "Hegel's Conception of the Family," *Polity*, 1981, vol. XIV, 5–28.

11 Hegel, *Philosophy of Right*, section 181.

Civil society constitutes people as "private persons," freeing them from the social bondage predominant in other societies and the communal purposes of the family. Each individual is a "particular"—each with her or his own set of needs and interests and for whom these needs and interests are her/his primary end. Further, the market as a central institution of civil society promotes individual self-expression and self-seeking. Like the Scots, Hegel celebrates this as an achievement of the modern era. Additionally, the market is central to the process of dividing labor (Hegel uses the "English pin factory" as an example in earlier writings) and the expansion of wealth. Work transforms nature into a variety of objects; the cultivation of labor, including the division of labor, produces skillful workers who far outpace the "lazy," "dull and solitary," "barbarian," or the "clumsy" and uneducated worker of other places and times.[12]

Along with the expansion of wealth comes the refinement and increasing individualization of needs—"an indeterminate multiplication and specification of needs, means, and pleasures, i.e. *luxury*."[13] Hegel follows the Scots' assumption that, prior to a commercial society, this pursuit of individuality and expansion of need is not possible for humans. Indeed, modern property rights and law cultivate and secure the pursuit of individuality.[14] It is at this point in history that we "allow particularity its freedom."[15] As Hegel summarizes, "the creation of civil society belongs to the modern world, which for the first time allows all . . . to attain their rights."[16]

Yet Hegel departs from the Scots in several respects. Though individuals appear as "particulars" in civil society, they stand "essentially in *relation* to other similar particulars," a relation that Hegel describes as "as a system of all-round interdependence."[17] Smith would agree but Hegel pushes further by arguing that this interdependence changes the character of human neediness itself; humans must respond to others' desires and needs. Need takes on a social or (in Hegel's terms) a "spiritual" character. Individual needs are not direct expressions of particularity, but are shaped within social relations—as "fashion and fancy," to quote Peter Stillman.[18] Likewise, people treat their role in a "system of needs" as an object of reflection; they come to understand

---

12 Hegel, *Philosophy of Right*, sections 197 addition and 198. Hegel refers to the pin factory in his earlier Jena texts: *System of Ethical Life and First Philosophy of Spirit*, Albany: State University of New York, 1979, pp. 247–8.

13 Hegel, *Philosophy of Right*, section 195. Hegel's analysis of consumption is much better developed than Smith's. Though not always consistent, Smith's account tends to turn on a two-class model—of those who receive subsistence and those who receive necessaries and luxuries, as we saw in the earlier chapter. The more likely influence here, says Waszek, *The Scottish Enlightenment*, p. 152, is Steuart.

14 Ibid., sections 217–21.

15 Ibid., section 185 addition.

16 Ibid., section 182 addition.

17 Ibid., sections 182–3.

18 Ibid., section 182, 191–4 and Stillman, "Partiality and Wholeness," p. 73.

and internalize the laws of political economy, making them not simply an impersonal procedure going on behind their backs, but a process in which they "determine their knowledge, volition, and action in a universal way."[19] In this manner, individuals also come to recognize the individuality of others—a reciprocity central to their very constitution as modern social beings.[20]

The contrast to Smith is subtle but significant. Smith understands the historicity of a commercial society, though his historical story turns on universal claims. He regards the historicity of civilized society as the unfolding of a fixed element of human nature—the desire to improve one's situation—and identifies key human sentiments (i.e., sympathy) as universal. However, the character of these fixed and universal elements differs by the kind of society or, more precisely, by the stage of development that society has reached.[21] Hegel historicizes human motivations and sentiments more thoroughly. In Stillman's words: "What economic thinking tends to accept as given, Hegel tends to analyze as the result of the shared experiences of a culture that produces common, intersubjective, shared attitudes and institutions."[22] Emphasizing Hegel's placement of political economy more fully within the realm of culture, if we can put it that way, helps us understand the distinctiveness of Hegel's critical analysis of liberal civil society. Nevertheless, Hegel's conscious emphasis on the social as opposed to the natural determination of practices puts into sharp relief his sudden reversal: he resorts to a "natural" principle—of race—in his understanding of history, as we explore below.

Like Ferguson, Hegel worries that market society produces atomism. Where "selfish ends" alone direct behavior, individuals refuse any constraints, however legitimate. This puts the society at the mercy of individual self-indulgence, "contingent arbitrariness, and subjective caprice." "Here," as Hegel describes the impact of individualization, "the ethical is lost in its extremes."[23] The danger is that political community may perish in the face of these "centrifugal forces."[24] Smith recognizes this possibility, but regards the mechanism of "justice" as adequate to stabilize a commercial society. Hegel

---

19 Hegel, *Philosophy of Right*, section 187. Hegel uses "The System of Needs" as a subheading for sections 189–208.
20 Ibid., section 193.
21 See Jacob Viner, *The Role of Providence in the Social Order: An Essay in Intellectual History*, Princeton: Princeton University, 1972, p. 84.
22 Stillman, "Partiality and Wholeness," p. 76. See Laurence Dickey, *Hegel: Religion, Economics and the Politics of Spirit, 1770–1807*, Cambridge: Cambridge University, 1987, 218, argues similarly that Hegel's viewpoint suggests a more "sociocultural orientation" to economic life. And Gareth Stedman Jones, "Hegel and the Economics of Civil Society," in Sudipta Kaviraj and Sunil Khilnani (eds.) *Civil Society: History and Possibilities*, Cambridge: Cambridge University, 2001, p. 106, suggests that, for Hegel, reason itself "was embodied in language and culture."
23 Hegel, *Philosophy of Right*, sections 184 addition and 185.
24 G. Heiman, "The Sources and Significance of Hegel's Corporate Doctrine," in Z. A. Pelczynski (ed.) *Hegel's Political Philosophy: Problems and Perspectives*, Cambridge: Cambridge University, 1971, p. 123.

too sees legal restraint as crucial to the *"undisturbed security* of *persons* and *property*,"[25] but deems this an inadequate reconciliation of individual freedom and the social good. Such a reconciliation requires something more—a conscious harmonization of the purposes of the individual and the nation.[26]

The "corporation" begins this reconciliation *within* civil society. Civil society involves not only individuals, but also corporate bodies. Perhaps following Smith, Hegel notes that work produces social wealth and that work is divided "into different branches according to its particular nature."[27] But each branch of work "comes into existence" not simply as a result of the workings of economic laws, but in the form of a legally recognized "association." Each "corporation has the right . . . to look after its own interests within its enclosed sphere." This involves not merely educating individuals into the trade and regulating their work once in the trade, but also promoting the "less selfish end of this whole."[28] The qualifier "less" indicates that Hegel does not believe that the joining of individuals into these larger wholes reproduces atomism at the level of interest group pluralism, to use a more contemporary term. The corporation is and does more. It increases the security of the livelihood of the individual in a capricious market but, more importantly, secures the *"honour of belonging to an estate."* Within the corporation, the individual loses his "isolation," taking on an ethical role beyond a "private end," such as the role of breadwinner for the family.[29] Since the corporation also plays a role in governing the society—as an organ of representation in an assembly of estates—the individual comes to understand the interdependence of the interests of the many corporations, the need for compromise, and the need for all to submit to public authority to secure their freedom. Through political activity the individual begins to find his way to identification with the state.[30] As Heiman puts it, the "doctrine of corporatism" is a key part of the institutional structure that transforms individual atoms into "more responsible political being[s]."[31]

Building on this, Hegel turns his attention to the State, where a full reconciliation becomes possible. What he means by the State is not simply the institutions of government that restrain and regulate individual behavior, but something more like what is conveyed by the term "political community."[32]

25 Hegel, *Philosophy of Right*, section 230.
26 See the accounts of Ilting, "Civil Society" and "The Structure," and Stillman, "Partiality and Wholeness."
27 Hegel, *Philosophy of Right*, section 251. See also sections 203–4.
28 Ibid., sections 251–3.
29 Ibid., sections 253–5.
30 Ibid., sections 256, 288–9, 302.
31 Heiman, "Hegel's Corporate Doctrine," p. 112.
32 See K.-H. Ilting, "Hegel's Concept of the State and Marx's Early Critique," in Z. A. Pelczynski (ed.) *The State and Civil Society: Studies in Hegel's Political Philosophy*, Cambridge: Cambridge University, 1984, pp. 94–5.

Here the image is the "citizen," not the "bourgeois,"[33] and we move closer to Ferguson's terrain. For Ferguson, the constraints of justice alone cannot restore the integrity of society; a good society requires a public spiritedness that takes us well beyond simply respecting the person and property of others. Hegel's position is similar. He draws on Roman law and medieval legal and institutional structures to construct his "corporation," but adapts them to the needs of modern civil society.[34] His notion of the State appeals to an ancient or republican idea(l) of the polity.[35] Like Ferguson, Hegel suggests that a modern market society can still aspire to the kinds of political community embraced by classical thinkers. In this respect, Hegel's political thinking continues to contain "pre-modern aspects."[36]

However, Hegel moves us well beyond Ferguson when he destabilizes and redefines the notion of freedom central to the Scots and an emerging liberalism. Acting without restraint is ultimately "self-defeating."[37] What Hegel means is that individual caprice must be limited by the very public purposes that make individuality possible. Earlier in the *Philosophy of Right*, he argues that impulsive and hedonistic actions do not make for a free, self-determining individual. Self-determining individuals "stand above" the "*immediately present . . . drive, desires and inclinations*" that might be thought to motivate the self; self-determination involves reflecting on those desires, making them subject to one's will rather than one's will being subject to them. It is to "determine and posit them as [one's] own," or to disown them as the case may be.[38] To be rational is not simply to calculate how to achieve one's desires, but rather to "work through the process of self-production both by going out of [one]self and by educating [oneself] inwardly."[39] In a more modern parlance, following Stillman, those scholars who limit the notion of freedom to the exercise of one's preferences without regard to anything but external constraint can "have little helpful to say to someone who is trying to discover, articulate, and follow a plan of life."[40]

If in a market society, individual actions are partially capricious, so are market forces themselves. Once immersed in civil society, the individual's livelihood and his family's subsistence are provisional; in Hegel's terms, their

---

33 Ilting, "Civil Society," p. 221; Hegel implies this distinction in *Philosophy of Right*, section 33.
34 See Heiman, "Hegel's Corporate Doctrine," pp. 115–21; Cary J. Nederman, "Sovereignty, War and the Corporation: Hegel on the Medieval Foundations of the Modern State," *Journal of Politics*, 1987, vol. 49, pp. 510–17.
35 See Ilting, "Hegel's Concept of the State;" Schlomo Avineri, *Hegel's Theory of the Modern State*, Cambridge: Cambridge University, 1972, pp. 15–24.
36 Neocleous, "Policing the System of Needs," p. 53.
37 Hegel, *Philosophy of Right*, section 184.
38 Ibid., section 11. That we may (or must) disown parts of the self explains in part why the other always lurks within the self.
39 Ibid., section 10 addition. See Dickey, *Hegel*, pp. 235–6.
40 Stillman, "Partiality and Wholeness," p. 72.

very "existence" is subject to "contingency."[41] Hegel focuses on the extremes of opulence and poverty. We will treat the issue of poverty in greater detail in the third section, but here we want to introduce Hegel's view of the market. He is less than convinced of market society's self-regulation; his Scottish tutor here is more Steuart than Smith.[42] Hegel speaks of government regulation as the power to police, which both constrains ill effects and cultivates positive social purposes.[43] The line between private concern and a public matter is always blurry; many contingencies intrude, like war, and the line depends always on the particular political and cultural constitution of the nation.[44] Hegel's unwillingness to police the boundaries of the political and the economic may reflect his less than full confidence that the "differing interests of producers and consumers" will be automatically reconciled. Where they are in "collision" (as for example in unfair restraints of trade and tainted products), Hegel calls for conscious regulation by an "agency that stands above both sides."[45] Smith allowed no such function for government. He assumed that the interests of competing groups—owners of stock and laborers—would be decided by the balance of forces arrayed on each side, a battle normally won by the capitalists. Indeed, Smith's government seems naturally to prohibit the "combination" of workers that might shift the balance of power somewhat. Smith condemns this imbalance, but offers no remedy.

Hegel pushes further in saying that government may need to assist and guide "large branches of industry" that are "dependent on external circumstances and remote combinations whose full implications cannot be grasped by the individuals who are tied to these spheres by their occupation."[46] Hegel signals that individuals do not necessarily make better economic decisions than the government. In this respect, Hegel might be channeling Steuart and some contemporary authors extend the parallel to link Steuart, Hegel, and Keynes.[47] These speculative linkages suggest that we should read Hegel's backing of government intervention as relatively constrained. His notion of the police supports individual freedom and promotes production of the wealth that is the substrate of individual freedom; he argues that the "aim of oversight and provisions on the part of the police is to mediate between the individual and the universal possibility for the attainment of individual

41 Hegel, *Philosophy of Right*, section 238.
42 A more ambiguous account of Steuart's influence can be found in Waszek, *The Scottish Enlightenment*, pp. 186–7, 196–204.
43 On the idea of the police, see Neocleous, "Policing the System of Needs," pp. 44–7.
44 Hegel, *Philosophy of Right*, sections 230, 234.
45 Ibid., section 235.
46 Ibid., section 236.
47 Pelczynski, "Introduction," p. 10. See also A. S. Walton, "Economy, Utility and Community in Hegel's Theory of Civil Society," in Z. A. Pelczynski (ed.) *The State and Civil Society*, p. 244.

ends."[48] Thus, Hegel justifies regulation of civil society, as did Smith and Steuart, in terms of what we might call market failure.[49] All three agree that the market creates wealth and realizes individual freedom but they differ markedly in their faith in self-regulation.

This conclusion misses Hegel's distinctiveness, however. Restraints on individual freedom in modern society come only partly in the form of external state regulation. Rather, the modern state, in its broadest sense, points to the immersion of the individual in an ethical community. The individual does not produce him or herself out of nothing. The self-determination and hence freedom of the individual occurs only within the confines of a particular cultural context—the whole array of norms and institutions that define a nation. The individual orients him or herself in that context, determining (that is, shaping and constraining) his or her activities in a way that makes the public purposes and goals of the political community part of the individual's life plan. For Hegel it is ethical life that keeps a market society from falling into an atomistic and unconstrained struggle among competing interests.[50] Since policing of the economy shapes ethical life, market failure cannot be the sole principle guiding intervention. Rather, intervention and regulation is justified because it serves ethical purposes such as individuation and self-realization.

We might take seriously, then, Laurence Dickey's comparison of Hegel, not to Keynes, but to Karl Polanyi. As we noted in earlier chapters, Polanyi argues that the economy's unleashing of private motives is destructive of human and natural relationships, unless it is embedded in a social-cultural world of institutions and practices.[51] Hegel also makes clear that a market society is necessarily embedded. For Hegel, the purpose of modern society is not primarily material, though economic advances do remove the weight of natural determination. The purpose of the market is to bring the individual into the institutions of "ethical life."[52] As Shaun Gallagher puts it, Hegel's "civil society is . . . not a disembedded economy;" it is "embedded in moral, legal, political, as well as familial dimensions of life." Unlike Marx, then, Hegel "resolves" the problems of modern life not in reference to some future,

48 Hegel, *Philosophy of Right*, section 236 addition.
49 See Waszek, *The Scottish Enlightenment*, pp. 203–4.
50 Dickey, *Hegel*, pp. 184–5; Ilting, "The Structure," pp. 94–7.
51 Ibid., pp. 195, 214–19. We stress Polanyi's cultural political economy in Naeem Inayatullah and David L. Blaney, *International Relations and the Problem of Difference*, New York: Routledge, 2004, ch. 5.
52 Hegel draws this contrast in *Philosophy of Right*, section 258. Hegel's motivations for healing this rend in the modern self are well analyzed by Robert Shilliam, "The 'Other' in Classical Political Theory: Re-contextualizing the Cosmopolitan/Communitarian Debate," in Beate Jahn (ed.) *Classical Theory in International Relations*, Cambridge: Cambridge University, 2006, 207–32.

transcendent form of social life, but from the beneficial intersection of the multiple domains of modern life.[53]

Even if we doubt, along with Marx, that the modern state can reconcile the strong republican ideals of political community with the operations of a capitalist economy, Hegel's insights remain acute. He insists that "economic relations are social in character." Looking back to Smith and forward to Marx, Hegel rejects an image of man as locked into a material struggle with nature in which he, collectively and inadvertently, produces social progress. Historical advance unfolds in a "spiritual" or, as we read it, cultural process. Hegel thereby steers us away from an account of economy as a "technical process." Economy is neither simply "a metabolism between man and nature" nor an auction of supply and demand; he emphasizes that it is a distinctly "normative sphere."[54] We have the seeds of a cultural political economy.

II. History as the Court of Judgment: Race, Time, and Genocide

World history provides the "capstone" of Hegel's discussion of civil society in the *Philosophy of Right*.[55] Modernity realizes a long historical struggle to reconcile individual freedom and political community. The influence of the Scots' progressive history is obvious.[56] Indeed, Hegel adapts Smith's "four-stages theory" for his own purposes. In his early writings, Hegel reforms "religious" ideals so that Christianity becomes consistent with the imperatives of the modern world. Specifically, he overturns a pessimistic view of human capacities for one in which humans realize progress on earth by assimilating some of God's characteristics. He understands that this shift must be consistent with the "real" processes of historical change. He affirms Scottish political economy as an account of the inevitable forces of change, making, as Plant puts it, the "development of urban life, labor, mutual dependence, state, and nation" into "part of the progressive trend in history."[57]

Hegel envisions this harmony of ideals and progressive forces in a "system of right" that he describes in *Philosophy of Right* as "the realm of actualized

53 Shaun Gallagher, "Interdependence and Freedom in Hegel's Economics," in William Maker (ed.) *Hegel on Economics and Freedom*, Macon: Mercer University, 1987, pp. 170, 173.
54 Richard Dien Winfield, "Hegel's Challenge to the Modern Economy," in William Maker (ed.) *Hegel on Economics and Freedom*, Macon: Mercer University, 1987, pp. 29–31. See also Christopher J. Arthur, "Hegel on Political Economy," in David Lamb (ed.) *Hegel and Modern Philosophy*, London: Croom Helm, 1987, pp. 108–9.
55 We draw this phrase from Donald J. Maletz, "History in Hegel's *Philosophy of Right*," *Review of Politics*, 1983, vol. 45, p. 210.
56 We take on the account of Dickey, *Hegel*, especially pp. 181–5, 237–41, 279–80, in this paragraph. See also Terry Pinkard, *Hegel: A Biography*, Cambridge: Cambridge University, 2000, chs. 1–3.
57 Plant, "Hegel and the Political Economy," pp. 101–2.

freedom." Freedom is not already present for humans in some state of nature at the beginning of history. Rather, freedom unfolds through human achievement—"the world of spirit produced from within itself as a second nature."[58] Spirit, or the human will, unfolds as a process of negation; it determines itself, but the determinate content that it posits also appears as a limit—as "finitude"; as a "difference"—that will embraces but moves beyond as it reconciles the particular and the universal.[59] Hegel refers to this process of unfolding as "dialectic:"

> The higher dialectic of the concept consists not merely in producing and apprehending the determination as an opposite and limiting factor, but in producing and apprehending the *positive* content and result which it contains; and it is this alone which makes it a *development* and immanent progression.[60]

This logical movement produces gain—each "determination . . . becomes continually richer in itself, so that the last determination is also the richest."[61] But this progression also takes place in time. As Hegel asserts elsewhere, "World History in general is the development of Spirit in *Time*."[62]

Hegel makes time unfold through space—across a succession of historical peoples, from the Oriental to the Greek and Roman, arriving at modern freedom finally with the role of the Germanic peoples.[63] Hegel would stress, however, that modern society unfolds as expressly *universal*, not the reflection of a particular national spirit or culture. We might say, contra Hegel, that what he envisions as universal is a particular modern, European culture. It is the shape of modern European consciousness that sets the agenda for the world-historical present. The moment of negation in European thought—its reflective critique that challenges all givens—brings us to a philosophy and practice of "right" that reconciles human freedom and political community and spurs development towards that reconciliation.[64] In Hegel's *Lectures in the Philosophy of World History*, Europe appears as the "absolute end of history."[65] All nations or peoples are henceforth judged by what they

---

58 These two quotations are joined in the original. Hegel, *Philosophy of Right*, section 4. See also Steven B. Smith, "Hegel's Discovery of History," *Review of Politics*, 1983, vol. 45, p. 187.

59 Hegel, *Philosophy of Right*, sections 4–7.

60 Ibid., section 31.

61 Ibid., section 32 addition.

62 G. W. F. Hegel, *Reason in History: A General Introduction to the Philosophy of History*, New York: Bobbs-Merill, 1953, p. 87.

63 Hegel, *Philosophy of Right*, sections 354–8.

64 Ibid., p. 471.

65 G. W. F. Hegel, *Lectures in the Philosophy of World History*, Cambridge: Cambridge University, 1975, p. 197. This is not to say that the unfolding of spirit has finally ended, but that, for as far as we can see, the European present provides the highest point of human achievement.

mean "for thought"—what they mean for critical European philosophy and an actualized practice of right in Europe.[66] As Hegel evocatively puts it in *Philosophy of Right*, the particularities of states and peoples, the "ceaseless turmoil" of events, the play of "passions, interests, ends, talents and virtues, violence, wrongdoing, and vices" all have their part to play in the "dialectic" of the "universal spirit." The process of movement "exercises its right—which is the highest right of all—over finite spirits in *world history* as the *world's court of judgment.*"[67]

In this set of claims, Hegel gives ethical meaning to the movement of nations and peoples as well as to the specific events of history. Violence and cruelty, kindness and creativity, etc., are not measured against the morality of individuals or groups, but relative to their role in history's deeper purpose—the actualization of freedom as a modern civil society and state. Hegel's understanding of events reveals the secularized theodicy central to his vision. Like Smith, he shows how evil and human suffering work to produce good results in modern society.[68] The complex machinations of "world history" must be understood in terms of movement towards its "ultimate purpose"—"the Idea in general, in its manifestation as human spirit" or, "[m]ore precisely . . . the idea of human freedom."[69] Thus, we can make sense of "the slaughter-bench at which the happiness of peoples, the wisdom of states, and the virtue of individuals have been sacrificed." These admittedly "monstrous sacrifices" have meaning and significance: they are the "events" that serve as "the means for realizing the essential destiny, the absolute and final purpose, or, what amounts to the same thing, the true result of world history."[70] History teleologically achieves its ultimate ends through a chain of "efficient causation," involving, in this case, conflict, war, suffering, and death.[71] This is not simply a necro-economics, as discussed in prior chapters, but a broader necro-ontology or necro-philosophy. We might see this as a secular sacralization of suffering and death.

For Hegel and the Scots, Europe represents the height of civilization to which all others must become reconciled, even if such development proceeds

---

66 Maletz, "History," p. 225.
67 Hegel, *Philosophy of Right*, section 340.
68 As Viner, *The Role of Providence*, p. 26, notes, progressive histories tend to take on religious valences, though in a secular form.
69 Hegel, *Reason in History*, pp. 20–1.
70 Ibid., p. 27.
71 That Hegel's teleology involves this kind of mechanism is demonstrated by Willem A. deVries, "The Dialectic of Teleology," *Philosophical Topics*, 1991, vol. 19, 51–70. Thus, the recent debate staged by Jaeger and Brooks about Hegel's "realism" may miss that Hegel lodges *Realpolitik* in a broader theory of the ethical purpose of history, though it is clearly not an embrace of a global civil society. Hans-Martin Jaeger, "Hegel's Reluctant Realism and the Transnationalisation of Civil Society," *Review of International Studies*, 2002, vol. 28, 497–517 and Thom Brooks, "Hegel's Theory of International Politics: A Reply to Jaeger," *Review of International Studies*, 2004, vol. 30, 149–52.

through cruelty and force. In partial contrast to Smith, however, Hegel specifies those destined for the slaughterhouse. While for Smith all peoples seemed called to progress, however that might be achieved, Hegel's account of the division of the human species into races suggests that some—like Africans and the Amerindians—stand outside of history altogether. Only world-historical peoples "play their part successively on the historical scene" and Hegel's account "is distinctively, indeed aggressively European"[72] and white, we might add, given the role assigned to "the Nordic principle of the *Germanic peoples.*"[73]

We may be overstating the case, given that Hegel's racial views are contested. Terry Pinkard, for example, describes Hegel as, like Kant, quite provincial and distinctly "Eurocentric," but not racist, despite his "rather painful and typical characterization of the kinds of traits typical of the different races."[74] Others stress his egalitarianism as evidence of his non-racialized stance, if not genuine anti-racism.[75] Hegel does note that "it is rightly said that genius, talents, piety, moral virtues and sentiments appear in all zones, under all constitutions, and political conditions." However, in the pages that immediately follow he asserts that the issue is neither the genius of individuals, for they remain trapped within the spirit of a people, nor a prevalent morality, but a capacity to be an actor in an historical "dialectic," to be a "world-historical people."[76] Elsewhere in the *Philosophy of Spirit* in the *Encyclopedia* (1817), Hegel similarly rejects the importance of debates about the singular or multiple origins of the species, suggesting that no clear distinctions could be drawn between races in terms of their reason and rights. Yet in his 1825 lecture course, he says that "[t]he question of racial variety bears upon the rights one ought to accord to people; when there are various races, one will be nobler and the other has to serve it."[77]

However much he gestures towards equality, we find it difficult to see Hegel as a global egalitarian. In *Philosophy of Right*, the notion of State is limited to the kinds of constitutional arrangements specific to modern, European societies. Consistent with emerging usage, Hegel believes a proper nation must have a State and distinguishes such a nation from a "family, tribe, kinship group, mass [of people], etc."[78] This contrast has more than

72 W. H. Walsh, "Principle and Prejudice in Hegel's Philosophy of History," in Z. A. Pelczynski (ed.) *Hegel's Political Philosophy: Problems and Perspectives*, Cambridge: Cambridge University Press, 1971, pp. 182, 188–9.
73 Hegel, *Philosophy of Right*, section 358.
74 Pinkard, *Hegel*, p. 493.
75 Joseph McCarney, *Hegel on History*, New York: Routledge, 2000, pp. 142–5.
76 Hegel, *Reason in History*, pp. 81–7.
77 Quoted in Robert Bernasconi, "With What Must the Philosophy of World History Begin? On the Racial Basis of Hegel's Eurocentrism," *Nineteenth-Century Contexts*, 2000, vol. 22, pp. 185–6.
78 Hegel, *Philosophy of Right*, section 349.

analytical import; it bears on which entities can be recognized as sovereign in international society: "Civilized nations" are entitled:

> to regard and treat as barbarians other nations which are less advanced than they are in the substantial moments of the state (as with pastoralists in relation to hunters, and agriculturalists in relation to both of these), in the consciousness that the rights of these other nations are not equal to theirs and that their independence is merely formal.[79]

Here Hegel invokes Smith's "four-stages theory" to describe the hierarchy of social forms. If conflict and war are characteristic of relations among peoples that recognize the right to independence, what can those groups or peoples who fail to gain such recognition expect? What place do they have in "world history"?

Hegel's answer to these questions is informed by a system of racial classification developed in *Lectures on the Philosophy of World History*.[80] Here Hegel naturalizes the differences in "character" assumed by peoples and nations. Though he explicitly rejects a theory of degeneration so popular for many early modern thinkers,[81] his racial classification turns on the division of the world into continents; natural forces operate differentially across continental space, shaping people and their prospects.[82] Hegel stops short of the kind of climatic determinism associated with Montesquieu, but nature is significant in shaping social possibilities; it is "the ground on which the spirit moves."[83] The impact of geography is particularly decisive at the extremes. Hegel argues that "neither the torrid nor the cold region can provide a basis for human freedom or the world-historical nations."[84] He elaborates:

---

79 Hegel, *Philosophy of Right*, section 351.

80 The proximate source of Hegel's racial categories may have been Kant's writings on geography. See Bernasconi, "Philosophy of World History," pp. 175–6.

81 Hegel, *Reason in History*, p. 72.

82 Jospeh McCarney, "Hegel's Racism? A Response to Bernasconi," *Radical Philosophy*, 2003, no. 119, 1–4, refuses the charge against Hegel and characterizes Hegel's position as a "geographical materialism." Benasconi, "Hegel's Racism: A Reply," *Radical Philosophy*, 2003, no. 119, 4–6, replies that this geographical theory is precisely Hegel's form of racism, that Hegel only allows certain continents/races to produce the "peoples" that are the true subjects of history. It seems to us that many of the defenders of Hegel do little more than suggest that he doesn't share the exact form of scientific racism so prevalent in the later nineteenth and twentieth centuries. As we have noted at the outset of this chapter, processes of othering, racialization included, are not fixed categories/practices; they are invented and reinvented across time and space. Hegel's account of race seems quite consistent with the emerging racial theories of the Enlightenment.

83 Hegel, *Lectures on World History*, pp. 152–4. See Benasconi, "Philosophy of World History," p. 186.

84 Hegel, *Lectures on World History*, p. 154.

Aristotle has long since observed that man turns to universal and more exalted things only after his basic needs are satisfied. But neither the torrid nor the frigid zone permits him to . . . acquire sufficient resources to allow him to participate in higher spiritual interests. . . . The frost which grips the inhabitants of Lappland and the fiery heat of Africa are forces too powerful . . . for man to resist, or to achieve . . . that degree of richness which is the precondition and source of a fully developed mastery of reality. In regions such as these, dire necessity can never be escaped or overcome; . . . where nature is too powerful, it does not allow itself to be used as a means. The torrid and frigid regions, as such, are not the theatre on which world history is enacted. In this respect, such extremes are incompatible with spiritual freedom.[85]

Only the European temperate zone can serve as a "theatre" for world history. Others—Africans and Amerindians in particular—experience a lethal off-stage fate. Given this understanding of human history, one that continues to bind us in many respects,[86] Donald Maletz suggests that the best "backward" peoples can expect is assimilation to the particular freedoms of modern civil society.[87] If some can expect assimilation through colonialism, Hegel sentences others to slavery and extermination.

Africans are pivotal in Hegel's world. Africa, he tells us, "has no historical interest of its own, for we find its inhabitants living in barbarism and savagery in a land which has not furnished them with an integral ingredient of culture." For Hegel, the capacity to effectively manipulate nature is central to the operations of the human spirit in history. He is careful to limit his remarks to "*Africa proper*," by which he means sub-Saharan Africa, excluding Egypt and coastal areas influenced by Europe. He does so in order to exclude Africa from world-historical areas or areas adjacent to past theatres of world history.[88]

For Hegel, the African falls short. Subsumed by his "immediate existence" in nature, "dominated by passion," the African is "nothing more than a savage" incapable of progress.[89] As mere aspects of nature, Africans cannot access their higher spiritual potential. They lack that true sense of religion in which one becomes aware "that there is something higher than man."[90] African religious practices are frenzied, convulsive, and bloody, including the murder of family and friends and drinking of blood.[91]

85 Hegel, *Lectures on World History*, p. 155.
86 The argument that a geographical determinism shapes the respective fate of continents continues to intrigue us. See Jared Diamond, *Guns, Germs, and Steel: The Fates of Human Societies*, New York: Norton, 1999.
87 Maletz, "History," p. 233.
88 Hegel, *Lectures on World History*, p. 109.
89 Ibid., p. 177.
90 Ibid., pp. 178–9.
91 Ibid., p. 180.

Just at the moment where we might marvel at how the Hegel of the *Lectures* could have anticipated the most caricatured Hollywood scenes of Africans, he provides a partial reprieve, conceding that this kind of "witchcraft . . . once prevailed in Europe too."[92] Here we witness a double displacement in which the external other and its internal intimate twin are both moved into a previous developmental time. European witchcraft is part of the past that still envelops Africans; both are excluded from the present.

Just as swiftly, Hegel returns to his caricature. Africans, he asserts, have no respect for human beings—either for themselves or for others. Their resulting contempt for justice and morality not only produces tyranny but also permits cannibalism, including the sale of "human flesh."[93] Their sense of empathy and social morality is so weak that parents readily sell their children, and when given a chance, children sell their parents. Indeed, the polygamous family is rooted not in the love that gives the family its central purpose, but is instead designed to produce children for sale.[94] Indeed, their deficient respect for life makes them indifferent to their survival: "they allow themselves to be shot down in thousands in their wars with the Europeans." Their tactics reflect "madness and rage"—"fanaticism" not bravery.[95] For Hegel, in contrast to Smith and Ferguson, there is none of the quasi-romantic temporal inversion that locates martial virtue in pre-modern peoples.

As if the conclusion could be in doubt, Hegel sums up his view of the African condition, using a racial not a geographical term:

> From all these various traits we have enumerated, it can be seen that intractability is the distinguishing feature of the Negro character. The condition in which they live is incapable of any development or culture, and their present existence is the same as it has always been.[96]

Africa lacks just that ethical life whose presence in Europe Hegel sought to capture in *Philosophy of Right*.[97]

This is a disturbing picture. All the more disturbing when one considers that Hegel not only opts for the most disparaging sources, but also draws on these selectively, studiously ignoring anything that might suggest the presence of human culture in Africa. Nor is Hegel merely a product of his times, since quite different views of Africa were available.[98] But Hegel needs Africa as an

---

92 Hegel, *Lectures on World History*, p. 181.
93 Ibid., p. 183.
94 Ibid., pp. 184–5.
95 Ibid., p. 185.
96 Hegel, *Lectures on World History*, p. 190.
97 The parallel for Smith is the lack of divided labor that characterizes savage society. See "Introduction and Plan of the Work," *Wealth of Nations*, pp. 1–4.
98 This point is made convincingly by Robert Bernasconi, "Philosophy of World History," pp. 171–4 and "Hegel at the Court of the Ashanti," in Stuart Brown (ed.) *Hegel After Derrida*, London: Routledge, 1998, 41–63.

inert beginning point. Since beginnings are the ground on which all else follows, a cultureless place/race is necessary on which to build the progressive plenitude of the spirit. Africa acts as Europe's "constitutive other," remaining outside of history proper but simultaneously serving as that history's baseline. As Bernasconi puts it, Africa serves as the "null-point or base-point" of humanity against which Hegel explores the role of history's real subjects.[99]

Astoundingly, Africans fare better than Amerindians. If Africans are a "null-point" for Hegel, they still manage to exhibit physical vigor and a potential for being taught. This potential is utterly unavailable to the natives of the Americas. In comparing Amerindians to Africans, Hegel asserts that "negroes are far more susceptible to European culture than the Indians." He cites examples:

> An English writer reports that, among the wide circle of his acquaintances, he had encountered instances of negroes becoming skilled workers and tradesmen, and even clergymen and doctors, etc. But of all the free native Americans he knew, he could think of only one who had proved capable of study and who eventually became a clergyman.

Even this individual, Hegel reports, "died afterwards as a result of excessive drinking."[100] Drawing upon themes of American degeneracy developed by Buffon and popularized by Cornélius de Pauw, Hegel asserts that "America has always shown itself physically and spiritually impotent, and it does so to this day." Even the flora and fauna of the Americas is inferior.[101] The Americans, consequently, are "like unenlightened children, living from one day to the next, and untouched by higher thoughts and aspirations."[102] Rather than advancing with European contact, these "[c]ulturally inferior nations"—also referred to as "tribes"—"are gradually eroded."[103] This "erosion" has meant that "few descendants of the original inhabitants survive, for nearly seven million have been wiped out." Furthermore, the cause of their "destruction" (*untergehen*—also translated as "perished" or "vanished") is what Hegel terms "the breath of European activity."[104] World history renders its verdict.

99 Bernasconi, "Philosophy of History," p. 52.
100 Hegel, *Lectures on World History*, p. 163.
101 Ibid., p. 163. See Gilbert Chinard, "Eighteenth Century Theories on America as Human Habitat," *Proceedings of the American Philosophical Society*, 1947, vol. 91, 27–57.
102 Hegel, *Lectures on World History*, p. 165.
103 Ibid., p. 163.
104 For the verb *untergehen*, there are different translations. We are using Nisbet's translation as "destruction," but others have used "perished" and "vanished." See Michael Hoffheimer, "Hegel, Race, and Genocide," *The Southern Journal of Philosophy*, 2001, vol. XXXIX, p. 37.

Such statements and Hegel's general treatment of Africans and Amerindians leads contemporary commenter Michael Hoffheimer to ask if Hegel meant to justify genocide:

> His imposition of a racial hierarchy on the colonial experience in America raises the question of whether he meant to offer a philosophical justification for the subjugation, displacement, and genocide of American Indians.[105]

Hoffheimer leaves this question open, but he nevertheless points to Hegel's language as an indication of his evasion of European responsibility:

> The phrase ["perished," "vanished" or "destroyed" at the "breath" or "whiff" of "European activity"] removed any European responsibility for this extinction or submersion. European activity was not the subject of the phrase, nor was responsibility ascribed by means of the passive voice.[106]

As we have seen, Europe as world historical actor is the tool of a deeper historical purpose: the realization of modernity. "The real hero of history is after all the spirit," as Walsh puts it.[107] European hands are bloodless; the responsibility for genocide rests on history as a "world court of judgment." Even if we accept these seeming evasions, we might nonetheless wonder about the merit of modern freedom if it is achieved at the cost of genocide.

If Americans are simply "disappeared" by Hegel, Africans suffer a more complex fate. Even if we absolve Hegel of justifying genocide, his open defense of slavery is difficult to fathom. In principle, Hegel strongly opposes slavery: "Slavery is unjust in and for itself, for the essence of man is freedom."[108] However, the pursuit of ideals cannot entail quantum jumps beyond the context of an historical moment. At a particular time and place, a specific form of slavery might be rational and necessary. Africans are a case in point. The African devaluation of life means that, for Hegel, "slavery is the basic legal relationship in Africa." Indeed, Hegel asserts that "[i]n all the African Kingdoms known to the Europeans, this slavery is endemic and accepted as natural."[109]

Quite significantly, the form of slavery practiced in Africa is arbitrary relative to the state organized slavery of world-historical peoples like the Greeks and Romans:

105 Hoffheimer, "Hegel, Race, and Genocide".
106 Ibid.
107 Walsh, "Principle and Prejudice," p. 193.
108 Hegel, *Lectures on World History*, p. 184.
109 Ibid., p. 183.

when [slavery] occurs within an organized state, it is itself a stage in the progress away from purely fragmented sensuous existence, a phase in man's education, and an aspect of the process whereby he gradually attains a higher ethical existence and a corresponding degree of culture. Slavery is unjust in and for itself, for the essence of man is freedom; but he must first become mature before he can be free.[110]

For immature and stateless African tribes, supplanting their form of slavery by slavery at the hands of those nations that possess a State is not only acceptable, it is a means for elevating their existence. For Africans, enslavement by Europeans "is a moment in the transition towards a higher stage of development."[111]

Hegel echoes this position elsewhere in his work. In the *Philosophy of Right*, he writes that "[s]lavery occurs in man's transition from the state of nature to genuinely ethical conditions; it occurs in a world where wrong is still right. At that state wrong has validity and so is necessarily in place."[112] In the *Encyclopedia*, he says: "To become free[,] . . . to acquire the capacity for self-control, all nations must therefore undergo the severe discipline of subjugation to the master."[113] Thus, while Hegel may make the injustice of slavery a continuing theme in his work, Hoffheimer notes that he also "would never unequivocally endorse the abolition of slavery."[114] We can see why: slavery for Hegel lifts lower races to culture, progress, and freedom. Hegel's answer to Kant's question about why the Tahitians bother to exist is that they and others exist to be civilized and, where that is not possible, to be swept away by the hand of history.

Hegel's denigration of Africans as a "null-point" also serves an additional function in his work. In *Philosophy of Right*, colonial expansion not only civilizes others, but also, as we shall see, is Hegel's solution for the problem posed by certain internal others—those Europeans immersed within the systematic poverty produced by civil society. If these Europeans can be exported to the colonies, then poverty at home and barbarism abroad both have colonization as their solution. Bernasconi suggests that, whatever Hegel intended, colonialism serves this double function in this thought.[115] We pursue this intuition in the next section.

---

110 Hegel, *Lectures*, p. 184.
111 Ibid.
112 Hegel, *Philosophy of Right*, para. 57 addition.
113 Quoted in Steven B. Smith, "Hegel on Slavery and Domination," *Review of Metaphysics*, 1992, vol. 46, p. 111.
114 Hoffheimer, "Hegel, Race, Genocide," p. 44. Going further, Bernasconi, "Philosophy of World History," p. 58, believes that Hegel provided "comfort and resources to those who rejected abolition." To support his claim, Bernasconi cites Hoffheimer's documentation ("Does Hegel Justify Slavery," *The Owl of Minerva*, 1993, vol. 25, pp. 118–19) of the use of Hegel in debates on the eve of the U.S. Civil War.
115 See Bernasconi, "Hegel at the Court," pp. 59–60.

III. Poverty and Imperialism: Salving the Wound of Wealth

As we have seen, Hegel conceives the economy in terms of its implicit and explicit ethical purposes. The capitalist economy within modern bourgeois society crucially promotes individuality, legal equality, and freedom. Hegel also recognizes that placing the market at the center of civil society threatens social disintegration through atomization of social life. Thus, the market is necessarily circumscribed by, and embedded within, the wider ethical imperatives of the family, civil society, and the state.

However plausible Hegel's reconciliation of the individual and community, most commentators agree that he failed in one respect: the problem of poverty.[116] This failure is not inconsequential, since Hegel's examination of poverty is considered to be especially astute.[117] As Shlomo Avineri argues, in a justly famous passage:[118]

> What is conspicuous in Hegel's analysis . . . is not only his far-sightedness but also a basic intellectual honesty which makes him admit again and again—completely against the grain of the integrative and mediating nature of his whole social philosophy—that he has no solution to the problem posed by poverty in its modern context. This is the only time in his system where Hegel raises a problem—and leaves it open.

As we will see, however, Hegel's failure leads him to go beyond the political community itself and give modern colonialism a central place within his political economy. As slavery is necessary to the purpose of world history, so colonialism is essential to the construction and maintenance of a modern political economy. Colonialism is an indispensable component in the totality that Hegel imagines as modernity.

Hegel suggests that poverty is created and unleashed by wealth creation itself and that therefore poverty is distinctively modern. This is an insight both profound and incisive. Hegel forewarns: "The important question of

---

116 Our account is inspired by Avineri, *Hegel's Theory of the Modern State*, ch. 7; Plant, "Hegel and the Political Economy," pp. 119–21; Thomas Wartenberg, "Poverty and Class Structure in Hegel's Theory of Civil Society," *Philosophy and Social Criticism*, 1981, vol. 8, 168–82; Ian Fraser, "Speculations on Poverty in Hegel's *Philosophy of Right*," *The European Legacy*, 1996, vol. 1, 2055–68; Robert Fatton, Jr., "Hegel and the Riddle of Poverty: The Limits of Bourgeoisie Political Economy," *History of Political Economy*, 1986, vol. 18, 579–600; Tsenay Serequeberhan, "The Idea of Colonialism in Hegel's Philosophy of Right," *International Philosophical Quarterly*, 1989, vol. XXIX, 301–18; and Gabriel Paquette, "Hegel's Analysis of Colonialism and Its Roots in Scottish Political Economy," *CLIO*, 2003, vol. 32, 415–32.

117 Hegel's work on the impact of the technical division of labor prefigures Marx's in some respects, but is less prescient perhaps, since he derived much from Smith and perhaps Ferguson.

118 Avineri, *Hegel's Theory of the Modern State*, p. 154.

how poverty can be remedied is one which agitates and torments *modern societies especially.*"[119] Hegel's analysis of the division of labor reveals civil society's darker side:

> ... the *specialization* and *limitation* of particular work also increase, as do likewise the *dependence* and *want* of the class which is tied to such work; this in turn leads to an inability to feel and enjoy the wider freedoms, and particularly the spiritual advantages, of civil society.[120]

But besides workers' inability to enjoy the freedoms of civil society, Hegel's argument indicates a deeper difficulty—the technological innovation unleashed by modern society displaces workers. This claim is closer to Marx's "General Law of Capitalist Accumulation" than to Smith's vision of capitalist harmony. While Hegel may miss the obvious point that innovation need not mean a net loss of jobs for the economy, he was aware of the dislocations associated with capitalist enterprise. Innovation generates new industries, causing older industries and jobs to become obsolete. While retraining programs might promise to match old workers to new jobs, it appears (apart from Sweden perhaps) that those who do lose their jobs are not likely to be the ones employed in newer industries. New industries tend to hire those closer to their location and mostly younger workers, who have more facility with whatever new skills might be required. Those laid-off from the older industry may retire early or fall into permanent unemployment; those who do find jobs may find their incomes substantially reduced.[121] The point is that Hegel's claim of "dependence and want" for workers appears more compelling when, in thinking about job loss and re-employment, we take the frictions of time and space more seriously. In addition, as we shall see, Hegel stresses not so much the absolute material lack some might face but more their sense of social dislocation and alienation—exactly the consequences of rapid economic change.

Though Hegel recognizes that some in civil society face "starvation,"[122] his argument does not depend on a definition of poverty as absolute immiseration. Rather, he points us to that "large mass of people" that "sinks below the level of a certain standard of living."[123] He focuses on the "subjective aspect of poverty" or what we might today call "relative poverty."[124] Like Sahlins, Hegel understands that scarcity and affluence must be measured against a

---

119 Hegel, *Philosophy of Right*, section 244. Our emphasis.
120 Ibid., section 243.
121 Louis Uchitelle, *The Disposable American: Layoffs and their Consequences*, New York: Vintage, 2007.
122 Hegel, *Philosophy of Right*, section 240 addition.
123 Ibid., section 244.
124 Ibid., section 242. Plant, "Hegel and the Political Economy," p. 119, argues that Hegel is quite "modern" in his account of poverty as a relative condition.

social standard of needs. A high level of social neediness, combined with minimal and insecure means, constitutes a feeling of deprivation and a potential severing of the ligaments of social life. With the latter comes a potential fracturing of the political community on which the actualization of modern freedom depends. As he puts it, those that fall into poverty, still

> are left with the needs of civil society and yet—since society has taken from them the natural means of acquisition . . .—they are more or less deprived of all the advantages of society, such as the ability to acquire skills and education in general, as well as of the administration of justice, health care, and often even of the consolation of religion.[125]

Consequently, the poor lose "that feeling of right, integrity, and honour which comes from supporting oneself by one's own activity and work."[126]

They lose their dignity but *not* their sense of entitlement; they assert "a right to demand a livelihood from society." As Hegel says, "within the conditions of society hardship at once assumes the form of a wrong inflicted on this or that class."[127] Thus, there is always the potential for the poor to form a "rabble," adopting "a disposition" of "inward rebellion against the rich, against society, the government."[128] The "rabble" represents for Hegel nothing less than a failure to integrate large masses of people into the modern political community. The obvious and not irrational refusal of the poor to acknowledge the benefits of participation in the wider community might be seen, in modern terms, as a legitimation crisis—a systematic failure to reconcile the individual freedom of modern civil society with ethical life.[129] In other words, poverty "threatens the existence of civil society itself"[130] and endangers his whole system. We can sense Hegel's urgency.

He explores and finds wanting a number of ways of dealing with poverty. The material burden of supporting the poor could be shifted to the wealthy or to a public source of wealth. "Almsgiving and charitable donations" do not seem an adequate solution to this problem since they are "contingent" and must be supplemented by public activities.[131] But government subsidies

125 Hegel, *Philosophy of Right*, section 241.
126 Ibid., section 244.
127 Ibid., sections 240 addition and 244 addition. Hegel is not alone in suggesting that poverty comes to be seen as a problem only under modern conditions. See Bronislaw Geremek, *Poverty: A History*, London: Blackwell, 1997, pp. 1–8; Gareth Stedman Jones, *An End to Poverty: A Historical Debate*, London: Profiles Books, 2004.
128 Hegel, *Philosophy of Right*, section 244 addition.
129 Plant, "Hegel and the Political Economy," p. 121 suggests the language of legitimation crisis. On Hegel's failure to deliver on the promise of the modern state, see also Serequeberhan, "The Idea of Colonialism" and Fatton, "Hegel and the Riddle of Poverty."
130 Wartenberg, "Poverty and Class Structure," p. 175.
131 Hegel, *Philosophy of Right*, section 242.

also fail the test. Having their needs fulfilled by the public dole, instead of by their own efforts, "would be contrary to the principle of civil society and the feeling of self-sufficiency and honor among its individual members."[132] As many commentators stress, this sense of self-sufficiency and honor is crucial, since modern civil society ties individuality and the capacity to share in cultural development directly to property ownership.[133]

A second possibility is that the state could provide employment directly through public works. Hegel dismisses this idea by employing what we now know as the "overproduction thesis." As he puts it, the "livelihood" of the public works employees "might be mediated by work ... which would increase the volume of production." But, he continues, "it is precisely in overproduction and the lack of a proportionate number of consumers ... that the evil consists."[134] Individuals are unemployed precisely because society produces more than can be consumed; supply outstrips demand. For the state to employ these individuals only worsens the problem since now still more will be produced without sufficient demand, resulting in still more poverty.

This point is contestable. Keynesian economics turns on the idea that a stimulus to demand, whether by direct income transfers or the provision of public works, reduces inventories, moves the animal spirits, and brings forth private investment that creates jobs. The consequence, monetarists might say, is not overproduction but excessive demand, generating inflationary spirals, an argument beyond Hegel's time perhaps. The more crucial argument, as Raymond Plant suggests, builds on Hegel's earlier point: welfare state provisions are difficult to sustain politically within the logic of a modern civil society because they sever the link between work and reward. Public assistance as social insurance effectively leaves out of social life those unable to contribute and makes them the recipients of charity, shame, and resentment.[135] If so, then Hegel's observation appears prescient

> This shows that, despite an *excess of wealth*, civil society is *not wealthy enough*, i.e., its own distinct resources are not sufficient—to prevent an excess of poverty and the formation of a rabble.[136]

And, paraphrasing Hegel, no society, no matter how wealthy, seems to have adequately resolved this problem.

Hegel considers a final "solution," one tied to his image of British, perhaps Smithian, political economy. He notes that in Britain

---

132 Hegel, *Philosophy of Right*, section 245.
133 Avineri, *Hegel's Theory of the Modern State*, p. 137; Wartenberg, "Poverty and Class Structure," p. 173.
134 Hegel, *Philosophy of Right*, section 245.
135 Plant, "Hegel and the Political Economy," pp. 120–1.
136 Hegel, *Philosophy of Right*, section 245.

the most direct means of dealing with poverty, and particularly with the renunciation of shame and honor as the subjective basis of society and with the laziness and extravagance which give rise to a rabble, is to leave the poor to their fate and direct them to beg from the public.[137]

Smith mostly evades this brutal consequence of poverty, diverting our attention to the even poorer savages. Because of this habitual evasion, we want to stress what may seem obvious, namely, that death—both social and biological—is the rabble's "fate" in modern society. Death points us to the Lacanian "real" of capitalist wealth production. Drawing on Warren Montag (as we did in Chapter 3), we can say that Hegel is describing a form of "necro-economics"—an economy premised on systematic human death.

Hegel cannot leave us with "necro-economics." That some "must allow themselves to die"[138] seems an unsatisfactory actualization of freedom in (European) civil society. Hegel is left with one strategy: if slavery can serve a progressive function in history, then perhaps colonialism can benefit the capitalist political economy. At this precise point he opens up his "closed-economy model,"[139] extending his analysis beyond the boundaries of an abstract civil society and onto the theatre of the world:

> This inner dialectic of civil society drives it—or in the first instance *this specific society*—to go beyond its own confines and look for consumers, and hence the means it requires for subsistence, in other nations which lack those means of which it has a surplus or which generally lag behind it in creativity, etc.[140]

Aware perhaps that he is unable to repair civil society's inner dialectic[141] of vast wealth and necro-economics, and unwilling to accept the consequences, Hegel reveals that the analysis of civil society is not merely a European abstraction, but embedded in a world where European and non-European nations are linked. As Tsenay Serequeberhan argues, Hegel "stealthily" suggests that colonialism is the "only viable solution to the fundamental

---

137 Hegel, *Philosophy of Right*.
138 Warren Montag, "Necro-Economics: Adam Smith and Death in the Life of the Universal," *Radical Philosophy*, 2005, no. 134, p. 16.
139 A. O. Hirschman, "On Hegel, Imperialism, and Structural Stagnation," in *Essays in Trespassing: Economics to Politics and Beyond*, Cambridge: Cambridge University, 1981, p. 168.
140 Hegel, *Philosophy of Right*, section 246.
141 Serequeberhan, "The Idea of Colonialism," p. 307, in considering the role of poverty for Hegel's conception of civil society observes: "It is the insoluble character of this difficulty which leads Hegel to endorse European colonialist expansion." For a response to Serequeberhan that gives a somewhat alternative interpretation, see Paquette, "Hegel's Analysis of Colonialism."

contradictions that emerge from the dialectic internal to civil society and the state."[142]

That Europe exports those who might otherwise become a (European) rabble is one side of Hegel's analysis of colonialism:

> This extended link also supplies the means necessary for *colonization*—whether sporadic or systematic—to which the fully developed civil society is driven, and by which it provides part of its population with a return to the family principle in a new country, and itself with a new market and sphere of industrial activity.[143]

Civil society reconciles the subjective freedom of individuals and the ethical life of political community, only if the rabble—that internal other—is spatially displaced to the colonies, where they may flourish in a new hive of civil society. Hegel seems to have mended the wound of wealth.

What effect does this civil-society driven colonization have on the natives who experience colonization? The answer to this question is the second side of Hegel's analysis of colonialism. We have already seen how Hegel's anthropology and theory of history prepare the ground for a policy of "domination that otherwise violates modern political right" as a necessary feature of modernity.[144] The extension of European political economy to the colonies not only gives the European rabble social purpose as colonial masters, it also, in a transubstantiation worthy of Christian rites, promises to give modern life to the historically moribund non-Europeans. As Hegel tells the story,[145] "industry," driven by the contradictions in a closed civil society, takes to "the *sea*" as its "natural element." Industry establishes "communication" and "creates trading links between distant countries, a legal relationship which gives rise to contracts"—the basis of property and modern individuality we might add. Hegel then delivers the punchline: "such trade is the greatest educational asset and the source from which commerce derives its world-historical significance." The contradictions of civil society as a closed system now appear dialectically transcended, revealing a "world-historical" purpose—to civilize the natives, to save them from the spiritual death of backwardness.

In this way, Hegel rescues both internal and external others from spiritual or physical death and gives them life. We might pause here. Recall that Hegel's account of history slates Amerindians for death through contact with Europeans, and Africans experience their spiritual rebirth only through the

---

142 Serequeberhan, "The Idea of Colonialism," p. 301.

143 Hegel, *Philosophy of Right*, section 248.

144 Richard Dien Winfield, "Postcolonialism and Right," in Robert R. Williams (ed.) *Beyond Liberalism and Communitarianism: Studies in Hegel's Philosophy of Right*, Albany: SUNY, 2001, p. 104, emphasizes Hegel's grasp of the necessity of "drawing a racial divide between indigenous peoples and their metropolitan masters" for justifying imperial domination.

145 Hegel, *Philosophy of Right*, section 247.

mediation of European slavery. We might also remind ourselves of Hegel's account of the costs of the realization of the world spirit, since violence and suffering surely would be part of colonial projects. Thus, hoping to evade a necro-economics of civil society, Hegel delivers us to a broader necro-philosophy. And, we might add, he cannot evade the former, since the inner dialectic of civil society remains unchanged when transported to the world stage.[146] The production of poverty is merely displaced onto the colonial world and, to pre-figure Marx and theories of dependency and the world-system, reappears as a global wound.

Colonialism thereby serves as bi-directional time travel for Hegel. The rabble, which Smith merely displaces into a previous stage of history, cannot be so readily displaced because the rabble is not a residue of a past stage but a necessary product of the capitalist machine; it is intrinsic to the modern. However, the rabble *can* be displaced spatially to the colonies and this displacement is consistent with the "right" established by a modern society where a racial divide places parts of humanity outside of world-history. The spatial displacement of the rabble has the effect of bringing the temporally displaced and racialized natives into modernity's pedagogic transit lounge. Here as modern missionaries try to soothe their pain, the natives can select one of three deaths: the biological death of extermination; the social death of bartering their culture for elements of modernity; or if they reject this barter, the temporal death of being severed from the greater, historical purpose of humanity.

Tying the European rabble to non-European natives via colonialism solves neither the problem of poverty nor the problem of what to do with those outside of history. Knotted together, however, both problems are finessed and repressed: one appears to evade "necro-economics," but merely displaces it outside of Europe; the other seems to rescue the native for history, but only via the operation of a "necro-history" that colonizes, assimilates, and exterminates.

IV. Conclusion: Beyond Universal History and Death

The Enlightenment seems to leave us with a peculiar combination of cosmopolitan ideals and racist practices.[147] Bernasconi muses:

> Declarations of universal rights were authored and pronounced by people who were apparently oblivious of whole classes of people to whom those

---

146 See Robert Siemens, "The Problem of Modern Poverty: Significant Congruences Between Hegel's and George's Theoretical Conceptions," *American Journal of Economics and Sociology*, 1997, vol. 56, 617–37; Serequeberhan, "The Idea of Colonialism," pp. 311–12.

147 See Susan M. Shell, "Kant's Concept of a Human Race," in Sara Eigen and Mark Joseph Larrimore (eds.) *The German Invention of Race*, Albany: SUNY, 2006, 55–72, for an intriguing account of the space created for racial differences in Kant's effort to embody his abstract characterization of reason.

rights nominally applied, but to whom hardly anyone thought to apply them.[148]

Such duplicity is hardly novel. Theorists often manage to overlook how their interests shape their thought. What *is* noticeable, if not completely original, is "the universal language that they brought to their cause," that European prejudices lend "themselves to a universalism that is not so much opposed to racism as it is an instrument of racism."[149] Abstract universalism and racism share a key feature: both proclaim universal standards without regard to the worth, the views, or the voices of others.

At the root of this pretense may be a desire to protect European identity from potential criticism. Perhaps all groups engage in such hypocrisy, but we think there is more to be said in this particular case. To secure the pure European identity envisioned by the Enlightenment, it first has to be constituted in a particular manner. Most important, the constitution of Europe must be freed of all internal and external boundary problems. Despite his construction of civil society as an amalgam of modern and pre-modern social elements, Hegel's broader historical theory purifies Europe of the pollution that comes from the overlaps with spatial/racial/temporal others.

Perhaps Hegel understood this. In his account of how the stages of development map onto nations, he notes:

> History is mind clothing itself with the form of events or the immediate actuality of nature. The stages of its development are therefore presented as immediate natural principles. These because they are natural, are a plurality external to one another, and they are present therefore in such a way that each of them is *assigned to one nation* in the external form of its geographical and anthropological conditions.[150]

Hegel seems to suggest that historical events do not, on their own, reveal their meaning. Humans connect events and secure meaning by giving these connections an inner coherence. This coherence is laid bare by applying the principles of a genuine philosophy of history and Hegel's version is the one by which humans come increasingly to grasp the unfolding of their history. The immanent unfolding of freedom in history sustains a logic that seems to have the world theatre as its "unit" of analysis. Such consciousness, however, becomes present not to the world as a whole, nor to a particular individual

---

148 Robert Bernasconi, "The Invisibility of Racial Minorities in the Public Realm of Appearances," in K. Thompson and L. Embree (eds.) *The Phenomenology of the Political*, Dordrecht: Kluwer, 2000, p. 171.

149 Ibid., pp. 171, 186.

150 Hegel, *Philosophy of Right*, section 346. Emphasis added. We use Knox's translation here. Nisbet's translation, though very similar, seems more obscure to our ears.

abstracted from a concrete society, but rather to "nations." It might be more accurate to say that what Hegel has in mind is that various stages of history map onto continents/races. The world spirit climbs stage by stage through the (assumed) boundaries of races and continents. We find that freedom and rationality begin with Asians and Asia, bypassing Americans and the Americas and Africans and Africa, and reaching their fullest development with Europeans and Europe. The full unfolding of freedom in Europe gives Europeans the right and pedagogic duty to intervene and colonize the rest of the world.

In drawing this picture of discrete boundaries, what does Hegel exclude? It appears that a particular nation, race, or continent cannot contain multiple stages. Hegel excludes, for example, the possibility of a nation containing internal others who might be living in a different stage. Smith allowed for just this possibility in considering the Scottish highlanders internal to Europe while believing that they lived in a different developmental time. Ferguson blurred the categories of the Scots' stadial theory even more fully and Steuart explicitly theorized a world of unevenly developed units. Hegel, by contrast, cannot allow continents or stages to overlap on the world theatre. For example, we might believe that Africa, Asia, and Europe, rather than being separated by discrete lines, have overlapping boundaries. What we call Egypt, Palestine, Turkey, or Greece, instead of residing in only one continent, might claim to be in all three. If so then all four countries—Egypt, Palestine, Turkey and Greece—can simultaneously be at the null point (Africa), beginning (Asia), and apex (Europe) of history. Our point is that Hegel has to finesse or evade spatial and temporal boundary problems in order to make plausible freedom's sequential unfolding in discrete non-overlapping spaces.

We do not wish to posture as pedants, however. We hope to avoid the mistakes of those trying a bit too hard to locate the fatal errors in Hegel's corpus, as well as the mistakes of those who wish away his flaws to preserve its coherence. Both miss the opportunity to think deeply with him. In that spirit we offer what we take to be the most important of Hegel's exclusions. First, what we find missing is an understanding of the interactive character of *global* encounter—that is, genetic and cultural intercourse, economic exchange, and all manner of contact through travel, trade, conquest, and migration that might constitute the character and spirit of nations, races, and continents.[151] We should not ignore, as does Duncan Forbes,[152] that, despite Hegel's vast historical knowledge of just such interaction, he seems to have overlooked the possibility that when a particular aspect of freedom transforms from the potential to the actual, its repercussions and reverberations might move beyond the boundaries he assigns them. Or, put differently, while

151 Tarak Barkawi and Mark Laffey, "The Postcolonial Movement in Security Studies," *Review of International Studies*, 2006, vol. 32, 329–52.
152 Duncan Forbes, "Introduction," in G. W. F. Hegel, *Lectures on the Philosophy of World History: Introduction*, Cambridge: Cambridge University, 1975, pp. xvi, xxiv.

it seems true that the rate of world interaction has increased exponentially, this does not mean that societies, regardless of geographic distance from each other, were hermetically sealed from each other prior to the modern era.[153] Their character and spirit may have emerged as much from interaction with others as from the dialectical unfolding of the spirit in relation to its "natural" environment. Hegel ignores such interactive influence.

Second, Hegel argues that the spirit only operates when humans are freed from subordination to nature, when they eliminate the coercion of physical need. He argues that the *modern* spirit lives only when individuals are freed from subordination to the social whole within which they find themselves in prior forms of society. We find this compelling at one level. The coercion of physical need can be debilitating, as can the demand that the individual submit to the whole. However, it is one thing to make such arguments for the relative advantages of modernity and quite another to claim that *only* in modern civil society can humans develop a critical consciousness of life's spiritual and aesthetic purpose. We do not accept that humans overcome the strictures of nature *first* and *then* develop cultural, aesthetic, and spiritual purpose. Do not humans develop their culture, aesthetics, and spirit *at the same time as* they interact with nature to meet their needs?[154]

Third, modern civil society, far from eliminating the coercion of neediness has in fact intensified it. Those who must work find themselves dependent on a capricious system that leaves them insecure, vulnerable to the shame of failing to support themselves, and cut off from the benefits of spiritual life. Modernity expands needs and, confirming our earlier reflections, it also generates scarcity and poverty, as Hegel himself stresses. If, as Hegel argues, it is modernity that produces poverty, then his stadial history of the world can be seen less as an attempt to arrange a hierarchy of cultures and more as the projection of a particularly modern lack. This lack points to the pedagogic work that freedom's modern bearers must still perform.

We are comfortable with the idea that Hegel fails to reconcile the tensions within civil society, but we are less certain that we can simply reject his theory of history. If European society necessarily seeks to resolve the problem of poverty through colonization and, if non-Europeans can only realize their full humanity by adopting European values (i.e., development), then we should shed no tears when a "necro-political economy" of cultural genocide flattens global social life. After all, life and death are dialectically related—a basic insight known to even the "basest" of cultures. The fuller pursuit of freedom requires that, paraphrasing Montag, others let their cultures die. If this is what freedom requires, then we ought indeed to let these cultures die, without belated salvage missions and without a lingering sense of regret. The

---

153 Little more needs to be done than gesture to the majesterial work of people like Janet Abu-Lughod, Eric Wolf, William McNeal, Andre Gunder Frank, and Amitav Ghosh.
154 See Marshall Sahlins, *Culture and Practical Reason*, Chicago: University of Chicago, 1976.

conversation could then end. We could then jettison the multicultural niceties that accompany the assimilationist practices of modernity. Accordingly, we could accept and perhaps even memorialize the deaths of those peoples and cultures that modern freedom requires. If it occurs to the reader that these days, either secretly or not so secretly, we already celebrate this "necro-ontology," then this speaks to the power of Hegel's prophetic realism. Lest we are misunderstood, we make this last observation flatly—absent sarcasm and without the slightest turn to irony.

6 Marx and temporal difference

Hegel's "speculative history," like Smith's before, provides a philosophical justification of civil society—a secular theodicy that explains the continuing presence of human malevolence as necessary to the promised achievements of a modern market society. We may turn away in horror from this suggestion. Our refusal to simply accept the wound of wealth might lead us to Marx who powerfully invokes the violence and suffering integral to modern progress. But Marx himself inherits a problem from Smith and Hegel: while he condemns the violence of modern capitalism, he also needs it. Most notably, Marx describes colonial conquest as a necessary moment in a historical process that leads us *beyond* civil society.[1] The crux of this chapter concerns how we can think of this "beyond." Marx mostly thinks of this "beyond" in temporal and teleological terms, but we can read his "beyond" in spatial and perspectival terms.

While Smith's historical thinking set the stage for Marx's political economy, the influence of Hegel is more direct and profound. Marx follows Hegel in endorsing a "speculative" historical style, even as he also resists it. Marx offers a totalizing and assimilative historical project, where he, as Teodor Shanin puts it, uses a "[d]iversity of stages" to explain "the essential diversity of forms" he identified in his political economy.[2] To this point, Marx simply reproduces the temporal displacements of Smith and Hegel, denying the coevalness of peoples beyond Western Europe. However, Marx's dominant historiography rests uneasily aside an alternative vision of history as an immanent and implicitly pluralizing project. As we will see, the role of difference in Marx's political economy and his assessment of the cultural worth of colonized peoples shifts as he moves back and forth between a speculative and teleological history, on one side, and a relatively more descriptive and comparative history, on the other.

---

1 Marx is hesitant to say much about post-capitalism, though he emphasizes the necessity and inevitability of movement beyond capitalism.
2 "Late Marx: Gods and Craftsmen," in Teodor Shanin (ed.) *Late Marx and the Russian Road: Marx and 'the Peripheries of Capitalism,'* New York: Monthly Review, 1983, p. 4.

We explore this tension between Marx's self-enunciated method in *Grundrisse* and his rather inconsistent application of that method in *Capital*. In *Grundrisse*, Marx argues that remnants of older social forms are subsumed within capitalism. Therefore the categories of the most advanced social form, in this case capitalism, contain the conceptual key to understanding less developed forms. But there is a second method. In *Capital*, Marx, like Polanyi, depicts alternative social forms without apparently subsuming them within a development sequence that has capitalism at its apex. Some might regard Marx's inconsistency on this score a logical weakness. But we see it also as an opening for differences that can resist, critique, and sustain an indifference towards capitalist expansion. We counterpose our alternative for rescuing historical difference in Marx to that offered by Dipesh Chakrabarty in *Provincializing Europe*. If Marx remains crucial to postcolonial critics of capitalist and imperialist modernity, as Chakrabarty stresses,[3] we contend that our exploration of Marx's methodological inconsistency suggests a more productive avenue for finding the place of historical and contemporary difference within his thought.

I. Secular Universal Time and Colonialism

Marx's writings are replete with accounts of human history unfolding in relatively fixed and universal stages of development. Though Marx's commitment to a stage theory is debated,[4] and various nuances and ambiguities are easy to locate, it is also easy to discern in his work, as Chakrabarty puts it, the operation of a "secular universal time."[5]

Marx's explicit references to a universal history parallel Smith's account in many respects.[6] In *The German Ideology* (1845–6), Marx and Engels trace out "the various stages of development in the division of labour" as "just so

---

3 Dipesh Chakrabarty, *Provincializing Europe: Postcolonial Thought and Historical Difference*, Princeton: Princeton University, 2000, p. 47.

4 See William H. Shaw, *Marx's Theory of History*, Stanford: Stanford University, 1978, pp. 1–4; Jon Elster, "Historical Materialism and Economic Backwardness," in Terrence Ball and James Farr (eds.) *After Marx*, Cambridge: Cambridge University, 1984, 34–58; Jorge Larrain, *A Reconstruction of Historical Materialism*, New York: Ashgate: 1992; Antonio Negri, *Marx Beyond Marx: Lessons on the Grundrisse*, South Hadley: Bergin and Garvey, 1984; and James D. White, *Karl Marx and the Intellectual Origins of Dialectical Materialism*, New York: St. Martin's, 1996.

5 Chakrabarty, *Provincializing Europe*, p. 48.

6 This is not to argue that Marx draws his historical theories directly from the Scots, though Ronald Meek, *Economics and Ideology: Studies in the Development of Economic Thought*, London: Chapman and Hall, 1967, 34–50, implies as much and Marx had read Smith prior to the composition of *Economic and Philosophic Manuscripts*. See also Stanley Moore, "Marx and Lenin as Historical Materialists," in Marshall Cohen, Thomas Nagel, and Thomas Scanlon (eds.) *Marx, Justice and History*, Princeton: Princeton University, 1980, pp. 217–18; and Etienne Balibar, *The Philosophy of Marx*, London: Verso, 1995, p. 80.

many different forms of ownership." Where people live "by hunting and fishing," or perhaps by herding and the beginnings of agriculture, the "division of labour at this stage is still very elementary" and "tribal ownership," the first stage, is dominant. Where tribes begin to congregate in cities, communal and private property begins to take hold alongside the extension of the division of labor—between "town and country" and between "industry and maritime commerce." The "third form of ownership," then, is "feudal or estate property," where some combination of "landed property with enserfed labour chained to it," and "small capital commanding the labour of journeymen" are established.[7] All these are prelude to a bourgeois stage where an extension of commerce and the development of manufacturing gradually "transformed all capital into industrial capital." We see the production of "world history for the first time," as "everywhere the same relations between the classes of society" are established.[8]

Even in their early work, Marx and Engels' account is more nuanced and complex than the Scots. But some things seem quite familiar. Marx and Engels argue "that a certain mode of production, or industrial stage, is always combined with a certain mode of co-operation, or social stage;" since "the multitude of productive forces accessible to men determines the nature of society, . . . the 'history of humanity' must always be studied and treated in relation to the history of industry and exchange."[9] For Marx, like the Scots, these stages define the direction of history. The "Preface" to *Critique of Political Economy*, for example, contrasts "older" modes of production with newer, "superior" ones that supersede them, driving humanity forward towards its end—a truly historical era.[10] Marx's statements in *The Manifesto* (1848) are more direct. He emphasizes "the most revolutionary part" played by the bourgeoisie, including putting an "end to all feudal, patriarchal, idyllic relations." The bourgeoisie certainly practice "naked, shameless, direct, brutal exploitation," but they have also spread a common system of social relations "over the whole surface of the globe," battering "down all Chinese walls" and drawing "even the most barbarian nations into civilisation."[11] The message seems clear: modern capitalism renders other forms of life obsolete. Of course, there is a twist: bourgeois society is also the most exploitative and sows the seed of its own supersession by communism.[12]

---

7 Karl Marx and Friedrich Engels, *The German Ideology, Part One*, New York: International Publishers, 1970, pp. 43–6.

8 Ibid., pp. 72–8.

9 Ibid., p. 50.

10 Karl Marx, *A Contribution to the Critique of Political Economy*, New York: International Publishers, 1970, pp. 20–2.

11 Karl Marx and Friedrich Engels, "The Manifesto of the Communist Party," in Robert C. Tucker (ed.) *The Marx-Engels Reader*, New York: W. W. Norton, 1978, pp. 474–7.

12 However, in the 1882 preface Marx admits that "the primeval common ownership of land" in Russia might be the basis for a "higher form of communist common ownership" and that

Marx's historiographic commitments are clearest in the *Grundrisse* (1857–8).[13] While Marx's stage theory disrupts the Scots' story of commercial society as a point of arrival, like Smith he largely erases difference with the sweep and inevitability of historical movement. Marx's "vast temporal plot," as Joan Cocks suggests, is governed by the rhythms of Hegel's dialectic: *Grundrisse* presents a dialectical schema of three stages that capture the moments of negation and transcendence involved in the movement of human history:[14]

> Relations of personal dependence (entirely spontaneous at the outset) are the first social forms, in which human productive capacity develops only to a slight extent and at isolated points. Personal independence founded on *objective* dependence is the second great form, in which a system of general social metabolism, of universal relations, of all-round needs and universal capabilities is formed for the first time. Free individuality, based on the universal development of individuals and on their subordination of their communal, social productivity, as their social wealth, is the third stage. The second stage creates the conditions for the third. Patriarchal as well as ancient conditions (feudal also) thus disintegrate with the development of luxury, of money, of exchange values, while modern society arises and grows in the same measure.[15]

Much of the *Grundrisse* gives content to this basic schema.

The first stage of human development—"personal dependence" connected to a limited development of the productive forces—appears in a number of historical variants paralleling Hegel's world historical actors: the Asiatic, the Roman, and the Germanic.[16] Here, Marx's sensitivity to difference exceeds that of the Scots, though what is common to these different forms is that

---

Russia might achieve communism without recapitulating the "historical evolution of the West." See ibid., pp. 470–2. Though a potential gesture towards difference, the pre-capitalist or pre-communist societies still remained backward and were to be superceded as prehistory. More precisely, Marx presents multiple paths to capitalism and/or communism, not multiple paths to human fulfillment, rooted in varying values and visions.

13 Karl Marx, *Grundrisse: Foundations of the Critique of Political Economy*, New York: Vintage, 1973.

14 Joan Cocks, "Hegel's Logic, Marx's Science, Rationalism's Perils," *Political Studies*, 1983, vol. XXXI, 583–603, makes very clear the relationship of Marx's schema and Hegel's *Logic*. The quotation is from p. 594. Marx's *Grundrisse* also is made centerpiece of Carol C. Gould's, *Marx's Social Ontology: Individuality and Community in Marx's Theory of Social Reality*, Cambridge: MIT Press, 1978.

15 Marx, *Grundrisse*, p. 158.

16 See the section entitled "Forms which precede capitalist production" (ibid., pp. 471–516). Marx mentions (p. 472) that, prior to these settled forms of existence, humans lived a "pastoral" or "migratory form of life."

"[e]ach individual conducts himself only as a link, as a member of this community,"[17] justifying lumping them into a single stage.

There appears to be less room for diversity at the second stage. Modern capitalism imposes uniformity by dissolving "all fixed personal [historic] relations of dependence in production." As for Hegel, human beings individuate themselves in a system of capitalist exchange: expanding and differentiating needs, constituting human beings as legal equals, and marking out a sphere of individual freedom.[18] In contrast to Hegel, however, the equality and freedom of exchange are largely illusory.[19] As Marx suggests, "not only has [the worker] produced the conditions of necessary labour as conditions belonging to capital; but also the value-creating possibility, the realization of which lies as a possibility within [the worker], now likewise exists as surplus value, . . . as capital, as master over living labour capacity"—as "an *alien power.*"[20] These "slaves of capital" perform a "simple" activity that can be conceived (and measured) as "labour time" in the production of surplus value and, hence, capital accumulation.[21]

Thus, with Hegel and Smith, Marx sees that capital accumulation expands human possibilities and contributes to "the development of a rich individuality."[22] But, like Ferguson, he emphasizes that this rich individuality comes with a tragic cost. The enhancement of human needs and capabilities "appears" also "as a complete emptying out, this universal objectification as total alienation, and the tearing down of all limited one-sided aims as sacrifice of the human end-in-itself to an entirely external end."[23] Capitalism produces history's cruelest and most complete exploitation and alienation, but also destroys pre-capitalist dependence, undeveloped needs, and limited productive capabilities. In this respect at least, bourgeois society appears as both progressive and degenerate. Marx supports *and* inverts the narrative of modern progress in Smith and Hegel.

The dialectic of history is complete with communism.[24] With communism, the "universality and the comprehensiveness of [the laborer's] relations

---

17 Marx, *Grundrisse*, p. 472.

18 Ibid., pp. 156, 241–3, 496.

19 Ibid., pp. 507–8.

20 Ibid., pp. 452–4.

21 Ibid., pp. 612–13. See also p. 325. On time, abstract labor, and capitalism, see Moishe Postone, *Time, Labor, and Social Domination: A Reinterpretation of Marx's Critical Theory*, Cambridge: Cambridge University, 1993, ch. 5.

22 Marx, *Grundrisse*, p. 325.

23 Ibid., p. 488. Sudipta Kaviraj, "Marxism and the Darkness of History," *Development and Change*, 1992, vol. 23, 79–102, emphasizes that Marx tempers his enlightenment vision with a tragic dimension.

24 There is some debate about whether Marx treats communism as a moment of completion. See Terrence Ball, "Marxian Science and Positivist Politics," in Terrence Ball and James Farr (eds.) *After Marx*, Cambridge: Cambridge University, 1984, pp. 243–4. There is little doubt communism completes the dialectic of historical movement in *Grundrisse*.

and his capacities" developed under capitalism become the worker's own possessions and expressions of his/her "free individuality."[25] Whatever we make of this claim, communism represents for Marx the fulfillment of an unfolding process where capitalism mediates two phases of fully communal or social individuality and this mediation involves two moments of negation. Capitalism first negates past backwardness by destroying pre-capitalist ways of life. And by providing the preconditions for human fulfillment while also denying their realization in social life, capitalism negates itself. The costs of this dual mediation are very high to those living through it—a human tragedy but a necessary one.[26] A key feature of that tragedy is colonialism. Who but Hegel, as we have shown, could put the point more plainly?

Indeed, Shlomo Avineri famously reads Marx as a student of Hegel's analysis of colonialism. For both Hegel and Marx history begins only when humans recreate nature to meet their own needs.[27] As Avineri suggests, Marx follows Hegel in regarding Africans and Asians as non-historical:

> The notion that Asia has no history is not, of course, of Marx's own making. While many eighteenth-century authors saw China as a model society, where order, stability, and obedience have been successively achieved through Oriental wisdom, Marx followed Hegel in rejecting such a view of the Celestial Empire as misleading romanticism. To Marx as to Hegel history means man's process of changing his environment; where there is no change, there is no history, and man remains a purely natural being.[28]

One can cull an abundance of passages that seem to confirm this interpretation. Of course, this is not our only concern; we hope also to demonstrate a fidelity to Marx's complex posture towards colonialism.

Two reports written for the *New York Daily Tribune* in 1853 are taken as exemplary of Marx's racism or orientalism. In "The British Rule in India," Marx highlights the absence of any internal or indigenous impetus to social revolution in India and, by implication, all of Asia:

> English interference having placed the spinner in Lancashire and the weaver in Bengal, or sweeping away both Hindu spinner and weaver, dissolved these small semi-barbarian, semi-civilized communities, by

25 Marx, *Grundrisse*, pp. 152, 158, 162, 611, and 704.

26 See Jeffrey Vogel, "The Tragedy of History," *New Left Review*, 1996, no. 220, 36–61.

27 On this Hegelian resonance in Marx, see also Irfan Habib, *Essays in Indian History: Towards a Marxist Perception*, London: Anthem Press, 2002, p. 16.

28 Shlomo Avineri, *Karl Marx on Colonialism and Modernization*, New York: Doubleday, 1968, p. 10.

blowing up their economical basis, and thus produced the greatest, and, to speak the truth, the only *social* revolution ever heard of in Asia.[29]

India is not only profoundly stagnant, but its social formation cripples any civilized human aspirations and possibilities: "idyllic village communities, inoffensive though they may appear, had always been the solid foundation of Oriental despotism." The "human mind" is confined, Marx says, "making it the unresisting tool of superstition, enslaving it beneath traditional rules, depriving it of all grandeur and historical energies." This "undignified, stagnatory, and vegetative life" also contains "in contradistinction, wild, aimless, unbounded forces of destruction," that render "murder itself a religious rite in Hindustan." If this is not enough, we must remember "that these little communities were contaminated by distinctions of caste and by slavery, that they subjugated man to the external circumstances, that they transformed a self-developing social state into a never changing natural destiny."[30]

Hegel could not have put it better (or is it worse?). And while Marx is no friend of capitalism, he nevertheless believes that it triggers India's (and by implication all of Asia's) emergence from a profound backwardness onto the theatre of human history. So great is the weight of ritualized inertia that Marx appears to forgive British colonialism the catastrophic consequences of its plundering:

> England, it is true, in causing the social revolution in Hindustan, was actuated only by the vilest interests, and was stupid in her manner of enforcing them. But that is not the question. The question is, can mankind fulfill its destiny without a fundamental revolution in the social state of Asia? If not, whatever may have been the crimes of England she was the unconscious tool of history in bringing about that revolution.[31]

Here, as for Hegel, actors become tools of a "vast" and tragic, "temporal plot."

As if taking a script directly from the apologists for Britain's empire, Marx argues in his second report, "The Future Results of British Rule in India," that British conquest began the job of "regenerating" India. It unified and modernized India by training a native army and creating political unity through the sword; by building the telegraph and establishing a free press; by imposing "private property in land—that great desideratum of Asiatic society;" by building educational and scientific institutions; and by bringing steamships and railways that shorten the distance between England and India as producers and consumers. Indeed, the day is not far off when India will be

---

29 Karl Marx, "British Rule in India," in Aijaz Ahmad (ed.) *On the National and Colonial Questions: Selected Writings*, New Delhi: LeftWord Book, 2001, p. 65.
30 Ibid.
31 Ibid., pp. 65–6.

"actually annexed to the Western world."[32] All is well that ends well, it seems.[33] It would seem there is not much to distinguish Marx from Hegel on either the diagnosis or the cure for Asian (and African) lethargy.

Marx's triumphant temprocentricism is modified, however, by a sense of lament and loss absent in Hegel: "There cannot, however, remain any doubt that the misery inflicted by the British on Hindustan is of an essentially different and infinitely more intensive kind than all Hindustan had to suffer before."[34] At another point, Marx seems mournful:

> England has broken down the entire framework of Indian society, without any symptoms of reconstitution yet appearing. This loss of the old world, with no gain of a new one, imparts a particular kind of melancholy to the present misery of the Hindu, and separates Hindustan, ruled by Britain, from all its ancient traditions, and from the whole of its past history.[35]

And, in an apparent inversion, Marx displays appreciation for Indian culture. He hopes for the eventual "regeneration of that great and interesting country, whose gentle natives are '*plus fins et plus adroits que les italiens*,' [More subtle and adroit than Italians]." Indians have displayed "a certain calm nobility" and "have astonished the British officers by their bravery." Their civilization also prefigures those in Europe.[36] We found no such reverence in Hegel, though Smith becomes wistful about the virtues of now superseded societies at some points, and Ferguson—more earnestly—hoped to restore such virtues in the present.

In marked contrast to Hegel's and Smith's optimism, however, Marx presents a blistering critique of capitalism that counters his earlier claim that happy days for India are just around the corner:

> The Indians will not reap the fruits of the new elements of society scattered among them by the British bourgeoisie, till in Great Britain itself the now ruling classes have been supplanted by the industrial proletariat, or till the Hindus themselves shall have grown strong enough to throw off the English all together.[37]

Indeed, in this historical drama, the bourgeoisie now appear as barbarians, not civilizers:

32 Karl Marx, "The Future Results of the British Rule in India," in Aijaz Ahmad (ed.) *On the National and Colonial Questions: Selected Writings*, New Delhi: LeftWord Book, 2001, pp. 70–1.

33 For a contemporary Marxist account of this kind, see Bill Warren, *Imperialism: Pioneer of Capitalism*, New York: Verso, 1981.

34 Marx, "British Rule," p. 62.

35 Ibid.

36 Marx, "Future Results," pp. 73–4.

37 Ibid., p. 73.

Bourgeois industry and commerce create these material conditions of a new world in the same way as geological revolutions have created the surface of the earth. When a great social revolution shall have mastered the results of the bourgeois epoch, the market of the world and the modern powers of production, and subjugated them to the common control of the most advanced peoples, then only will human progress cease to resemble that hideous pagan idol, who would not drink the nectar but from the skulls of the slain.[38]

Even in the reports most often cited to demonstrate his disregard for cultural difference, Marx's tonal complexity once again distinguishes him from Smith and Hegel.

Marx may even begin to lose faith in colonialism as a generator of progressive change by the 1850s.[39] His later reports and letters indicate that his sympathies for the working class carried over to non-European peoples. In passages from *Capital*, Marx makes no attempt to hide capitalism's brutal necro-economics: "If Money, according to Augier, 'comes into this world with a congenital blood-stain on one cheek,' capital comes dripping from head to toe, from every pore, with blood and dirt."[40] And in direct reference to colonies, he writes:

The discovery of gold and silver in America, the extirpation, enslavement and the entombment in mines of the indigenous population of that continent, the beginnings of the conquest and plunder of India, and the conversion of Africa into a preserve for the commercial hunting of blackskins, are all things which characterize the dawn of the era of capitalist production.[41]

This passage suggests that imperialism recapitulates the process of initial or "primitive accumulation," with its "blood and dirt." Only a few pages later, though, Marx highlights the difference between capitalism's operation at home and in the colony:

At home, in the mother country, the smug deceitfulness of the political economist can turn this relation of absolute dependence [between the

38 Marx, "Future Results," pp. 74–5.
39 Some point to the first war of Indian independence in 1859 as the key event. See Aijaz Ahmad, "Introduction," in *On the National and Colonial Questions*, pp. 8–9, 18–20; Sunita Kumar Ghosh, "Marx on India," *Monthly Review*, 1984, vol. 35, 39–53. August Nimtz, "The Eurocentric Marx and Engels and Other Related Myths," in Crystal Bartolovish and Neil Lazarus (eds.) *Marxism, Modernity, and Postcolonial Studies*, Cambridge: Cambridge University, 2002, p. 65, believes that the trigger was the failed European revolutions of 1848–9, though this fails to explain the 1853 essays.
40 Karl Marx, *Capital: A Critique of Political Economy. Volume I*, New York: Vintage, 1977, p. 926.
41 Ibid., p. 915.

capitalist and the worker] into a free contract between buyer and seller. ... But in the colonies this beautiful illusion is torn aside.[42]

In the colonies, capitalists must separate producers from their means of production so that their labor enriches capitalists instead of themselves. This separation requires the use of force, backed by the "power of the mother country."[43]

Consistent with this, as August Nimitz recounts, Marx and Engels' later attitudes on Algeria reveal an abrupt about-face:

> ... a month before the *Manifesto* was published Engels applauded the French conquest of Algeria and defeat of the uprising led by the religious leader Abd-el Kader saying that it was "an important and fortunate fact for the progress of civilization." Nine years later in 1857 he had completely reversed his stance and now severely denounced French colonial rule and expressed sympathy for religious-led Arab resistance to the imperial power.[44]

Similarly, Marx once believed that the prerequisite of the liberation of Ireland was the overthrow of capital in England. But by 1871, Marx and Engels had "abandoned ... their earlier optimism about the exemplary role of English workers."[45] Indeed, Marx comments that the "English working class ... will never be able to do anything decisive here in England before they separate their attitude towards Ireland ... from that of the ruling classes."[46] In an 1870 letter to Meyer and Vogt, Marx makes clear that, instead of showing the way to the backward, the fate of English workers is completely tied to the emancipation of Ireland—that "the national emancipation of Ireland is ... the first condition of their own social emancipation."[47]

Finally, Marx came to believe that colonization of India produced what we might call "underdevelopment:" "By ruining handicraft production of finished articles in other countries, machinery forcibly converts them into fields for the production of its raw material." Marx notes that India was thus "compelled to produce cotton, wool, hemp, jute and indigo for Great Britain" and a "new and international division of labor springs up, one suited to the requirements of the main industrial countries."[48] Thus, the develop-

---

42 Karl Marx, *Capital: A Critique of Political Economy. Volume I*, p. 935.
43 Ibid., p. 931.
44 Nimtz, "The Eurocentric Marx," p. 68.
45 Ibid., p. 73.
46 Quoted in Ibid. See also Ahmad, "Introduction," p. 16.
47 "Marx to Sigfrid Meyer and August Vogt," in Ahmad (ed.) *On the National and Colonial Questions*, pp. 223–4.
48 Marx, *Capital*, pp. 579–80. See also Nimtz, "The Eurocentric Marx," p. 73; and Ghosh, "Marx on India," p. 45.

ment of railways, that impetus to commerce, served only to reinforce this colonial division of labor and "increased the misery of the masses."[49] The imposition of private property, that symbol of capitalist modernization, appears now as regressive: "the extinction of the communal ownership of land was only an act of English vandalism that pushed the indigenous people not forward but backward."[50] Marx came to believe that only indigenous, internal development would create regeneration and therefore the necessary prerequisite to real progress is independence and self-government.[51] Here Marx shifts from classical Marxism to a neo-Marxism.

We are left with questions nonetheless. What would indigenous, internal development look like? Can tragedy be avoided and a necro-philosophical turn evaded? Given Marx's account of "primitive accumulation" as bloody and dirty and capitalism as the most total exploitation, it is difficult to imagine a pleasant fate for the masses, however indigenous their capitalist development. Perhaps indigenous forms of social production might be the basis for the transition to communism, though it remains unclear how to achieve the rich individuality of the communist subject without destroying pre-capitalist relations of "personal dependence." Marx did study an array of ethnographic writings late in his life, trying to locate "democratic and equalitarian" elements in "Archaic communal forms," though he died still embracing an evolutionary account.[52] Our own contemporary experience of actually existing forms of "socialist development" in Africa and Asia give us little room for hope in this regard. Nor does Marx's own summary account of how history unfolds: "In actual history, it is a notorious fact that conquest, enslavement, robbery, murder, in short, force play the greatest part."[53] Hegel's prophetic realism appears in Marx as historical observation.[54]

II. Marx's Temporal Assimilationism

Marx's dominant historical accounts seem to deny the other a place in the present, subjecting that other to destruction or perhaps to colonization. An initial reading of his elaborate methodological discussions in *Capital* (1867) and *Grundrisse* reinforce this picture. Marx's dominant historical account is not contingent or accidental—a feature of his work that might be sloughed

---

49 "Marx and Engels, *Selected Correspondence*, Moscow: Progressive Publishers, 1965, p. 318, cited in Ghosh, "Marx on India," p. 45.

50 Marx, "Brief an V.I. Sassulitsch, Dritter Entwurf," cited in Ghosh, "Marx on India," p. 46.

51 Ghosh, "Marx on India," p. 51. See also Ahmad, "Introduction," *On the National and Colonial Questions*, p. 15.

52 See Lawrence Krader, "Introduction," *The Ethnological Notebooks of Karl Marx*, Assen: Van Gorcum, 1972, pp. 1–3.

53 Marx, *Capital*, p. 874.

54 Balibar, *Philosophy of Marx*, pp. 98–9, suggests this continuity with Hegel.

off, while preserving its radical integrity. Rather, this temporal displacement of the non-capitalist other is central to his method.

In the preface to the first, German edition of *Capital*, Marx compares his method to that of a physicist. The physicist isolates natural processes as if they were occurring in a "pure state," or barring that, observes processes as they occur in their "most significant form." Following this analogy, Marx begins the study of capitalism with its most developed form, namely England, the "*locus classicus*" of capitalism. He immediately warns the German reader, however, that what happens to the English will also happen to the Germans and this tale told *of* England is also told *for* Germany:[55]

> Intrinsically, it is not a question of the higher or lower degree of development of the social antagonisms that spring from the natural laws of capitalist production. It is a question of these laws themselves, of these tendencies winning their way through and working themselves out with iron necessity. The country that is more developed industrially only shows, to the less developed, the image of its own future.[56]

As with Smith, we are treated to "natural laws" of capitalism, in which the "more developed" shows the path (if not exactly serving as a model) that the "less developed" must traverse by an "iron necessity." And, as with Hegel, England and Germany are not treated as locations within global capitalism with possible mutual conditioning and interactive effects. Of the authors we have surveyed, only Steuart is openly sensitive to how development in one country or region may condition the development of others. For Marx, much like Smith, the development of capitalism is internal to the boundaries of England and these tendencies and laws, with minor variations, will unfold also in Germany.

Marx admits to one crucial difference between England and Germany. English capitalism is developed enough to spawn forms of resistance while, in continental Western Europe, "we suffer not only from the development of capitalist production, but also from the incompleteness of that development."[57] Marx then spells out what we take to be his dominant understanding of the relationship between the past and the present:

> Alongside the modern evils, we are oppressed by a whole series of inherited evils, arising from the passive survival of archaic and outmoded modes of production, with their accompanying train of anachronistic social and political relations. We suffer not only from the living, but from the dead. *Le mort saisit le vif!* ["The dead man clutches onto the living!"][58]

---

55 Marx, *Capital*, p. 90.
56 Ibid., pp. 90–1.
57 Ibid., p. 91.
58 Ibid.

Past modes of production are "archaic" and "outmoded" and their social and political relations are "anachronistic." Far from thinking that the remnants of the past can be of value—even if just to provide a sense of perspective on the present—the remainders or survivals of past social forms must be, and will be, submerged as the logic of capitalism unfolds. Germany's mixed mode—capitalism and archaic pre-capitalism—is not a possible alternative, as Polanyi or perhaps even Steuart might suggest, but instead a double disadvantage: Germany suffers from the ill-effects of capitalism as well as from the incompleteness of its development.

Still, "[o]ne nation can and should learn from others,"[59] as Marx suggests, but this learning cannot divert the nation from the necessary historical path:

> Even when a society has begun to track down the natural laws of its movement—and it is the ultimate aim of this work to reveal the economic law of motion of modern society—it can neither leap over the natural phases of its development nor remove them by decree. But it can shorten and lessen the birth-pangs.[60]

Thus, "countries," "nations," or "societies"—not continents, as in Hegel— are the containers for the "economic law of motion of modern society." In this, Marx is closer to Smith. Learning by one country can at best only reduce the birth-pangs of capitalism, not help chart a different path, a different economy. As Balibar concludes, Marx's task is "thinking the materiality of time" and it is difficult to imagine his thought without a notion of progressive development centering on the capitalist stage of development.[61]

When Marx takes exception to political economy or to Hegel, it is not to question their commitment to theories of development or progress. Indeed, he charges Smith and other early political economists with an inattention to history. Political economy, says Marx, ignores the "historical character" of categories and practices, abstracting from the "real development" of social forms. With "the results of the process of development ready to hand," political economists treat contemporary social practices as expressions of the "fixed quality of natural forms of social life."[62] He singles out Smith for misunderstanding the "form of value" that "stamps the bourgeois mode of production as a *particular kind* of social production of a historical and transitory character." Smith's mistake is not a simple one, but results from treating value as "external to the nature of the commodity itself"—as a reflection of an "eternal natural form of social production."[63] If Smith is not historical

59 Marx, *Capital*, p. 92.
60 Ibid.
61 Balibar, *Philosophy of Marx*, pp. 81, 83–4.
62 Marx, *Capital*, p. 168.
63 Ibid., p. 174 fn 34. Our emphasis.

enough, Marx is more positive about Hegel. In the "Postface to the Second Edition" of *Capital* (1873), he avows himself a "pupil of that mighty thinker," suggesting that it is necessary to demystify, not reject, Hegel's dialectic. What is at fault is not the form of Hegel's dialectic, which reveals to us the "general forms of motion in a comprehensive and conscious way," but it's content that makes the "process of thinking ... the creator of the real world."[64] For Marx, the *form* of Hegel's dialectic reveals to us the general pattern of historical movement.

In *Grundrisse*, Marx gives his developmentalism a deeper and more rigorous defense. He opens *Grundrisse* with the issue of beginnings. Like Ferguson, Marx argues that the idea of the "individual and isolated hunter and fisherman" is really "the anticipation of 'civil society'" in which "the individual appears detached from the natural bonds etc. which in earlier historical periods make him the accessory of a definite and limited human conglomerate." Even Smith falls into the trap of projecting his "ideal" form of being "into the past."[65] Marx works to overcome the false idealization of the isolated individual of civil society found in the Scots' "conjectural history" by suggesting that "individuals producing in society ... is, of course, the point of departure."[66] But this phrase hardly settles the issue.

What does it mean to begin with the society as a whole? We might begin by describing various features of the social whole, such as the population, branches of production, exports and imports, commodity prices, and other aspects of what Marx calls the "real and the concrete." Such "concrete" descriptions add up to no more than "a chaotic conception of the whole." But this muddled set of descriptions does presuppose a set of analytical categories that are the real object of analysis. The presupposition of these categories by political economy explains why Marx can build on the work of political economists. The "real and the concrete" lead the theorist to a necessary process of conceptual abstraction that, Marx argues, allows identification of the "simplest determinations." With these simpler categories in hand, "the journey would have to be retraced until I had finally arrived at the population again, but this time ... as a rich totality of many determinations and relations."[67]

We take Marx to mean that detailed descriptions of social life do not speak for themselves and must be integrated by a "speculative" method that binds the narrative with a purpose. We need an analytical support system (composed of categories arranged as a totality of determinations) that constitutes those facts as relevant for our apprehension. Understanding that system—its categories and their necessary interrelations—is the precondition

64 Marx, *Capital*, pp. 102–3.
65 Marx, *Grundrisse*, p. 83.
66 Ibid.
67 Ibid., p. 100.

for understanding a society since this system of thought gives shape to the descriptions. Taking descriptions or facts at face value, without going through this more rigorous analytical process, produces only superficial understandings of capitalism.

Marx ties this "scientifically correct method" to Hegelian logic: the social whole is constructed as a unity of many opposed categories by complex processes of mediation, or, as Marx puts it, the "concentration of many determinations, hence unity of the diverse."[68] He accepts this intimacy with Hegel, though he apologizes for the "idealist manner of the presentation, which makes it seem as if it were merely a matter of conceptual determinations and of the dialectic of these concepts."[69] Indeed, he wishes to avoid and overturn what he thinks of as Hegel's mystical idealism. The problem is that

> Hegel fell into the illusion of conceiving the real as the product of thought concentrating itself, probing its own depths, and unfolding itself out of itself, by itself. . . . But this is by no means the process by which the concrete itself comes into being.[70]

Economic categories have material preconditions and material consequences, including shaping the consciousness of actors who sustain concrete social practices. Thus, the "concrete social totality is a totality of thoughts, . . . but not in any way a product of the concept which thinks and generates itself outside of or above observation and conception." Marx stresses that the "real subject," that is, society, "retains its autonomous existence outside the head" and "the theoretical method" takes the existence of society as "presupposition."[71]

Society thereby plays a dual role in Marx's method. On the one hand, it provides the material for description, the "real and the concrete" that is reducible to simpler categories or abstractions via a scientific method. On the other hand, lest we fall into Hegel's idealist trap, we must remember that the theorists who perform the "correct scientific method" live in a specific society—a society which produces the problems that serve as the foundations of their thought. Thus, Marx sees the theorist as an historically situated being. Even the most prophetic theorist is unable to uncover society's secrets beyond those exhibited by the society's level of social development.

Having distinguished his method from Hegel's, Marx moves from concerns about the relationship between "society" and the categories by which "society" is apprehended to the question of the historical emergence of these

68 Marx, *Grundrisse*, p. 101. Martin Nicolaus discusses the influence of Hegel on the *Grundrisse* at great length in his "Foreword," to Marx, *Grundrisse*, pp. 24–44.
69 Marx, *Grundrisse*, p. 151.
70 Ibid., p. 101.
71 Ibid., pp. 101–2.

categories and their relationship to actual historical processes. He asks: if these abstractions, or "simpler categories," are not simply the product of the mind of the theorist, do they, like society, have "an independent historical or natural existence predating the more concrete ones?"[72] What is the relationship between "simpler categories" and the historical development of society?

Marx's rather important discussion of the category "labor" in *Grundrisse* produces the rhythm of his argument.[73] He lists labor as a basic category— among the "simple relations"—around which a concrete conception of an economic system may be built by adding additional determinations.[74] From the point of view of the present, we can see that this analytical category possesses a transhistorical status, though it is only realized in concrete form in the specific determinations of a particular form of society. That is, "labour in general" is the central, common element in all "wealth-creating activity" but it always takes on a particular social form: "All production is appropriation of nature on the part of an individual within and through a specific form of society."[75] At the same time, the general or abstract category "presupposes a very developed totality of real kinds of labour"—a situation, as in capitalism, where labor itself becomes abstract or, as Marx puts it, takes on an "[i]ndifference towards any specific kind of labour."[76]

Marx acknowledges that the relationship between the general category and past and present forms of labor might seem ambiguous:

> Labor seems quite a simple category. The conception of labor in this *general form*—labor as such—is also immeasurably old. Nevertheless, when it is economically conceived in this simplicity, "labour" is as modern a category as are the relations that create this simple abstraction.[77]

Labor is simple and old, but it achieves its "full intensity" or "full (intensive and extensive) development" only within the relations of a modern society.[78] Marx resolves this ambiguity by announcing the "rule" that "the most general abstractions arise only in the midst of the richest possible concrete development."[79]

72 Marx, *Grundrisse*, p. 102.
73 Negri, *Marx Beyond Marx*, pp. 47–50, shows that the category of labor is central to Marx's account of a "determinate abstraction." Marx gives similar (if somewhat confusing) accounts of the historical movement of money and possession or property as categories within determinate social practices. See Marx, *Grundrisse*, pp. 102–3.
74 Marx, *Grundrisse*, pp. 100–1.
75 Ibid., pp. 104, 187.
76 Ibid., p. 104.
77 Ibid., p. 103.
78 Ibid., pp. 102–3.
79 Ibid., p. 104.

This rule is not a matter of speculative thought for Marx; he treats it as an aspect of actual historical development or at least as an abstraction that is possible to make only in an advanced society.[80] Indeed, "this abstraction of labor as such is not merely the mental product of a concrete totality of labors;" "[i]ndifference towards specific labors corresponds to a[n actual] form of society" only with capitalism, "in which individuals can with ease transfer from one labor to another, and where the specific kind is a matter of chance for them, hence of indifference." In capitalism, labor becomes an actual abstract entity or, as Marx says, "[n]ot only the category labor, but labor in reality has here become the means of creating wealth in general, and has ceased to be organically linked with particular individuals in any specific form."[81]

Marx pushes to a key conclusion:

> This example of labour shows strikingly how even the most abstract categories, despite their *validity*—precisely because of their abstractness— *for all epochs*, are nevertheless, in the specific character of this abstraction, themselves likewise *a product of historic relations*, and possess their *full validity only for and within these relations.*[82]

The abstract categories by which the theorist grasps the logic of societies past and present are available only when the most advanced society produces actually existing abstraction in its social relations.

Let us pause and assess. Marx introduces two notions of simple or abstract labor. On the one hand, the category "labor" appears as an abstraction, a basic generalization that captures something common to all forms of production: humans must interact with nature in order to meet their needs. On the other hand, the category "abstract labor" appears as historically specific—a genuinely simple, mechanical activity that is indifferent to its various particular uses. The first abstraction—labor as human interaction with nature—is transhistorical in two respects: it is common to all historical social formations *and* it stands outside of history, present at the beginning and end of time, where all social developments appear as particular forms of the timeless original. The second—labor as the commodity labor-power—arrives only near the end of history where all previous forms of the category are lesser in a scale of forms.[83] It is not clear to us, however, if it is legitimate to say that the simple, transhistorical category, what Marx calls "labour as such," is the same as actual "abstract labour" in capitalism, though Marx links the two as a key principle of his method. Nor is it immediately apparent how "validity

---

80 White, *Intellectual Origins*, pp. 162–72, stresses Marx's distinction between an abstraction arrived at speculatively and a real abstraction constituted by social processes.
81 Marx, *Grundrisse*, pp. 104–5.
82 Ibid., p. 105. Emphasis added.
83 R. G. Collingwood, *An Essay on Philosophical Method*, Oxford: Clarendon, 1933, p. 89.

... for all epochs" relates to "full validity only for and within these [historic capitalist] relations," though Marx commands the theorist (and credits him/her with the ability) to move between these two notions of abstract labor. We return to this issue below.

In *Grundrisse*, Marx argues that theorists in an advanced capitalist society are uniquely able to perform the analytical abstraction (an act of abstracting) that allows them to arrive at the actual "simple category" of labor. It is only with this simplification, achieved in and appreciated by the theorist of the advanced society, that we can begin to capture the logic of the present and, at the same time, the logic of *all* prior forms of society. Marx expresses this equation in a rather famous passage:

> Bourgeois society is the most developed and most complex historic organization of production. The categories which express its relations, the comprehension of its structure, thereby also allows insights into the structure and relations of production of all the vanquished social formations out of whose ruins and elements it builds itself up, whose partly still unconquered remnants are carried along within it, whose mere nuances have developed explicit significance within it, etc. Human anatomy contains a key to the anatomy of the ape. The intimations of higher development among the subordinate animal species, however, can be understood only after the higher development is already known. The bourgeois economy thus supplies the key to the ancient, etc.[84]

Marx thereby locates the starting point of his analysis not just with any social whole, but with the specificities of modern capitalism.

One does not begin with the past to understand the present. One does not explore economic categories in the sequence of their historical appearance, as we have done to some extent in this book. One begins with the present to understand the past: the "sequence [of categories] is determined, rather, by their relation to one another in modern bourgeois society, which is precisely the opposite of that which seems to be their natural order or which corresponds to historical development."[85] The most developed and most complex historic organization of production, namely bourgeois society, is a totality that contains within it simple categories, such as labor. These simple categories come into full intensity and full development only in the most complex and developed society. It is not just that the most advanced capitalist states reveal the future to the less advanced, but that all less advanced modes of society can be understood *only* in terms of their movement towards capitalism. The more developed form—capitalism in this case—engulfs and assimilates the lesser developed within itself. Despite mentions of "unconquered

84 Marx, *Grundrisse*, p. 105.
85 Ibid., p. 107.

remnants," "nuances" and the ambiguities surrounding simpler or more complex categories, Marx's account appears as universalistic and teleological as Smith's or Hegel's.

Marx's dominant historical stories and his account of his method appear therefore to be mutually reinforcing in rendering non-capitalist social forms as pre-capitalist, as historically backward, or as "remnants" within a capitalist space.[86] Everything is understood from the perspective of capitalism—its reproduction, its historical role, and the analytical simplifications that make it possible as a form of social production. In this respect, Marx's work is not only temporocentric as we have used the word, but "capitalocentric" in the sense elaborated by Gibson-Graham. In capitalocentric thinking, they explain, the non-capitalist is located at the periphery of our understanding; it lacks "the fullness and completeness of capitalist 'development.' " "Noncapitalism" likewise cannot share the time of the capitalist: it "is the before or the after of capitalism." Capitalism is the "pinnacle of social evolution" up to this point. It is a "unified," if internally contradictory, "system or body" that "confers meaning upon subjects and other sites in relations to itself, as the contents of its container, laid out upon its grid, identified and valued with respect to its definitive being." Capitalism serves as the " 'hero' of the industrial development narrative, the inaugural subject of 'history,' the bearer of the future, of modernity, of universality."[87] So it seems for Marx.

III. Rescuing Marx for Postcolonial Critics?

Dipesh Chakrabarty would admit that Marx leaves little space for difference. He writes that "Marx's use of categories such as 'bourgeois' and 'prebourgeois' or 'capital' and 'precapital' " places him as among the philosophers that "read into European history an entelechy of universal reason."[88] For Marx,

> [t]he prefix *pre* here signifies a relationship that is both chronological and theoretical. The coming of the bourgeois or capitalist society, Marx argues in the *Grundrisse* and elsewhere, gives rise for the first time to a history that can be apprehended through a philosophical and universal category, "capital." History becomes, for the first time, *theoretically knowable.*[89]

---

86 However obscure comments about pre-capitalist "remnants" may appear, this idea gained life as scholars attempted to use Marx's categories to describe complicated articulations of capitalism with other modes of production. See Aidan Foster-Carter, "The Modes of Production Controversy," *New Left Review*, 1978, no. 107, 47–77.

87 J. K. Gibson-Graham, *The End of Capitalism (as we knew it): A Feminist Critique of Political Economy*, Minneapolis: University of Minnesota, 2006, pp. 6–8.

88 Chakrabarty, *Provincializing Europe*, p. 29.

89 Ibid., pp. 29–30.

History can be known because "differences among histories" are "invariably overcome by capital in the long run."[90]

Yet Chakrabarty reminds us that Marx's writings were crucial to *Subaltern Studies*, helping to constitute a key moment in "anti-imperial thought."[91] He wagers that there is enough ambiguity in Marx's work that a world understood in Marxist terms "may once again be imagined as radically heterogeneous."[92] In service of this goal, Chakrabarty returns to Marx's use of "abstract labor" and his deployment of the relationship between capital and history. Marx uses the term "abstract labor" to capture how capitalism extracts from diverse "peoples and histories . . . a homogenous and common unit for measuring human activity." For Marx, "abstract labor" seems to be the means by which "capital sublates into itself the differences of history," but Chakrabarty proposes an alternative reading of Marx that resists this sublation or assimilation of difference.[93]

Chakrabarty starts, as Marx does in *Capital*, with exchange. Commodities are exchanged only if their uses are different. However, exchange requires an equation where differences reveal an underlying commonality. The basis for this equation, Marx asserts, is "human labor in the abstract."[94] Marx claims in *Capital*, as he did in *Grundrisse*, that abstract labor emerges *only* in a bourgeois society, *only* in a society in which "the concept of human equality had already acquired the permanence of a fixed popular opinion."[95] In the first seven chapters of *Capital*, Marx tends to define abstract labor in natural or physicalist terms—as bodily motions where physical energy is expended. Though Marx sometimes treats this naturalized conception as the simple or transhistorical category realized by capitalism that allows us to understand the history of human social production, Chakrabarty immediately, and in our estimation correctly, realizes that this understanding of abstract labor is problematic.[96] Where we talk about a distinct stage of *social* production, the substance that equates the two different commodities in exchange must be a *social* substance, not merely physical energy. Physical energy must be harnessed and transformed within processes that produce *socially* meaningful and usable products. While human energy is necessary to labor, it is not sufficient to capture the role of labor in any specific form of economy, including capitalism.

Chakrabarty recognizes, as we explained above, that Marx also speaks of the "abstract" in "abstract labor" as the act of abstracting—as a deductive

90 Chakrabarty, *Provincializing Europe*, p. 47.
91 Ibid.
92 Ibid., p. 46.
93 Ibid., p. 50. James White, *Intellectual Origins*, p. 169, points to Marx's idea that labor in its varieties is subsumed under capital.
94 Marx, *Capital*, p. 128.
95 Ibid., p. 152.
96 Chakrabarty, *Provincializing Europe*, p. 53.

activity performed by an analyst of modern capitalism: "Sometimes Marx writes as if abstract labor was what one obtained after going through a conscious and intentional process—much as in certain procedures of mathematics—of mentally stripping commodities of their material properties."[97] He refers the reader to this passage from *Capital*:

> If then we disregard the use-value of commodities, only one property remains, that of being products of labor. . . . If we make abstraction from its use-value, we also abstract from the material constituents and forms which make it a use-value. It is no longer a table, a house, a piece of yarn or any other useful thing. All its sensuous characteristics are extinguished. Nor is it any longer the labor of the joiner, the mason or the spinner, or any other kind of particular productive labor. With the disappearance of the useful character of the products of labor, the useful character of the kinds of labor embodied in them also disappears; this in turn entails the disappearance of the different concrete forms of labor. They can no longer be distinguished, but are all together reduced to the same kind of labor, human labor in the abstract.[98]

Chakrabarty immediately resists this aspect of Marx's self-understanding, however. In the later parts of *Capital* that discuss the discipline of the factory, he claims Marx "does not visualize the abstraction of labor inherent in the exchange of commodities as a large scale mental operation" but the actual historical activity of abstract laborers in industrial production. "Abstraction happens in and through practice," as Chakrabarty puts it; "It precedes one's conscious recognition of its existence."[99] The "abstract" in "abstract labor" remains ambiguous.

Interestingly, Chakrabarty claims that "abstract labor" is both description and critique. Abstract labor, he says, "reproduces the central feature of the hermeneutic of capital—how capital reads humanity."[100] We take Chakrabarty to mean that capital reads human activity as reducible to nothing more than what it needs from the human—that s/he can become a living cog in the machine, the homogeneous labor plugged in as an appendage to machine production. Capital reads human activity as reducible to the commodity labor-power. Chakrabarty does *not* embrace this language of labor-power as a commodity, however. He turns instead to rather vague formulations, calling the commodity labor-power "the labor of abstracting" or "abstract living labor."[101] Chakrabarty means to indicate that Marx uses this

97 Chakrabarty, *Provincializing Europe*, p. 54.
98 Marx, *Capital*, p. 128.
99 Chakrabarty, *Provincializing Europe*, p. 55.
100 Ibid., p. 58.
101 Ibid., pp. 58 and 60.

language *to describe* how abstract labor has been transformed from different particular labors (such as weaving, baking, smithing, etc.) to the kind of labor that is indifferent to its particularities; and that Marx uses this language *to critique* the way the particularities of each human existence is necessarily ignored in capitalist production, often at great cost to the worker. Thus, "abstract labor is also a critique of the same hermeneutic because it—the labor of abstracting—defines for Marx a certain kind of unfreedom. . . . This despotism is structural to capital; it is not simply historical." The term "despotism" points to a long historical process of "class struggle," where the labor process of industrial production is imposed on workers despite their resistance. We can see, then, that capital contains "resistance" within its structural relationships, "as something internal to capital itself."[102]

Chakrabarty turns to Marx to suggest that capital posits just as many limits as it overcomes.[103] Marx, he says, "locates resistance in the very logic of capital"—in its very "being" or reproduction as capital, not in relation to its historical emergence or "becoming" as capital.[104] Chakrabarty emphasizes that Marx locates the sources of such resistance not in the encounter between modernizing capitalists and the habits of a pre-capitalist working force, but within "the very logic of capital." "Resistance is the Other of the despotism inherent in capital's logic," not a relationship between capitalism and alternative modes of being.[105]

The contradiction between capitalist despotism and resistance within capitalism is not Marx's only concern, however. He also turns his method to the material unfolding of history. In *Grundrisse*, as Charkrabarty notes, Marx suggests that the logic of capital points *"to the real history of the relations of production"*—to "empirical" realities "which point towards a past lying behind this system."[106] For Chakrabarty, these remarks open a space for difference in the relations between "being" and "becoming." He finds two competing accounts of history in Marx's work.

In the first account, the "being" of capital is capital in its full development, whereas "becoming" is the historical process by which it comes to this fullness of "being." Chakrabarty points out that "[b]ecoming is not simply the calendrical or chronological past that precedes capital but the past that the category retrospectively posits."[107] Marx notes that capital "posits the conditions for its realization"[108] and Chakrabarty takes this to mean that

102 Chakrabarty, *Provincializing Europe*, p. 58.

103 Ibid. See Marx, *Grundrisse*, p. 410.

104 Chakrabarty, *Provincializing Europe*, p. 58. Negri, *Marx Beyond Marx*, p. 51, makes the same point.

105 Chakrabarty, *Provincializing*, p. 59.

106 Marx, *Grundrisse*, pp. 460–1. Chakrabarty's quotation (*Provincializing Europe*, p. 62, our emphasis) reads "a past lying *beyond* this system," though he apparently uses the same translation.

107 Chakrabarty, *Provincializing Europe*, p. 62.

108 Marx, *Grundrisse*, p. 459.

"becoming" includes those events that are the necessary prerequisites to capital's own "being"—a kind of time retrospectively posited by capital. For example, there would be no workers available to capital if labor still had living connections with either land or tools. Capitalist production posits a pool of workers "freed" from the means of production as its prerequisite and thus enclosures and proletarianization are a necessary feature of capitalism's "becoming." The historical pre-conditions of capital's "being" form the structure of *the* story of capital's "becoming" in what Chakrabarty calls "History 1." As he puts it: "this is the universal and necessary history we associate with capital. It forms the backbone of the usual narrative of transition to the capitalist mode of production."[109]

"History 2," in contrast, opens us to different elements in the past—those antecedent to capital, which might be part of a story of its ancestry but are not strictly necessary for the "being" of capital. Chakrabarty quotes from Marx's *Theories of Surplus Value* (1862–3):

> The commercial and interest-bearing forms of capital are older than industrial capital, which, in the capitalist mode of production is the *basic form* of capital relations dominating bourgeois society. . . . In the course of its evolution, industrial capital must therefore subjugate these forms and transform them into derived or special functions of itself. It encounters these older forms as *antecedents*, but not as antecedents established by itself, not as forms of its own life-process. In the same way as it originally finds the commodity already in existence, but not as its own product, and likewise finds money circulation, but not as an element in its own reproduction.[110]

Here, the contemporary "being" of capital faces elements of past societies that are not posited by capital in the form they assume in its "own life process." These "older forms" must be transformed, subjugated, converted or appended to (or into) the logic of capital. Marx's "History 2," Chakrabarty observes, "writes into the intimate space of capital an element of deep uncertainty" and "double possibilities." Social practices we find in the present—that we associate with capitalism itself—are not necessarily "central to capital's reproduction"; they might just as well be aspects of social structure that are indifferent to its reproduction. "History 2s are thus not pasts separate from capital," Chakrabarty emphasizes; "they inhere in capital and yet interrupt and punctuate the run of capital's own logic."[111]

The flow of events in Marx's work allow two historical stories: one comprising elements that are the logical/historical preconditions of capital

---

109 Chakrabarty, *Provincializing Europe*, p. 63.
110 Karl Marx, *Theories of Surplus Value, Volume 3*, Moscow: Progress Publishers, 1979, p. 468.
111 Chakrabarty, *Provincializing Europe*, p. 64.

(History 1) and another with elements that are not logical/historical preconditions but which capital nevertheless incorporates, internalizes, and transforms
(History 2). We see why Chakrabarty takes such pains to underscore that
capital's internalization process was never total or complete, that it meets
resistance. While capital uses its resources, including force, to "subjugate
and destroy the multiple possibilities that belong to History 2," there is no
certainty that "the subordination of History 2s to the logic of capital would
ever be complete."[112] Thus, "History 2" points to that which is never or "not
yet," fully internalized. Prior to its encounter with capital, we might think of
such a history not only as pre-capitalist, since it has not been absorbed into
capitalism, but also as acapitalist, since it seems indifferent to the "being"
and "becoming" of capital suggested by "History 1." Those " 'remnants' of
'vanished social formations' that are 'partly still unconquered' " that Marx
refers to in parts of *Grundrisse* that we quoted above, signal, Chakrabarty
writes, that "a site of 'survival' of that which seemed pre- or non-capitalist
could very well be the site of an ongoing battle."[113]

Chakrabarty cannot afford to make too much of this opening. He recognizes that Marx's equivocations have created ambiguity. "Marx himself," he
says, "warns us against understandings of capital that emphasize the historical at the expense of the structural or the philosophical."[114] This warning
reinforces Marx's dominant method, where capitalism shows the future to the
backward. Chakrabarty's most compelling suggestion comes, however, when
he (but not Marx) treats the being and becoming of capital not as mutually
exclusive, but also as overlapping:

> "Becoming," the question of the past of capital, does not have to be
> thought of as a process outside of and prior to its "being." If we describe
> "becoming" as the past posited by the category "capital" itself, then we
> make "being" logically prior to "becoming." In other words, History
> 1 and History 2, *considered together*, destroy the usual topological dis-
> tinction of the outside and the inside that marks debates about whether
> or not the whole world can be properly said to have fallen under the sway
> of capital. Difference, in this account, is not something external to cap-
> ital. Nor is it something subsumed into capital. It lives in intimate and
> plural relation to capital, ranging from opposition to neutrality.[115]

History 2 is inside capital. Since it is unconquered and may be unconquer-
able, it resists capital. The non- or pre- or acapitalist elements of History
2 are a "category charged with the function of constantly interrupting the

---

112 Chakrabarty, *Provincializing Europe*, p. 65.
113 Ibid.
114 Ibid.
115 Ibid., pp. 65–6. Emphasis ours.

totalizing thrusts of History 1."[116] The recovery of History 2 seems to resist the "capitalocentrism" that we find central to Marx's dominant historical accounts and methodological self-understanding. Chakrabarty himself points at something like this conclusion:

> The idea of History 2 allows us to make room, in Marx's own analytic of capital, for the politics of human belonging and diversity. It gives us a ground on which to situate our thoughts about multiple ways of being human and their relationship to the global logic of capital.[117]

Thus, Chakrabarty stages an encounter where "the universal history of capital and the politics of human belonging are allowed to interrupt each other's narrative." This means that "[c]apital brings into every history some of the universal themes of the European Enlightenment." However, "various History 2s . . . always modify History 1;" they "interrupt and defer capital's self-realization" and "act as our grounds for claiming historical difference."[118]

Perhaps so. But what kind of space is there for difference if History 2 only *modifies* History 1? It seems as if the logic of dialectical unfolding can be interrupted but not refused. This strikes us as a rather one-sided encounter.

IV. Marx's Alternative Historical Forms

That Chakrabarty only interrupts the unfolding of Marx's History 1 suggests that he may not have pushed deeply enough into the problems of Marx's method. Even as he resists Marx's "secular universal time," Chakrabarty does not challenge the way Marx encloses his analysis of categories within a "scale of forms" in which the highest term "sums up the whole scale to that point."[119] As Marx puts it, the "sequences" of categories from previous societies "are determined . . . by their relation to one another in bourgeois society."[120] A diversity of forms is thereby assimilated into an historical sequence as they were with Smith. There is another possibility that seems to open more space for difference. In apparent contrast to his expressed method, we might recover the transhistorical aspect of categories that Marx deployed in order to expose diversity as temporally coeval with capitalism. Recovering this method may allow us to liberate the hidden diversity assimilated within the scale of forms.

We draw the notion of "scale of forms" from R. G. Collingwood's *An Essay on Philosophical Method*. Collingwood's project attempts to rescue the notion of "system" (drawing loosely on Hegel) for philosophy. As with Marx,

---

116 Chakrabarty, *Provincializing Europe*, p. 66.
117 Ibid., p. 67.
118 Ibid., pp. 70–1.
119 Collingwood, *Philosophical Method*, p. 89.
120 Marx, *Grundrisse*, p. 107.

Collingwood wants to avoid the common temptation to resolve all differences into unities. But, again along with Marx, he also refuses a picture of disconnected distinctions or facts that contribute to a "mere differentiated chaos." What both Collingwood and Marx seek is "the articulated unity of an ordered system"[121] or, as Marx put it in a passage we quoted, "the unity of the diverse."

Collingwood explains that applying any category necessarily engages differences in both degree and kind. These two registers of difference are intimately connected:

> When the variable, increasing or decreasing, reaches certain critical points on the scale, one specific form disappears and is replaced by another. A breaking strain, a freezing-point, a minimum taxable income, are examples of such critical breaking points on a scale of degrees, where a new specific form suddenly comes into being. A system of this kind I propose to call a scale of forms.[122]

It is not just that everything "may be looked at from the two points of view of quality and quantity," as Marx stresses in his analysis of the commodity in *Capital*. It is also that the very process of establishing a quantitative equivalence between use-values changes the very nature of value, transforms goods into commodities, and forms a central feature of a qualitatively distinct form of life.[123] Similarly, in *Grundrisse* Marx explains that capital is not just the stored up results of production over time (quantitative change), but the addition of a "specific quality" that transforms money into capital.[124] Later in *Capital*, Marx describes the qualitative transformation of money into capital as both an historical transition and as a process functioning within capitalism itself that allows us, from the vantage point of the present, to understand past forms.[125]

This relationship of quantity and quantity is arrayed, says Collingwood, across an entire "scale of forms," in which the lower reveals not the general category in its fullest extent, but a "specific kind" that is surpassed by the higher category. In phrases that seem to mirror Marx: "[t]he lower promises more than it can perform;" "it professes to exhibit" the fullness of the category, "but it cannot in reality do so in more than approximate and inadequate manner;" that fullness can "genuinely be achieved only by the next higher term."[126] Recall the "Preface" to *Contribution to Critique of Political Economy*, where Marx uses language that suggests that shifts

---

121 Collingwood, *Philosophical Method*, p. 8.
122 Ibid., p. 57.
123 Marx, *Capital*, ch. 1.
124 Marx, *Grundrisse*, p. 86.
125 Marx, *Capital*, pp. 247–57.
126 Collingwood, *Philosophical Method*, pp. 86–7.

between modes of production occur where quantitative changes reach a breaking point—where each social formation exhausts its productive potentials and a new form is born.[127] And just as in Marx's methodological assertions in *Grundrisse*, where the lower species "can be understood only after the higher development is already known," Collingwood asserts that "[w]herever we stand in the scale, we stand at a culmination . . . because the specific form at which we stand is the generic concept itself, so far as our thought conceives it."[128] For Marx, this logical progression is reproduced across time. Just as the Great Chain of Being—where a scale of forms ascends from the least perfect to the most perfect—was temporalized to produce stages of development or evolutionary sequences,[129] as we saw with Smith, so a "scale of forms" is temporalized (in History 1) by Marx as a conjoint sequence of categories and modes of social production.

We can observe some slippage in Marx's method that produces more than just the historical remnants of History 2. This slippage opens a kind of rupture that permits the coevality of diverse forms. As in *Grundrisse*, Marx gives a triple existence to categories that he regards as the determinants of complex and developed wholes: (1) as derived from an analytic/mental process of simplification from complex wholes—the act of abstracting; (2) as elements of actual less developed historical societies; and (3) as coming to their fullest intensity and realization while also showing their simplest expression in the development of modern society. Thus, it is only in the most advanced society that we can see fully the "scale of forms" involved: the "abstract" in "abstract labor" combines the simple or generalizable category—muscles at work for a purpose—with the capitalist construction of "abstract labor" as the commodity labor-power. Marx tries to conjoin these two notions of abstraction but we can see the gap between them appearing early on in the *Grundrisse* and opening further in *Capital*. That gap opens the space for what we call Marx's method of "alternative historical forms."

"Production in general," Marx suggests in *Grundrisse*, "is an abstraction, but a rational abstraction in so far as it really brings out and fixes" the elements common to each form of production. This is not to forget the key differences between modes of production, but to see that "the elements that are not general and common . . . must be separated out from the determinations that are valid for production as such." We can imagine "production as such" because of a "unity" that is common to all social production: "the identity of the subject, humanity, and of the object, nature."[130] Given that "[a]ll production is appropriation of nature on the part of an individual

---

127 Marx, *Contribution to the Critique*, pp. 20–1.
128 Collingwood, *Philosophical Method*, p. 89.
129 The key source is Arthur O. Lovejoy, *The Great Chain of Being: A Study of the History of an Idea*, Cambridge: Harvard University, 1964. chs. VI and IX.
130 Marx, *Grundrisse*, p. 85.

within and through a specific form of society," property also comes to appear as one of the "characteristics which all stages of production have in common, and which are established as general ones by the mind."[131] As we saw above, the simpler, more general, categories allow the theorist to conceive of determinations that help understand human production in specific and in general.

If we read closely, Marx seems to indicate that the relationship between the general category and its specific manifestations in varying forms of society is a relationship between the general and the particular, where the general reflects a material relationship common to all social forms. The general is what remains after one sorts out the social elements that give each mode its specific character and those that serve as a material precondition common to all forms of social production.[132] Marx's language suggests that this sorting of the general and particular depends on the analyst's capacity to take a *comparative* perspective, *not* on taking the perspective of the most advanced form of society as he suggests at other points.

It is necessary and sufficient only that the theorist has available diverse forms of production for comparison and that the sorting is guided by a materialist method that allows a clear distinction between what is precondition and what is social form. In principle, at least, the general category—the "rational abstraction"—might be made at any point in time by a skilled analyst and would give that analyst a perspective that was liberated from the narrow vision of any particular society.[133] More precisely, this "rational abstraction" allows the analyst to explode claims that a particular society's mode of production is timeless and natural. Marx himself understood the power of this relativizing move to refuse the universalizing prejudices of bourgeois society. He rails against the point of departure of the "isolated" individual, "the unimaginative conceits of the eighteenth-century Robinsonades," and "Rousseau's *contrat social*," all of which confuse the specificity of "civil society" for the natural condition of human kind.[134]

The power of this relativising strategy has been demonstrated more recently by Karl Polanyi. Polanyi, perhaps following Marx, makes a distinction that

---

131 Marx, *Grundrisse*, pp. 87–8.

132 Ibid., p. 85.

133 Marx might object that it is only the social theorist conditioned by the highest stage of social development that can comprehend the "scale of forms" of categories that capture earlier developments. His statements about Aristotle in *Capital* are indicative. Even "the giant thinker," who was able to see much of the qualitative change involved in converting use-value to exchange-value, could not quite imagine the notion of value associated with capital. See Marx, *Capital*, pp. 151, 175. That Aristotle receives a more positive reading by Karl Polanyi, "Aristotle Discovers the Economy," in George Dalton (ed.) *Primitive, Archaic, and Modern Economies: Essays of Karl Polanyi*, Garden City: Anchor, 1968, 78–115, may indicate more about their differing view of historical others than Aristotle's capabilities.

134 Marx, *Capital*, p. 83.

allows him to refuse what he calls "the economistic fallacy"—the "logical error" involved in confusing "a broad generic phenomenon" with "a species with which we happen to be familiar" and, specifically, "of equating the human economy in general with its market form."[135] To avoid this error, Polanyi distinguishes between "substantive" and "formal" meanings of economy. The substantive conception highlights what is common to all forms of economy: the process of providing the livelihood of human beings or, in terms close to Marx's, "the interchange with his natural and social environment, in so far as this results in supplying him with the means of material want-satisfaction." By contrast, the formal meaning of economy derives from the logical character of the means-ends relationship institutionalized in market societies, as is apparent in words such as "economical" or "economizing." Polanyi uses this distinction to establish a "perspectivism" that opens up the social sciences to the study of difference—to the varied "empirical economies of the past and present."[136] Market logic appears as but one form among many, not the category revealing the meaning of prior forms. Here the emphasis is not on establishing logical priority or historical sequences, but on exposing the diversity of economic experience.

Marx applies this method of "alternative historical forms" in *Capital*. In Chapter 7, he suggests that we must abstract from the specific features of capitalist society in order to expose "the general character of that production. We shall therefore, in the first place, have to consider the labor process independently of any specific social formation."[137] This passage comes as a bit of a surprise to anyone committed to Marx's enunciated method. Was not the historical and general understanding of categories to be understood through the fully developed (and simplest) categories in the most complex and developed society? Marx seems to be doing the opposite here, namely, using the most general and least specified meaning of labor as its real content and then asserting that this general formulation takes on different forms in different social formulations.

Marx implicitly uses this method when he works through a series of definitions to arrive at the proper general determination of labor. "Labor is, first of all," he says,

> a process between man and nature, a process by which man, through his own actions, mediates, regulates and controls the metabolism between himself and nature. . . . He sets in motion the natural forces which belong

---

135 Karl Polanyi, *The Livelihood of Man*, New York: Academic Press, 1977, pp. 4–5.
136 Karl Polanyi, "The Economy as Instituted Process," in George Dalton (ed.) *Primitive, Archaic, and Modern Economies: Essays of Karl Polanyi*, Garden City: Anchor, 1968, pp. 139–40. The term "perspectivism" comes from Tzvetan Todorov, *The Conquest of America: The Question of the Other*, New York: Harper and Row, 1984, pp. 185–93, 240.
137 Marx, *Capital*, p. 283.

to his body, his arms, legs, head and hands, in order to appropriate nature in a form adapted to his own needs.[138]

Marx makes clear that he aims to produce a notion of great historical generality. We must, he says, "presuppose labor in a form in which it is an exclusively human characteristic," having moved beyond animal instinct only after an "immense interval of time."[139] From this idea of labor as human, Marx moves directly to the idea of labor as purposive activity. In a famous passage, Marx argues that

> what distinguishes the worst architect from the best of bees is that the architect builds the cell in his mind before he constructs it in wax. At the end of every labor process, a result emerges which had already been conceived by the worker at the beginning, hence already existed ideally.[140]

However conscious this purpose, the laborer "must subordinate his will to it." And, as Marx argues, this "subordination is no mere momentary act:"[141]

> Apart from the exertion of the working organs, a purposeful will is required for the entire duration of work. This means close attention. The less he is attracted by the nature of the work and the way it has to be accomplished, and the less, therefore, he enjoys it as the free play of his own physical and mental powers, the closer his attention is forced to be.[142]

Marx seems to equate labor that expresses "freeplay" with labor that requires forced attention because in both cases a purposive ideal is being executed and realized. Labor is purposive regardless of whether an ideal motivates the worker, as an expression of human species-being or whether the purpose is foreign or alien to the worker.[143]

This equation creates a general category of human labor that allows multiple forms. In the first case, where the purposive activity motivates the worker, labor is artisanal in character. The attention one brings to the laboring activity and which permeates this activity is, at least to some degree, "a

138 Marx, *Capital*. See also pp. 132, 133, 150, 169, and 172.
139 Ibid., p. 284.
140 Ibid.
141 Ibid.
142 Ibid.
143 We refer here to Marx's understanding of labor as "species activity" in *The Economic and Philosophic Manuscripts*, New York: International Publishers, 1964. This distinction becomes crucial for Marx's understanding of communism and the direction of historical movement. See R. N. Berki, *Insight and Vision: The Problem of Communism in Marx's Thought*, London: J. M. Dent and Sons, 1983. This distinction, here submerged, at other points is deployed to teleological purpose.

free play of physical and mental powers." And, as important, the attention and purpose the laborer brings to the activity is, to some degree, the laborer's own. Labor, in the latter case, is more akin to the "real and concrete" abstracted entity—the commodity labor-power. The attention given to the activity is necessary precisely because the purpose is not immediate and not directly the laborer's own.

Another way to grasp this distinction is by examining the temporal orientation of the two forms of labor. When the laborer is performing artisanal activity—weaving, tailoring, smithing—the laborer's temporal orientation combines both future and present. One aspect of an artisan's attention is directed towards producing a commodity for sale and thus is focused on the future in which s/he hopes to find a buyer. Another aspect of his/her attention includes a degree of creativity and individual expression in producing the product, what Marx calls "free play," and to that degree s/he is present-oriented. When there is no artisanal element in production, however, and the laborer's purpose contains nothing of his/her own, then s/he is using the activity as a means to an end of earning wages for future consumption. Here the future is the determining element in the immediate purpose. This laborer is in effect abstracting from the present and the "free play of his physical and mental powers" in order to perform the activity.

This contrast suggests two different forms of labor corresponding to two different forms of production. First, Marx seems to be working with what we, along with others, would call "simple commodity production."[144] In simple commodity production, there are property rights and a market in commodities, but no market for labor. There is, however, a social division of labor in which each producer owns his own means of production. In this world, capital does not exist in its fullest sense, nor do we see machine production. Thus, within this social division of labor, particular labors are still *different* particular labors. Labor in the "simple commodity economy" has irreducible characteristics that are tied to the specific tools of production and the personalities of the workers. There is nothing yet of the homogeneous labor that comes with machine production, a labor market, and class divisions that Marx describes in some detail in later chapters in *Capital*.

Once we turn to capitalist commodity production based on machinery and large-scale industry, a second form of labor animates the text. From Chapter 15 onwards, *Capital* is full of passages that describe labor as mind*less* or purpose*less* activity. The descriptions are stark:

> Factory work exhausts the nervous system to the uttermost; at the same-time it does away with the many sided play of muscles, and confiscates every atom of freedom, both in bodily and intellectual activity. Even the lightening of labor becomes an instrument of torture, since the

---

144 Joseph McCarney, *Hegel and History*, New York: Routledge, 2000, p. 188.

machine does not free the worker from work but rather deprives the work of all content.[145]

> ... the instruments of labor appear as a means of enslaving, exploiting and impoverishing the workers; the social combination of processes appears as an organized suppression of his individual vitality, freedom, and autonomy.[146]

And the contrast between the two modes of laboring is stark: "In handicrafts and manufacture, the worker makes use of a tool; in the factory, the machine makes use of him."[147] Though production is purposeful, the worker appears as little more than "an appendage of the machine," as Marx put the point elsewhere.[148] As a mere appendage, no laborer's labor is any different from any other's. It is just so much abstract labor to be put to use by capital to produce any use-value, any commodity.

This contrast exposes once again the tension between different notions of abstraction and a tension between Marx's expressed method and his actual analysis of key political economic categories, like labor. Abstracting from the specifics of modes of production, we might negate the particularities of forms of labor so that what is left is the human physical energy put to work for a purposive activity. Purposive labor, which implies a social process, serves thereby as a generalization that allows us to see the similarities and differences of varied forms of social life. Marx himself speaks this way. Even when he shifts the context from the artisanal labor of a simple commodity economy to the abstract homogeneous labor of machine production under capitalist commodity production, it is still so much human energy put to work purposively.

This notion of abstraction runs directly contrary to Marx's expressed method in *Grundrisse* and *Capital*. What Marx presents us with here is not a "scale of forms," where the abstract labor of capitalism serves as the most advanced category, but a general category, labor as purposive activity, which *reveals the diversity of forms* that laboring takes on. Once again, we see Marx introduce a "perspectivism" into political economy—a denaturalizing or relativizing move. However much Marx deploys this perspectival move, we wish to stress that he does not want to leave us with a coeval diversity of historical forms. His vision of historical stages requires that a diversity of forms, once exposed, be translated, as it is in Smith, into the logic of a "vast temporal plot." And, consequently, his notion of rational abstraction as an intellectual move cannot simply deliver us to a "perspectivism" that opens us

145 Marx, *Capital*, p. 548.
146 Ibid., p. 638.
147 Ibid., p. 548.
148 Marx and Engels, "Manifesto of the Communist Party," p. 479.

to difference. It must be conflated with and subordinated to the abstraction achieved in the way of life of the most advanced form of society.

There is something problematic in attempting to resolve this tension in Marx's method by returning to the notion of labor as simply physicalist, the movement of arms and legs, without regard to human productive purpose, as we hinted in our discussion of Chakrabarty. The general category, physical movement, might serve as an abstraction from all forms of labor (or is it all forms of human activity that involve movement of arms and legs?), and still also appear as the category of the most developed social form, since it seems to mirror the abstraction of labor inherent in capitalism. Here the analyst situated in a capitalist society abstracts away and negates the particularity of the labor/laborer. Simultaneously, capital has created that commodity, labor, which has the ability to abstract itself into all kinds of particular labors—into a homogeneous substance, no more than the movement of arms and legs, which can be applied to any production process. The parallel seems precise.

Marx's understanding of his method would seem to sanction this equation. However, one might think, as we do, that Marx (and Chakrabarty who follows him in this) are eliding something in equating abstract thought with capital's transforming of particular different labors into abstract homogenous labor and calling them both "abstract labor." Marx (and Chakrabarty) hide that Marx shifts back and forth between two general conceptions of labor that can capture the diversity of social forms. Abstract labor appears in *Capital* as both a conception of human energy connected to a productive purpose and as a commodity where labor is simplified, homogeneous. By eliding these two conceptions or switching back and forth between them, Marx preserves two key features of his methodological injunctions. He preserves his point of departure as social production and social labor, not natural movement abstracted from human purposefulness. And he can continue to subordinate social labor to an historical scheme that requires the most advanced and general category to be "real and concrete" abstract labor—the commodity labor-power.

But Marx is inconsistent in defending this second point as his methodological starting point.[149] Contrary to the methodological claims he makes elsewhere, at one point in *Capital* he explicitly sanctions beginning with the general determinants of *social* production as a transhistorical reality:

> The labor process, as we have just presented it in its simple and abstract elements, is purposeful activity aimed at the production of use-values. . . .
> It is the universal condition for the metabolic interaction between man and nature, the everlasting nature-imposed condition of human existence, and it is therefore independent of every form of that existence,

---

149 Terrell Carver, "Marx's Two-fold character of Labour," *Inquiry*, 1980, vol. 23, 349–56, makes a comparable point.

or rather it is common to all forms of society in which human beings live. We did not, therefore, have to present the worker in his relationship with other workers; it was enough to present man and his labor on one side and nature and its materials on the other. The taste of porridge does not tell us who grew the oats and the process we have presented does not reveal the conditions under which it takes place, wither it is happening under the slave-owner's brutal lash or the anxious eye of the capitalist, whether Cincinnatus undertakes it in tilling his couple of acres, or a savage, when he lays low a wild beast with a stone.[150]

Here Marx's stated method takes a decidedly different turn from his temporal assimilationism. In the method of "alternative historical forms" that he embraces here, the analyst searches for a general meaning for labor that would fit very different historical and social contexts—slavery, a dictator of Rome cultivating his own small farm, or a savage in a state of nature. The theorist then makes such a category the basis of analysis and shows that in different social contexts each meaning of labor is a variation on that general category. Thus labor as "exertion of human organs with a purpose" would be the general meaning of "abstract labor" of which the artisanal labor of the simple commodity economy and the abstract homogeneous labor, i.e. the commodity labor-power of capitalist commodity production would be variations. The power of this version of the category "labor as such" is its capacity to relativize; it allows us to identify and compare the similarities and differences of multiple forms of social production and social labor. Here we are no longer led by the need for assimilative developmentalism. Instead, we can contemplate a coeval diversity of forms.[151]

That Marx is committed at some level to both of these methods speaks to his relative ambiguity about the benefits of modernity and bourgeois society—at least as compared to the other theorists we have examined in these chapters. Marx seems to open spaces for a political economy of difference, comparable perhaps to Steuart, but he also defends a temporocentric schema closer to Smith and Hegel. More than this we do not think we can say.

V. Closing Thoughts

Marx closely connects his critique of capitalism to the promise of a post-capitalist society. His historical stories and his clearest and most elaborated

---

150 Marx, *Capital*, pp. 290–1.
151 Some might object that Marx's later ethnographic studies, especially his fascination with the Russian communes, pushed him in precisely this direction. See Krader, *The Ethnological Notebooks*, p. 6; the essays in Shanin, *Late Marx and the Russian Road*; Balibar, *Philosophy of Marx*, pp. 106–8; and White, *Intellectual Origins*, p. 358. Perhaps Marx had given up his unidirectional, meta-historical theories by the late 1870s and the distinction we draw between Marx and Polanyi is unfounded.

statements of method suggest a developmental schema that pushes humanity towards a post-capitalist future. Critique and temporocentrism are wired together, such that the ambiguous status of capitalism secures its position as a tragic moment in a "vast temporal drama." The "perspectivism" that Polanyi embraces and Marx shares as a recessive moment suggests a different possibility. Polanyi sees the various forms of economy as different, not simply earlier stages of our contemporary market society. Rather than temporally distancing himself from the other, these forms appear as alternatives, throwing our image of market society into relief and raising doubts about its necessity. If these doubts about the necessity of capitalism exhausted what Polanyi offers us, if he suggested no more than that we might live and have lived differently than we now do, we might be tempted to turn back to Marx's picture of the necessity of a different and better future. However temporocentric, whatever the tragic consequences of his historical scheme, at least Marx gives us some clear political/ethical direction. But there is more to Polanyi.

Polanyi's refusal of the "economistic fallacy" opens us up to critical self-reflection and provides us a stock of resources previously denied. References to certain transhistorical categories—the "substantive" notion of economy, "social production" or "labor as such"—produce the perspectivism that helps us displace the temporal distance of a "scale of forms" into a coevality of diverse forms. As Nandy suggests, making the past available to us "as an open-ended record of the predicaments of our time" gives us access to alternative values and visions for re-imagining our future that had previously been treated as temporally superseded.[152] Further, our own categories and our very selves are altered by the confrontation with difference as coeval. Sharing time with others disrupts the very notion of historical development. Our capacity to stand in the same time as the other requires, perhaps ironically, that we let go of the modern desire that Fasolt described in Chapter 1 to put everything into its historical place. The general, the eternal, gives us an access to difference that our modern historicism denies to us. It gives us access to a past that continues to intrude into the present; that interrupts our certainties—even our so certainly held uncertainties that are now fashionable. We will explore this theme further in the final chapter.

---

152 Ashis Nandy, *Time Warps: Silent and Evasive Pasts in Indian Politics and Religion*, New Brunswick: Rutgers Unversity, 2002, p. 1.

7   Savage times

In the European conversation about the diversity of social forms, the Scottish Enlightenment's use of the four-stages theory was a critical moment. Smith worked to close this conversation by contrasting the poverty of the savage with the abundance and therefore unquestionable superiority of modern commerce. But such conversation resists closure, as we have seen. For Smith, the savage serves also as a critical mirror, revealing a wound that tainted his providential optimism. Steuart extends the conversation. He resists the image of history as a harmonious and uniform machine, directing our attention to the conflicts, the disorder, and the potential suffering of common people in an era of commerce. He hopes, nevertheless, that the modern state, if attuned to difference, can mitigate unruly economic processes. While Steuart leaves us only with the resources of a modern capitalist society, Ferguson expands our vision by incorporating "past" values. He counters the dark side of modern progress—imperial warfare and the corruption of domestic society—with the manly virtues of earlier ages. By disrupting Smith's stadial scheme, Ferguson is able to deploy the "past" as a critical resource, but he only juxtaposes the savage past to commerce. He seems unable to treat other forms of life as sources of institutional innovation, as does Marx's alternative historical forms and Polanyi's ethnographic IPE. Hegel learns from the Scots and, like Ferguson, does not flinch when charting the sinister side of modern progress. Hegel is matchless in revealing the violence at the heart of the modern *culture* of political economy. His insight, his prophetic realism as we put it, threatens to break the project of modern progress. And, yet, in Hegel's hands, modernity's pernicious side becomes subsumed within the progressive (albeit dialectical) march of history towards a culture of individuality and freedom. The wound of wealth is both revealed in its starkest form—genocide, slavery, immiseration—and absolved as necessary to modern progress. Marx extends Ferguson's appreciation of the violence of modern capitalism, but he also shares much with Smith and Hegel. Marx's explicit method forecloses the past from polluting the present: the most advanced country shows the future to others while only the analyst situated in a capitalist society can comprehend the meaning of other, prior societies. We are left enmeshed in the culture of modern capitalism, aware of its advantages, but haunted by its massive costs. Nevertheless, Marx himself seems to recognize the need to open space for what he thought of as pre-capitalist difference, but which we might easily think of as non- or acapitalist alternatives. This recessive moment in Marx re-opens the political economic conversation to new resources and allows us to imagine an ethnographic IPE.

I. The Savage as Critical Present

Our language has become anachronistic: we can no longer use the term "savage" without a sense of irony. Even so, the category "hunter-gatherer" still remains vital if somewhat contested for anthropologists. Jonathan Friedman explains that the evolutionary notions of human progress that typically inform our thinking also periodically break down. This breakdown gives rise to a "culturalism" (or "primitivism") that overturns the reign of civilized standards by emphasizing the diversity of human experience and the contemporary relevance of allegedly past values and visions.[1] To return to where we began—with Trouillot—the savage and the particular utopian fantasies associated with political economy are co-constructions. We continue to insist that we are not savages, but we can never quite shake the doubts about the life we have embraced and the many savageries that it perpetuates. Nor can we completely reject the alternative vision that the savage represents. We might say that the savage, as the constitutive other of an internationalized political economy, retains a necessary position within the utopian slot filled by political economy. Thus, an examination of savage times has implications for contemporary thinking about time, space and economic life—for rethinking political economy.

For the anthropologist, the situation is perhaps inverted; political economy appears as the other against which the savage is understood. Indeed, Alan Barnard traces the origins of this anthropological category directly to the Scottish Enlightenment and Smith's theory of stadial development.[2] Similarly, Mark Pluciennik sees the hunter-gatherer as a figure created within that intellectual drama in which progressive history emerged. Notions of progress eclipsed "earlier historical theories—of degeneration (from creation or a primordial Golden Age) or cyclical theories of recurrence and return, or the sacralized linear time of the Christian tradition." The rise of political economy as a discipline and way of life is a key moment in the invention of progress.[3]

---

1 Jonathan Friedman, "Civilizational Cycles and the History of Primitivism," *Social Analysis*, 1983, no. 14, 31–50.
2 Alan Barnard, "Hunting-and-Gathering Society: An Eighteenth-Century Scottish Invention" in Alan Barnard (ed.) *Hunter-Gatherers in History, Archaeology and Anthropology*, Oxford: Berg, 2004, 31–41.
3 Mark Pluciennik, "The Meaning of 'Hunter-Gatherers' and Modes of Subsistence: A Comparative Historical Perspective," in Alan Barnard (ed.) *Hunter-Gatherers in History, Archaeology and Anthropology*, Oxford: Berg, 2004, pp. 20–1, 27–8. See also Pluciennik,

The savage emerges as a category of political economy's "universal history" that the Scots helped to initiate and which was crucial to the later construction of anthropology as a discipline in the mid- to late-nineteenth century.[4]

Current disciplinary boundaries mostly hide this story of the mutual constitution of anthropology and political economy. The continuing co-construction of the savage and political economy and the lurking presence of an alternative, savage domain of values are invisible especially to economists and political economists whose very position as arbiters of civilization depend on this blind spot. Most contemporary anthropologists are more acute. Detailed studies of hunter-gatherers question any easy dismissal of these societies as backward or as temporally superseded. As a result, anthropologists have become increasingly aware of the hunter-gatherer's radical potential. They inform us that hunter-gatherer societies live an alternative experience of time and space that can reshape our understanding of contemporary capitalism.

Contemporary anthropologists consistently trace renewed concern with hunting and gathering societies to a 1966 conference, "Man the Hunter."[5] Marshall Sahlins (in)famously intervened at this conference, introducing the idea of "the original affluent society."[6] Many of the reflections on hunter and gatherers since are, in one way or another, responses to Sahlins.[7] And, since

"Archaeology, Anthropology and Subsistence," *Journal of the Royal Anthropological Institute*, 2001, vol. 7, 741–58, and "The Invention of Hunter-Gatherers in Seventeenth-Century Europe," *Archaeological Dialogues*, 2002, vol. 9, 98–151.

4 Thomas R. Trautmann, "The Revolution in Ethnological Time," *Man*, 1992, vol. 27, 379–97. Adam Kuper emphasizes the later period in *The Invention of Primitive Society: Transformation of an Illusion*, London: Routledge, 1988.

5 The collection of papers was published as Richard B. Lee and Irven DeVore (eds.) *Man the Hunter*, Chicago: Aldine, 1968. Since that time, a series of conferences on hunting and gathering societies suggest the continuing vitality of this domain of inquiry, though one rife with debate about the purity of types, the diversity of forms, and the historicity of peoples often treated as living in another time. See Alan Barnard and James Woodburn, "Property, Power and Ideology in Hunter-Gathering Societies: An Introduction," in Ingold, Riches, and Woodburn (eds.) *Hunters and Gatherers*, pp. 4–5; Catherine Panter-Brick, Robert H. Layton and Peter Rowley-Conwy, "Line of Enquiry," in Panter-Brick, Layton, and Rowley-Conwy (eds.) *Hunter-Gatherers: An Interdisciplinary Perspective*, Cambridge: Cambridge University, 2001, 1–11; and Richard B. Lee, "Art, Science, or Politics? The Crisis in Hunter-Gatherer Studies," *American Anthropologist*, 1992, vol. 94, 31–54.

6 An initial published version appeared in *Man the Hunter*. An elaboration of his thinking appeared in Marshall Sahlins, *Stone Age Economics*, New York: Aldine, 1972, pp. 1–40.

7 See, for example, Nurit Bird-David, "Beyond 'the Original Affluent Society': A Culturalist Reformulation," *Current Anthropology*, 1992, vol. 33, 25–47; Peter Rowley-Conwy, "Time, Change and the Archaeology of Hunter-Gatherers: How Original is the 'Original Affluent Society'?," in Panter-Brick, Layton, Rowley-Conwy (eds.) *Hunter-Gatherers: An Interdisciplinary Perspective*, 39–72; John Gowdy (ed.), *Limited Wants, Unlimited Means: A Reader on Hunter-Gatherer Economics and the Environment*, Washington, D. C.: Island Press, 1998.

it is possible, says Barnard, to locate in Sahlins the resonance of Scottish theories of political economy of centuries past,[8] we might see his intervention as a continuation of the debates about wealth and poverty engaged by Smith, Steuart, and Ferguson. We might say that the Scots established the "historiographical preconditions" that make Sahlins' inquiries possible and that give his critique its potential bite.[9]

Indeed, Sahlins consciously challenges modernity's claim of ascending affluence. He denies to Smith and other moderns the image of hunter-gatherers as the most dismal characters of the dismal science: "Having equipped the hunter with bourgeois impulses and Paleolithic tools, we judge his situation hopeless in advance." Sahlins questions this "bourgeois ethnocentrism" by suggesting that "hunting and gathering economies" represent "the original affluent society."[10] By recognizing the affluence of the hunter-gatherer, we can "deny that the human condition is an ordained tragedy, with man the prisoner at hard labor because of a perpetual disparity between his unlimited wants and his insufficient means."[11]

Lest we think the problem is the "primitive" tools—the supply side of the equation—Sahlins insists that the evidence shows that hunter-gatherers meet their needs with minimal investment of time, interacting so efficiently with their environment that they enjoy abundant leisure: "people do not work hard. . . . Moreover, they do not work continuously."[12] We are back to Smith's flashing insight that savages have time to sing and dance. Thus, Sahlins stresses that "scarcity is not an intrinsic property of technical means. It is a relation between means and ends."[13] Hunter-gatherers create affluence by assuring that their needs remain within their means.

Thus, "[w]ant not, lack not," to emphasize the demand side, is the creed that sustains affluence instead of perpetual scarcity—what Sahlins evocatively calls "a Zen strategy" or "Zen road" to affluence.[14] For hunting and gathering societies, possessions are burdensome and accumulation of wealth is discouraged because subsistence depends on mobility.[15] In modern conditions of the anti-Zen road, even great wealth accumulation is insufficient, since the multiplication of needs exceeds the accumulation of means. Smith sensed but repressed this problem, while Ferguson and Steuart fretted about it. Sahlins delivers a judgment consistent with Hegel's recognition of poverty as a modern condition:

---

8 Barnard, "Hunting and Gathering Society," p. 42.
9 We draw this term from James Chandler, *England in 1819: The Politics of Literary Culture and the Case of Romantic Historicism*, Chicago: University of Chicago, 1998, p. xv.
10 Sahlins, *Stone Age Economics*, pp. 3–4.
11 Ibid., p. 1.
12 Ibid., pp. 14–32; the quotation is on p. 17.
13 Ibid., p. 5.
14 Ibid., pp. 11, 12.
15 Ibid., p. 34.

The world's most primitive people have few possessions, *but they are not poor*. Poverty is not a certain small amount of goods, nor is it just a relation between means and ends; above all it is a relation between people. Poverty is a social status. As such it is the invention of civilization. It has grown with civilization, at once as an invidious distinction between classes and more importantly as a tributary relation—that can render agrarian peasants more susceptible to natural catastrophe than any winter camp of Alaskan Eskimo.[16]

Sahlins brings the savage mirror to the face of the civilized. Savage life, instead of inevitably vindicating modern, commercial society, as it does for Smith, exposes the wound within that society: our wealth is paired with perpetual scarcity.[17]

In a later work, Sahlins trains the ethnological lens on modern, market society itself: A "native anthropology of Western society" reveals a distinctive and dismal cosmology that centers on scarcity—on the constant effort involved in the "melioration of our pains."[18] This cosmology informs economics' emphasis on scarcity and desire, but cuts still deeper. In contrast to many societies, Sahlins' European natives see the origins of evil in an "inherently wicked humanity, banished from the presence of God to a purely natural and antithetical world of thorns and thistles." Saint Augustine, for example, imagines that the "punishment" was implicit in the crime: in putting his desires before obedience to God, "man became the slave to his own needs."[19] Completing the circle, Sahlins continues:

> Still God was merciful. He gave us Economics. By Adam Smith's time, human misery had been transformed into the positive science of how we make the best of our eternal insufficiencies, the most possible satisfaction from means that are always less than wants. It was the same miserable condition envisioned in Christian cosmology, only bourgeoisified, an elevation of free will into rational choice, which afforded a more cheerful view of the material opportunities afforded by human suffering.[20]

Adding insult to injury, Sahlins tellingly quotes another informant, prominent neoclassical economist Lionel Robbins, to suggest that this linkage is more than subconscious:

---

16 Sahlins, *Stone Age Economics*, pp. 37–8.
17 Jenny Edkins makes this point central to her argument in *Whose Hunger? Concepts of Famine, Practices of Aid*, Minneapolis: University of Minnesota, 2000.
18 Marshall Sahlins, "The Sadness of Sweetness: The Native Anthropology of Western Cosmology," *Current Anthropology*, 1996, vol. 37, p. 395.
19 Ibid., pp. 396–7.
20 Ibid., p. 397.

We have been turned out of Paradise. We have neither eternal life nor unlimited means of gratification. Everywhere we turn, if we choose one thing we must relinquish others which, in different circumstances, we would wish not to have relinquished. Scarcity of means to satisfy ends of varying importance is an almost ubiquitous condition of human behavior. Here, then, is the unity of the subject of Economic Science, the forms assumed by human behavior in disposing of scarce means.[21]

Sahlins' conclusion, then, is fitting: "The Economic Man of modern times was still Adam."[22] But the savage is not Adam; the savage lives in affluence. We might shed the Adamic curse, hints Sahlins, if we could but learn from the savage.

II. Beyond Sahlins: The Times of a Cosmology of Sharing

Few authors are satisfied fully with Sahlins' account of "the original affluent society" and their efforts to refine that account contribute to a clearer and more variegated picture of hunter-gathers. In a key article, James Woodburn suggests that Sahlins has over-generalized. There are "two types of [hunter-gatherer] economic systems," operating according to different notions of time: "those in which the return for labour (the yield for labour) is delayed and those in which it is, in general, immediate."[23] In systems where the consumption of goods is delayed or where the production process takes some time to generate consumable goods, Sahlins' vision seems mostly askew. Consistent with Ferguson's assessment, the delay of consumption seems related to a sense of scarcity, *not* abundance. Organizational measures taken in response to scarcity entail the accumulation of property assumed by modern theories of progress.[24]

By contrast, in systems where goods are almost always immediately consumed, we can find something close to "original affluence:"

> They do not accumulate property but consume it, give it away, gamble it away or throw it away. Most of them have knowledge of techniques for storing food but use them only occasionally. . . . They tend to use portable, utilitarian, easily acquired, replicable artifacts—made with real skill but without hours of labour—and avoid those which are fixed in one place, heavy, elaborately decorated, require prolonged manufacture,

---

21 Lionel Robbins, *An Essay on the Nature and Significance of Economic Science*, London: Macmillan, 1952, p. 15, quoted in ibid.
22 Sahlins, "The Sadness of Sweetness," p. 397.
23 James Woodburn, "Hunters and Gatherers Today and Reconstruction of the Past," in Ernest Gellner (ed.) *Soviet and Western Anthropology*, New York: Columbia University, 1980, p. 97.
24 Ibid., pp. 97–8.

regular maintenance, joint work by several people or any combination of these. The system is one in which people travel light, unencumbered, as they see it, by possessions and by commitments.[25]

Where needs are few and means are abundant, there is little concern with careful planning or matching labor/material inputs and production processes with neediness across time.[26] Immediate return systems are thereby "strongly oriented to the present," suggesting a relative "lack of concern about the past or future."[27] Here there is little evidence of the condition of scarcity that necessitates either an economy of time, requiring a division of labor, or improvement across time, spurred by that division of labor.

Others have modified and reinforced Sahlins' work by including a deeper appreciation of features of social organization and cosmology.[28] Leacock and Lee describe the subsistence practices of hunter-gatherers as "total sharing" or "generalized reciprocity."[29] Reciprocity appears at the heart of hunting and gathering "economy," but it takes a form quite distinct from the equivalences established by market exchange. There is no measuring of "precise material rates" of exchange and none of the "higgle-haggle"—the truck and bartering—of the market that Smith attributed to the earliest state of human society.[30] Individuals and kin groups create obligations by structuring reciprocity into a system of social relationships that extends across the seasons and the spaces on which they move, forage, and socialize. Such obligations require sharing by those who have more at a given point, thus increasing the security of subsistence of all and, importantly, helping to preserve the way of life.[31] These relations of reciprocity are embedded in a

25 Woodburn, "Hunters and Gatherers Today," p. 99. See also Alan Barnard, *The Hunter-Gatherer Mode of Thought*, Buenos Aires: Anales de la Academis Nacional de Ciencias, 2000, p. 9.
26 Woodburn, "Hunters and Gatherers Today," pp. 100–1, notes that hunter-gatherers of this kind are, nonetheless, skillful users of their environment. In a later correction, Alan Barnard and James Woodburn, "Introduction," in Tim Ingold, David Riches, and James Woodburn (eds.) *Hunters and Gatherers: Property, Power and Ideology*, Oxford: Berg, 1988, pp. 21–2, suggest that it is not that needs are kept in check, since group members often complain they are hungry, but that production targets are kept low, minimizing the need for large labor/material inputs.
27 Woodburn, "Hunters and Gatherers Today," p. 106.
28 Catherine Panter-Brick, Robert H. Layton, and Peter Rowley-Conwy, "Lines of Inquiry," in Panter-Brick, Layton, and Rowley-Conwy (eds.) *Hunter-Gatherers: An Interdisciplinary Perspective*, Cambridge: Cambridge University, 2001, p. 4. See also Barnard, "Introductory Essay," in Alan Barnard (ed.) *Hunter-Gatherers in History, Archaeology and Anthropology*, Oxford: Berg, 2004, p. 6.
29 Eleanor Leacock and Richard Lee, "Introduction," in Leacock and Lee (eds.) *Politics and History in Band Societies*, Cambridge: Cambridge University, 1982, p. 8.
30 Marshall Sahlins, *Stone Age Economics*, pp. 277–8.
31 See Polly Wiessner, "Risk, Reciprocity and Social Influence on !Kung San Economics," in Leacock and Lee (eds.) *Politics and History in Band Societies*, Cambridge: Cambridge University, 1982, 61–84.

"moral hierarchy of *virtu*" that provides meaning, creates social expectations, and sets limits on behavior.[32] Here, Ferguson's virtues are not just invoked as platitudes but institutionally embodied.

We can understand this "moral hierarchy of *virtu*" better if we locate these practices of sharing in a deeper account of hunter-gatherer cosmology. Nurit Bird-David, drawing on a range of hunter-gatherer groups, constructs this world view. In so doing, she rejects any attempt to reduce hunter-gatherer economic systems to the technical imperatives of an interchange with nature.[33] Their economic strategies are not simply, and not in their own view (as she emphasizes), insurance policies in the face of a hostile environment. Rather, they require little insurance since their environment appears to them as "giving," not stingy; means are experienced as abundant not scarce. Thus, a band "economic system tends to be characterized by modes of distribution and property relations that are constructed in terms of giving, as within family," not in terms of exchange, as between strangers or legal persons.[34] The notion of "giving" serves as a "local economic model" that governs everyday interactions with *both* nature and other people and shapes hunter-gatherer social practices. It might be better, she muses, to distinguish the economic ways of life of various groups not in technical terms or as successive modes of subsistence, as in Smith or Marx, but in terms of world views—in terms of groups' "distinct views of the environment" and the alternative ways of life these enable.[35] Time is turned back into space and hunter-gatherers appear as co-eval instead of temporally displaced.

Bird-David elaborates her points through an extended reflection on Sahlins' idea of "the original affluent society." By focusing more on the cultural ideas of hunter-gatherer bands, "original affluence" appears as a product of particular "cultural representations as much as objective, ecological conditions." In brief, the notion of a giving environment extends broadly to inform a "cosmic economy of sharing," embracing both "human-to-human and nature-to-human sharing."[36] In Bruno Latour's terms, the hunter-gatherer sees the "common production of societies and natures" as inseparable.[37] The value of sharing lies principally in its occurrence and recurrence, not in the value of the resources involved in the immediate act. And, as Bird-David notes, hunter-gatherers tend to "explain experiences which could

---

32 Sahlins, *Stone Age Economics*, p. 277.
33 See Nurit Bird-David, "The Giving Environment: Another Perspective on the Economic Systems of Gatherer-Hunters," *Current Anthropology*, 1990, vol. 31, 189–96; "Beyond 'The Original Affluent Society:' A Culturalist Reformulation," *Current Anthropology*, 1992, vol. 33, 25–47; "Sociality and Immediacy: Or, Past and Present Conversations on Bands," *Man*, 1994, vol. 29, 583–603.
34 Bird-David, "The Giving Environment," p. 189.
35 Ibid., pp. 190, 195.
36 Bird-David, "Beyond 'The Original Affluent Society'," pp. 28–30.
37 Bruno Latour, *We Have Never Been Modern*, Cambridge: Harvard University, 1993, p. 141.

be at odds with this cultural representation," such as a paucity of game or foraging sources during a season or individual hording, "as temporary, accidental, and remediable exceptions."[38] Such anomalies are inconsistent with the cosmological experience of hunter-gatherers and are relegated to the margins.[39]

This is not necessarily a Zen strategy to affluence as Sahlins's analogy suggested. Polly Wiessner observes that hunter-gatherers often covet possessions, including those made possible by modern industrial production, which have entered their circuits of reciprocity. There is social pressure to circulate goods that are desired by others, though the recipients, being subject to the same pressure, rarely hold onto the coveted objects for long.[40] Tensions may arise when some individuals appear to hoard goods, but these are usually managed with cajoling, open criticism, or, in rarer cases, with threats of possible social isolation.[41] Though they may keep needs quite limited, hunter-gatherers, by contrast with their Zen counterparts, "delight in abundance when circumstances afford it." What they consistently want and demand is "a share" of what the natural/social environment provides to them as a group. "They thus restrict their material wants, but in a way which one does within a sharing relationship." As Bird delivers the punchline, this is "a 'sharing way' to affluence."[42]

A "giving environment" supports quite different notions of property, as Smith himself would have appreciated, that is, if we can call these practices a form of property. Fred Myers suggests that Pintupi aborigines' relations with objects are nested within their relations with other individuals; possessions are seen less as a relationship of individual ownership and more as markers affirming social identity.[43] However, since hunting-and-gathering societies coexist with other and wider systems of property and conditions of abundance/scarcity, the temptation to make exclusive claims on objects is strong and must be resisted by the kinds of social pressures that restrict needs and sustain abundance (something only Ferguson recognized). Colin Scott confirms this in his study of the Cree. The Cree have long integrated white traders as partners in relations of generalized reciprocity, rather than themselves being incorporated as individuals into fully commercial relations. The Cree strongly police this boundary; to cross the line is to fall into a white man's way of behaving, which is "identifiable as sub-human and

---

38 Latour, *We Have Never Been Modern*, pp. 29–30.
39 Economics appears, then, as the constitutive outside of forager cosmology.
40 Wiessner, "!Kung San Economics," pp. 80–2.
41 Leacock and Lee, "Introduction," p. 9.
42 Ibid., pp. 31–2.
43 Fred Myers, "Burning the Truck and Holding the Country: Property, Time and the Negotiation of Identity among Pintubi Aborigines" in Tim Ingold, David Riches, and James Woodburn (eds.) *Hunters and Gatherers: Property, Power and Ideology*, Oxford: Berg, 1988, pp. 54–5.

monstrous."[44] Thus, even many of the commodities produced and valued in the capitalist relations where "time is precious" are symbolically reconstituted as they enter the group so as not to disrupt the social and temporal relations of the hunter-gatherer.[45] Again, the time of the modern is not allowed to disturb a "giving environment."

This system of sharing/property has important implications for the "productive" activities of hunter-gatherers. We put the term in quotation marks because some political economists might distinguish what hunter-gatherers do from production.[46] This is not to say that hunter-gatherers do nothing to consciously modify their environment. Woodburn reports that many hunter-gatherers alter the environment in which they forage: burning to attract game or replenish grasses, altering migration patterns to allow land to regenerate, or limiting hunting to allow stocks to revive.[47] Despite this, the general consensus is that hunter-gatherers exhibit "an apparent underproduction and a general lack of material accumulation."[48]

Even this conclusion presumes some standard of economization, of optimization, against which the lack of the hunter-gatherer may be determined, but which is mostly foreign to their way of life. Robin Torrence resists this imposition: the effort of hunter-gatherers to achieve their goals does not "involve maximization of some property such as energy or reproductive success."[49] Rather, we might say following Sahlins and Bird-David that hunter-gatherers experience the cosmos differently. Work is not an economy of time, in which a paltry nature requires that we calibrate labor inputs according to our needs. We have already referred to Woodburn's characterization of "immediate-return" societies which do not calculate the relation of current consumption versus future returns. Indeed they have no basis for such temporal comparisons. Maurice Godelier's discussion hints at this feature of hunter-gatherers when he notes the lack of an "all-purpose currency" in hunter-gatherer groups. No currency serves as a universal measure and store of value, or catalyzes an explicitly economic rationality, since such groups do not organize their

44 Colin Scott, "Property, Practice and Aboriginal Rights Among Quebec Cree Hunters," in Tim Ingold, David Riches, and James Woodburn (eds.) *Hunters and Gatherers: Property, Power and Ideology*, Oxford: Berg, 1988 p. 41.

45 Marshall Sahlins, "What is Anthropological Enlightenment? Some Lessons of the Twentieth Century," *Annual Review of Anthropology*, 1999, vol. 28, pp. vi–ix.

46 Leacock and Lee, "Introduction," p. 7, wonder if the we can apply the notion of "mode of production" to band societies.

47 Woodburn, "Hunters and Gatherers Today," pp. 100–1.

48 Bruce Winterhalder, "The Behavioural Ecology of Hunter-Gatherers," in Catherine Panter-Brick, Robert Layton, and Peter Rowley-Conwy (eds.) *Hunter-Gatherers: An Interdisciplinary Perspective*, Cambridge: Cambridge University, 2001, p. 13.

49 Robin Torrence, "Hunter-Gatherer Technology: Macro- and Microscale Approaches," in Catherine Panter-Brick, Robert Layton, and Peter Rowley-Conwy (eds.) *Hunter-Gatherers: An Interdisciplinary Perspective*, Cambridge: Cambridge University, 2001, p. 74.

activities according to calculations across chronological time.[50] Maximizing one's productivity or accumulating wealth lacks relevance. And, where a "giving environment" and a "sharing perspective" are assumed, as Wiessner explains, working long hours to pile up goods only increases the demands for sharing that cannot be refused.[51]

What is most striking, given our interest in the temporal assumptions of the political economy tradition, is that hunter-gatherers do not organize their lives around an idea of development. Their sense of time differs. For the Pintupi, as Fred Myers suggests, objects appear more as signs and less as use-values. It is precisely this lack of use-values that leads Smith, Steuart, and Marx to characterize savages as impoverished. However, foragers' exchanges or transactions produce an abundance of meaning; they are opportunities to say something about oneself while re-establishing group identity across time and in relation to a place.[52] As Sven Lindqvist describes Australian aboriginal societies, "[t]he eternal truths of religions are expressed in the surrounding landscape." "The landscape," he stresses, "carries with it the narrative of its creation;" "a permanently present mythical history" shapes hunter-gatherer "lives and society" and this mythical history is re-enacted and eternal truths reproduced by the actions of living people.[53] Both Myers and Lindqvist highlight that hunting and gathering groups experience and participate in time in terms of continuity, not disjuncture. Because the past is not separated from the present or the future, human society cannot be imagined in terms of some unfolding or developmental logic. Rather, ritual action creates and recreates time and the cosmos as the present.

In this way, hunter-gatherers directly counter the Enlightenment conceptions of history described in earlier chapters. As Myer explains, they tend to deny "creative significance to history" and resist "the erosions of time." Their view "represents all that exists as deriving from a single, unchanging, timeless source." Indeed, this notion of continuity or timeless time is precisely what makes possible autonomous action for the foragers occupying this social world.[54] They know how to go on in society because the scripts of behavior of their life as foragers are highly stabilized and because the larger group, each smaller family grouping, and each individual achieve some degree of autonomy of action in the decentralization that this way of life makes possible.[55] There is no centralized authority to which individuals and groups are subordinated, yet they carry with them a set of understandings and norms that reproduce a relatively stable way of life. This

---

50 Maurice Godelier, *Rationality and Irrationality in Economics*, New York: Monthly Review, 1972, pp. 43–5.
51 Wiessner, "!Kung San Economics," pp. 78–82.
52 Myers, "Burning the Truck," pp. 55, 74.
53 Sven Lindqvist, *Terra Nullius*, New York: New Press, 2007, pp. 167, 182, 197.
54 Fred Myers, *Pintupi Country, Pintupi Self: Sentiment, Place and Politics among Western Desert Aborigines*, Washington, D.C.: Smithsonian Institution, 1986, p. 52.
55 We develop this theme more fully below.

is an order without an authoritative orderer, the Scots might say, and a way of life involving minimal coercion, we would add. The "spontaneous order" of hunter-gatherers also indicates that chaos is not the sole alternative to linear notions of progress as the modern faith in development suggests.[56] By contrast, modern notions of agency are situated within a theory of restless (and violent) change—of economic and social improvement linked to broader structures of global economic inequality and political hierarchy.

III. Savage Times and a Critique of Contemporary Global Political Economy

The ethnographic archive casts a different light on the savage—a light that necessarily falls also on its co-constitutive partner, political economy. John Gowdy argues that studies of hunter-gatherers shift our understanding of economy by revealing that "the economic notion of scarcity is a social construct, not an inherent property of human existence."[57] He stresses that our current market society conditions the modern individual's constant dissatisfaction, persistent sense of deprivation, and constant drive for more.[58] But once freed from the ontological supposition of scarcity,[59] we might learn that neither human happiness nor human freedom is necessarily related to abundance. We can thereby resist the ethical blackmail of today's anti-poverty efforts which tie economic growth to scarcity alleviation. And we can turn our attention instead to issues of inequality by shifting social life away from market-driven competitive acquisitiveness and towards greater sharing and the institutions that support it. We accept that some things may be lost in this shift; competition has its social purposes.[60] But we need not emphasize growth to the exclusion of issues of inequality.

We might also come to think of work in a different way. By setting limits on need, foragers circumscribe the extent and pace of work and limit their production targets. Thinking like foragers, we might adjust our social institutions so that they circumscribe our neediness, allowing us to decrease working time

---

56 J.-A. Mbembé, *On the Postcolony*, Berkeley: University of California, 2001, p. 17.

57 John Gowdy, "Hunter-Gatherers and the Mythology of the Market," in Richard B. Lee and Richard Daly (eds.) *The Cambridge Encyclopedia of Hunters and Gatherers*, Cambridge: Cambridge University, 1999, pp. 391–3. See also John Gowdy, "Introduction: Back to the Future, Forward to the Past," in John Gowdy (ed.) *Limited Wants, Unlimited Means: A Reader on Hunter-Gatherer Economics and the Environment*, Washington, D. C.: Island Press, 1998, pp. xv–xxxi.

58 Gowdy, "Mythology of the Market," p. 391.

59 We may not be freed from particular scarcities conditioned by time and place as Nicholas Xenos warns in *Scarcity and Modernity*, New York: Routledge, 1989. Being freed from the weight of an ontological condition that justifies self-regulating markets to maximize economic growth and the restless promotion of development is a relief nonetheless.

60 See Naeem Inayatullah and David L. Blaney, *International Relations and the Problem of Difference*, New York: Routledge, 2004, ch. 4.

and alter its pace in accordance with sociable rhythms.[61] We further learn from hunter-gatherers that "no necessary connection exists between production by individuals and distribution to individuals."[62] But here there is no surprise. Smith and Marx both argue that those who produce surplus are not necessarily those who receive it. Even Friedrich Hayek acknowledges that in modern society rewards are often unconnected to levels of effort or skill, although he is quick to add that such illusory connections are a productive deception.[63] The real contrast is that hunter-gather societies do not require this pretense; they de-legitimate principles that justify abundance for some and scarcity for others. None starve in a hunting and gathering society unless all are starving. There is no means to translate resources into hierarchical mechanisms of control that exclude some from access to the means of living. Such mechanisms of *concentrated* power and control over the character and remuneration of work are social creations that must be legitimated; they can also be de-legitimated and altered.

Smith, Steuart, and Ferguson often use savage societies as a model of human society in its most basic and impoverished form. Beginning with hunter-gatherer practices, we might treat as equally basic the idea that resources or knowledge, though produced individually or in small groups (relative to the population of society), are also social resources that may be pooled and shared. We might sustain social solidarity by strengthening the existing, rather intricate mechanisms of pooling and sharing, such as income transfer programs, social insurance, and community organized self-help. We could secure not just the livelihood of each member but sustain a relative equality of consumption.[64]

We might also intensify our appreciation of people's connection with local "landscapes." If, like hunter-gatherers, our work and transactions connect our lives to places with a relative stability, we might resist treating individuals as easily movable factors of production. If, nevertheless, our livelihoods continue to rely on potentially footloose capital, we might restructure incentives so as to limit mobility and short-term thinking while setting some restrictions on the relocation of production facilities.

This list cannot overcome all of life's impossibilities, nor could these actions taken together eliminate the wound of wealth. We do not pretend to think beyond human tragedy. Nevertheless, thinking with the savage is

---

61 Gowdy, "Mythology of the Market," p. 393.
62 Inayatullah and Blaney, *International Relations and the Problem of Difference*, p. 391.
63 Friedrich Hayek, *Law, Legislation, and Liberty, volume 2: The Mirage of Social Justice*, Chicago: University of Chicago, 1976, p. 74. A less generous reading is that this pretense is part of the dominant ideology that obscures the real operation of a market society.
64 Gowdy, "Mythology of the Market," pp. 393–6. We might notice Amartya Sen's reference in *Development as Freedom*, New York: Anchor, 1999, pp. 49–50, to the role of the growth of an ethos of sharing in the construction of the welfare state in early twentieth-century England. We also might look at Ha-Joon Chang's defense of knowledge as a communal property. See *Globalisation, Economic Development and the Role of the State*, London: Zed, 2003, ch. 8.

another way of encircling the wound of wealth. And thinking beyond the boundaries of our capitalist wisdom might allow us to mitigate some of capitalism's worst consequences.

Readers still might rightly think that all of this is rather romantic. To speak about learning from the savage is to engage in the very anachronism that a modern historical sensibility forbids.[65] In a later article, Sahlins pushes back this modern prejudice about history as well, challenging the idea that Enlightenment supersedes an unenlightened past.[66] For Sahlins, the ethnographic record suggests not the inevitable eclipse of hunting and gathering, but its survival, adaptability, and progress in an era where capitalism has emerged as a world-system.[67] Indeed, localized ways of life have come to see themselves as "cultures"—as distinct forms of life that will survive and adapt, evolve according to their own decisions, and claim a place among the diverse peoples of the world.[68] Thus, it is the idea of hunter-gatherers as superseded—as backward survivors of an earlier era destined for inevitable destruction—that now appears as superstition; as part of the dimness of Enlightenment thinking that might be corrected by the light of ethnographic observation. The temporocentrism of the moderns—that they show others their future—appears as mere prejudice. Sahlins suggests that a form of savagery follows from this Enlightenment superstition, namely "the terror that Western imperialism has inflicted on so many peoples" in the name of initiating them into a progressive history. In case we think imperialism is a time past, he suggests that we, like Hegel, continue to greet modernity's global civilizing mission with a "cheerful sense of cultural tragedy."[69]

Anthropology, claims Sahlins, can overturn modern political economy's temporal displacement and its cheerful tragedy. The savage, who never left the present, needs to be returned to the present; needs to be seen as coeval with modern societies. A number of implications follow. Where the savage is coeval, we may see ethnographies of hunter-gatherers as elements of "a redemptive cultural critique,"[70] as Gowdy also emphasizes. By disrupting modern prejudices, we might see that "[l]ocal societies of the Third and Fourth Worlds *do* attempt to organize the irresistible forces of the world-system according to their own system of the world—in various forms and with varying success."[71] What Sahlins wishes to emphasize, however, is that hunter-gatherers, even in this era of "late capitalism," continue to live "by

---

65 The extent to which these ideas are also modern ones is testament to the overlapping of selves and times we discuss below.
66 Sahlins, "Anthropological Enlightenment," pp. i–xxiii. See also Barnard, "Mode of Thought," pp. 20–1.
67 Sahlins, "Anthropological Enlightenment," pp. vi–ix.
68 Ibid., pp. viii–ix.
69 Ibid., pp. ii–iv.
70 Ibid., p. v.
71 Ibid.

hunting and gathering."[72] They survive, Sahlins suggests, not because of their isolation from modern societies, and not in spite of modernity, but by adapting elements of modern technologies and social practices to their own purposes.[73]

More precisely, Sahlins gestures towards Eric Wolf's recasting of the anthropological task in light of the global effects of western imperialism: there are no "pristine peoples." We live in a world not of isolated peoples and societies but of interconnection. He argues that Wolf misses one crucial point, however. Wolf "neglected to draw the complementary conclusion about the cultural differences the ethnographers had nonetheless discovered and described;" "If the indigenous peoples were not without history, it was because they were not without their culture."[74] In a world-system that threatens to destroy many local forms of existence, peoples and localities have come to speak of "*their* culture, or some near local equivalent." Their culture forms the basis for their own "engagement" with the world near and far, their own pursuit of "what they consider good things," and their own notion of what it means to "develop man," a term distinct from "development."[75] Sahlins describes this less as resistance to a global hegemony and more as an active "indigenization of modernity." This indigenization shifts our vision from a world capitalist system, however much this captures part of our experience, to a vision of the "new planetary organization of culture" as a "Culture of cultures."[76] The global in global political economy takes on a new shape. As Enrique Dussel argues, we might rethink the world-system as a situation of "trans-modernity" in which multiple "universal cultures" now take their place alongside "European and North American culture." Transmodernity is a vision of a "more human and complex world, more passionate and diverse, a manifestation of the fecundity that the human species has shown for millennia."[77] Spaces are overlapping in precisely the way Hegel had to refuse. And our IPE textbooks, our contemporary philosophies of right, might place the cosmologies of the hunter-gatherer and the global financier not as a succession in time, but as alternative visions of local and global space.

---

72 Sahlins, "Anthropological Enlightenment," p. vi.

73 Ibid., pp. vi–vii, xix–xx.

74 Ibid., p. xii.

75 Ibid., p. x. Emphasis added. Some might describe this as a form of hybridity, but Jonathan Friedman, "*Plus Ça Change?* On Not Learning from History," in Jonathan Friedman and Christopher Chase-Dunn (eds.) *Hegemonic Declines: Present and Past*, Boulder: Paradigm, 2005, p. 93, resists this language. He suggests that we not take for granted the kind of purity prior to contact that this notion presumes. He adds that hybridity is an attribution given by an observer, not the experience of the group itself.

76 Sahlins, "Anthropological Enlightenment," pp. ix–x. Sahlins draws the last phrase from Ulf Hannerz, "Cosmopolitans and Locals in World Culture," *Theory, Culture, and Society*, 1990, vol. 7, 237–51.

77 Enrique Dussell, "World-System and 'Trans'-Modernity," *Nepantla: Views from South*, 2002, vol. 3, pp. 236–7.

IV. Conclusions: A Dialogue of Times

Economic life is embedded in social institutions that themselves exist within particular cosmologies *of* time (not *in* time as some pre-existing grid).[78] If so, then challenging the reign of free markets and free trade involves not simply more successfully maximizing our use of scarce time, but altering our very notions of how time emerges and flows. As we have seen, hunter-gatherers preserve practices of sharing and maintain conceptions of a giving environment by placing them in the continuities of a timeless social space. In this way, they restrict the kinds of change modernity offers; they restrict the introduction of scarcity and inequality. Needs are limited and production targets are constrained in order to regulate and balance the time directed to production versus other social activities. And where economic activities are not allowed to colonize vast swathes of social space, production and consumption-related social hierarchies are minimized.

Mircea Eliade reports that human creativity has been directly related to the invention of the historical past.[79] As Fasolt and Kosselleck explain in our Introduction, when modern individuals are no longer subordinated to the authority of institutions that stretch changelessly across time, they become freer to imagine and make a better world. Political economy uses this modern notion of historical progress to rebuke the very savage we have celebrated here. The unimaginative stasis of savage society is associated with a poor, degraded life. For the Scots, Hegel, and Marx, the savage neither works hard enough nor saves sufficiently to generate the surplus marking economic progress and civilization. The temporal structure of savage society is associated with a lack of division of labor, a lack of wealth, and a lack of social improvement. James Woodburn notes the same disapproving tone in colonial officials who condemned foragers for indulging in the moment rather than saving for the future.[80] Development economists and World Bank documents sing the same song, as they decry the lack of an incentive structure that spurs hard work, investment, and development.[81]

Though we accept Sahlins' point that there is nothing natural about market societies and they come with many disadvantages, we also want to acknowledge the personal weight that these arguments carry for us. In a timeless time, one of us might find himself in the rice fields with his Punjabi ancestors. The

78 We extend and adapt Karl Polanyi's point in *The Great Transformation: The Political and Economic Origins of Our Time*, Boston: Beacon, 2001.

79 Mircea Eliade, *The Myth of the Eternal Return or Cosmos and History*, Princeton: Princeton University, 1971, p. 156.

80 James Woodburn, "Hunters and Gatherers Today," p. 100.

81 The World Bank, *Attacking Poverty: World Development Report 2000/2001*, New York: Oxford University, 1999; William Easterly, *The Elusive Quest for Growth: Economists; Adventures and Misadventures in the Tropics*, Cambridge: MIT, 2002; Hernando de Soto, *The Mystery of Capital: Why Capitalism Triumphs in the West and Fails Everywhere Else*, New York: Bantam, 2000.

other knows that somewhere in the past, standing behind several hundred years of yeoman farmers and small-town, German burghers, lies serfdom. Even so, we can no longer align ourselves with economists. While acknowledging that the unleashing of human "progress" generates benefits, we follow Ashis Nandy in *also* envisaging other times and places as critical resources. The proscription against anachronism prohibits the kind of "[t]ime-travel" that potentially "reshapes the past and the future" or holds up the past and future "as mirrors to the present." Instead, we "attempt to read the past as an essay on human prospects" and draw on the "ability to live with one's constructions of the past and deploy them creatively." Nandy warns that where we foreclose political and ethical recourse to various "pasts" (including those now being lived), we impair our capacity to imagine alternative "visions of the future."[82]

Also powerful is Mircea Eliade's imaginative reconstruction of the savage's indictment of modern claims to individual agency:

> To these criticisms raised by modern man, the man of the traditional civilizations could reply by a counter criticism that would at the same time be a defense of the type of archaic existence. It is becoming more and more doubtful, he might say, if modern man can make history. On the contrary, the more modern he becomes—that is, without defenses against the terror of history—the less chance he has of himself making history. For history either makes itself (as the result of the seed sown by acts that occurred in the past . . .) or it tends to be made by an increasingly smaller number of men who not only prohibit the mass of their contemporaries from directly or indirectly intervening in the history they are making . . ., but in addition have at their disposal means sufficient to force each individual to endure, for his own part, the consequences of this history, that is, to live immediately and continuously in dread of history.[83]

In a progressive history, modern individuals endure as much as they create. Individual agency is stunted exactly at the point where modernity promised its full flowering. Eliade thereby strikes a nerve since the Scots' notion of history as natural history—a product of unintended consequences or social laws—had already placed human agency at some risk. And where historical progress is so intertwined with conquest and suffering, a healthy "dread of history" seems warranted.

---

82 Ashis Nandy, *Time Warps: Silent and Evasive Pasts in Indian Politics and Religion*, New Brunswick: Rutgers University, 2002, pp. 1, 5. We wonder if the past or future can serve as a mirror for a timeless-time. But perhaps we occupy multiple temporalities simultaneously, as we suggest below.

83 Eliade, *Myth of the Eternal Return*, p. 156.

The savage might push the point further, says Eliade. The "man of the archaic civilizations" lives an existence that is both free and creative: "We know that the archaic and traditional societies are granted freedom each year to begin a new, a 'pure' existence, with virgin possibilities. . . ." In this way, he explains that "archaic man recovers the possibility of definitively transcending time and living in eternity." The past is not foreclosed to the present and the future is not laden with "dread." "Furthermore," Eliade elaborates, "archaic man certainly has the right to consider himself more creative than modern man, who sees himself as creative only in respect to history. Every year, that is, archaic man takes part in the repetition of the cosmogony, the creative act *par excellence*." While moderns make history (to the extent that history is under anyone's control, as Eliade warns), the archaic thinkers see themselves as "creative on a cosmic plane," participating in the constant reproduction of the eternal.[84]

If participating in a timeless time allows continual recreation of the world, it also provides strong social moorings that give individuals a clear idea of how to go on in social life: how to establish social status; how to ensure livelihood; how to treat family and kin; and, in general, how to connect means and ends. In that respect, a stable social environment is quite conducive to sustaining meaningful action, and social change is dislocating and disruptive of meaning and action, especially where forces beyond one's control rapidly alter the social environment in which one secures livelihood.

Karl Polanyi makes social dislocation central to his political economy and to his reading of the temporal conceptions of liberal political economists.[85] Whatever the benefits of market society (which Polanyi admits), the social changes wrought by market society create "a catastrophic dislocation of the lives of the common people."[86] Such dislocations go beyond change in incentive structures to which already rational economic actors readily and quickly respond. Rather, they are transformations in forms of life. Past modes of working, thinking, and social connection suddenly became outmoded. The rhythm and time of social life are radically altered with dire consequences: "the old social tissue was destroyed" leaving a "veritable abyss of human degradation."[87]

As shocking is the utter disregard for this suffering. Polanyi traces this heedlessness directly to liberal philosophy's failure to understand "the problem of change:"

> Fired by an emotional faith in spontaneity, the common-sense attitude toward change was discarded in favor of a mystical readiness to accept

---

84 Eliade, *Myth of the Eternal Return*, pp. 157–8.
85 We draw particularly on ch. 3 of *The Great Transformation*.
86 Ibid., p. 35.
87 Ibid., pp. 35, 41.

the social consequences of economic improvement, whatever they might be. The elemental truths of political science and statecraft were first discredited then forgotten. It should need no elaboration that a process of undirected change, the pace of which is deemed too fast, should be slowed down, if possible, to safeguard the welfare of the community. Such household truths of traditional statecraft . . . were in the nineteenth century erased from the thoughts of the educated by the corrosive of a crude utilitarianism combined with an uncritical reliance on the alleged self-healing virtues of unconscious growth.[88]

This uncritical belief in both the inexorability and virtues of economic progress—this Smithian theodicy or Hegelian necro-philosophy—blinds us to the violence in the "rate of change." This rate is critical in determining "whether the dispossessed could adjust themselves to changed conditions without fatally damaging their substance, human and economic, physical and moral."[89] An unquestioning belief in economic laws, such as the instantaneous reallocation of the factors of production (to add our gloss on Polanyi's point), ignores the frictions implied by the fact that these factors of production are human beings, living particular ways of life, rooted in particular places.[90] Creative destruction, to appeal to a recently revived notion, is not only creative.[91] To ignore this point is to repeat again and again a cycle of liberalization that fosters violent, dislocating change and a counter movement for social protection of those dislocated that Polanyi so aptly captures. A narrower implication of this view gives some credence to the savage's point. To link a meaningful life to a progressive history—to human creativity and improvement—is to ignore a component of the eternal: that a life of meaning is difficult to sustain in a world of dislocation.

Polanyi implies that we need not polarize modern and savage views of time. The "dread of history" that the archaic man experiences is not eased by attaining a supposedly modern historical sensibility. Rather, as Eliade suggests, our sense of ourselves as historical beings leaves us vulnerable to historical changes beyond our control. But modern and savage times overlap and this overlap generates opportunities for uncovering political and ethical resources for re-imagining the world. Nandy warns that it is a mistake to foreclose traveling between the savage time of the eternal with its repetition of the re-creation of the cosmos and the modern time of creative self-transformation with its creative destruction. In the tension between repetition

---

88 Polanyi, *The Great Transformation*, p. 35.
89 Ibid., p. 39.
90 Ibid., p. 40.
91 The term is drawn from Joseph Schumpeter, *Capitalism, Socialism and Democracy*, New York: Harper Colophon, 1975, ch. vii. For a more contemporary deployment of the language, see Tyler Cowen, *Creative Destruction: How Globalization is Changing the World's Cultures*, Princeton: Princeton University, 2002.

and innovation we can locate alternative visions of social life and the possibility of moderating the dislocations of change.

Nandy, Sahlins, and Polanyi converge on the idea that the times of the savage and the modern overlap. Bruno Latour latches onto something like this when he suggests that "a 'comparative anthropology' reveals that the modern is not simply the winner in a fight with past forms of life. Rather, the Ancients and the savages win as often as the modern."[92] Enlightenment announces the human capacity to understand and manipulate the cosmos. However, accessing this power to manipulate the social/natural cosmos may simultaneously deprive us of any engagement in the process of re-creating the eternal and subordinate many to the creative destructions we have wrought. We seem hopelessly conflicted, but Latour suggests that this conflict reflects the narrowness of the modern perspective itself. As the savage has long known, subject and object overlap, as does freedom and determinacy.[93] The "modern world—marked by the arrow of time" where the present breaks "definitively with the past"—forgets, as anthropologists often do not, that modern temporal structures are only one alternative among many in facing life's impossibilities.[94] Though the (perpetual) promise of modernization obscures this fact, every act and event is "polytemporal;" every space is a mixture of times.[95] As Mbembé evocatively puts it: "every age . . . is in reality a combination of several temporalities."[96] We might imagine, then, a "polytemporal" global political economy—a world of mixed times. Recognizing that we always occupy "a mixture of times" allows attention, at once, to Sahlins' "culture of cultures" and to economic practices that mix the logic of possession and accumulation associated with "delayed returns" with the sharing associated with "immediate returns." Recognizing our polytemporality allows recalibrating our political economic realities, bringing our ideals more into line with the (im)possibilities of life.

92 Latour, *Never Been Modern*, p. 10.
93 Ibid., pp. 51–5, 64.
94 Ibid., pp. 67–8.
95 Ibid., pp. 71–4.
96 Mbembé, *On the Postcolony*, p. 15.

Epilogue

Johannes Fabian stresses that our notion of space and time "is a carrier of significance, a form through which we define the content of relations between Self and the Other."[1] By the time of the Enlightenment, Kim Hutchings tells us, "our grasp of the world is inescapably structured through time and space ... conceived in Newtonian terms."[2] Fabian shows how applying a social analogy from this physics means two bodies cannot occupy the same space at the same time.[3] And, we might add, why a single body cannot occupy two times in the same space. Yet our exploration of the time of political economy and the savage reveals both: two temporally separable bodies occupying the same space at the same time and a body living two different times simultaneously in a single space. The modern solution to this problem of simultaneous occupation, as we have seen, is either the physical or social eradication of one body by the other or the separation of the two bodies—as in a kind of apartheid. When these solutions weigh too heavily against the modernist self-referential notion of the equality of human beings, then a more subtle, third solution is available, namely, temporal displacement. In this move the dominant body ignores its co-presence with others and then displaces them into a different developmental time. Others are placed in a temporal transit lounge to await their lessons from time-traveling experts who stage this pedagogic encounter.

In previous work, we offered Francisco de Vitoria's treatment of Amerindians as one of the clearest theoretical origins of this temporal displacement.[4] This book has traced this temporal displacement from the ethnologies of Lafitau, who, along with Charlevoix, greatly influenced the Scottish Enlightenment, and through the influence of Smith, Steuart, and

1 Johannes Fabian, *Time and the Other: How Anthropology Makes its Object*, New York: Columbia University, 1983, p. ix.
2 Kimberly Hutchings, *Time and World Politics: Thinking the Present*, Manchester: Manchester University, 2008, p. 3. We cannot do justice to this excellent but recent work.
3 Fabian, *Time and the Other*, pp. 28–30.
4 Naeem Inayatullah and David L. Blaney, *International Relations and the Problem of Difference*, New York: Routledge, 2004, ch. 2, "Intimate Indians."

Ferguson to Hegel and Marx. We suspect that this temporal displacement is modernity's deepest legacy. It marks Europe not only as a separate continent, but also as a separate and progressive temporal site—a site of imperial pedagogical practices imposed for others' benefit and a site of imperial knowledge that divines the world's future. Europe begets itself as an oracle as much as a continent.

Such temporal displacement finds its high (or low) point in Hegel's theory of history. Even Marx, who reversed his verdict on the British colonization of India, sustains the Hegelian developmental schema and its temporal displacements. We want to suggest that this temporal displacement, like the ethics of capitalism, has an appeal that goes beyond a combination of force and ideology. We did not address why this displacement might be appealing to both displacer and displaced in this book. But without some small effort to study the attractions of temporal displacement, we fear we will return to the moment where trumpets and drums will have to be sounded to declare the need for another new IR/IPE.

Moving Towards Economics?

One of our teachers, David Levine, a Hegelian who hopes to put Marx back on his head, jokingly asks: "What are economists good for?" Or "Why do we need economists?" He would stop the lecture, ponder his own question for a few minutes, and answer: "We need economists to bring us bad news." If we didn't need to hear bad news, we wouldn't create economists.

There surely is more to it, but Levine is on to something. Becoming an economist has two possible appeals. Economics attracts us because it works to remove the veil of material life—that part of life that most modern wealthy parents do so much to hide from their children. Economics is the world of real adults, bringing home the news that behind our ideals and high-minded words is the base motive of self-interest operating through a system of interactions that produce a largely unintended social order. Of the people who become economists, too many take inordinate pleasure in bursting our illusions—perhaps in response to having had their own illusions betrayed. Their disdain for everyday and childlike understandings of life and their self-deluding fantasies takes on a parental character. They assume the role of parental pedagogue for us all.

This parental stance isn't the only path that follows from piercing the veil of material life. Starting with a child's attentive awe, we might soak up the depth and complexity of social relations. We would go further and say that the adult world—where much goes on behind our backs—is *not* inconsistent with a child's playfulness. This overlap of stern parent and childish play points us to the idea that the value and insight the science of economics brings us is something we already possess. We have known it all along. We carry such knowledge with us in the form of fables, stories, poems, aphorisms, and common knowledge passed from mouth to mouth and across generations by all kinds of everyday folk. If so, then it is not only the temptation to sit upon a parental pedagogue's perch that leads us to economics. Our ethnological impulse—the desire to know otherness both within and beyond ourselves—can also take us there.

The Abundance of Scarcity

The performing economist's favored trick is the production of scarcity—the coin suddenly vanishes and what we see is a bare hand. But unlike magicians, the economist's trick is designed to appeal not to the child, but to the modern adult in us. The content of scarcity is simple: there is only so much stuff while our needs are never ending; never ending needs with limited stuff, and presto, scarcity. It seems so compelling—especially if, like most modern affluent children, we were led to believe that resources just magically appear, disappear, and reappear.[5] Colonial officials performed that same trick for various childish peoples.

Calling scarcity an economist's trick is not quite fair. In a given time, at a given place, with a defined set of priorities—needs overrun resources. Scarcity, as we suggest earlier, is not a social fact with which one can really argue. (But, like Joseph Conrad's "idea," we can bow and make sacrifices to it and then build a kind of imperialism around it.) To reject scarcity, to pretend it does not exist, to wish it away, well, that seems immature at best, if not altogether pathological.

And yet, there *is* a trick here. We can name it: it's the immaculate appearance of scarcity abstracted from any specific time/place/culture. We can see this trick in our everyday lives. When I regretfully say "no thank you" to a request by a friend, I couch it in the following terms: "I would like to do what you ask, but I don't have the time to do it." Here I am employing scarcity; not enough hours in the day and all that. . . . But, to say that I wish I had more time to do the things I wanted, or to say that I don't have the time to do x, y, or z, is to also say that x, y, and z are not particularly high on my list of priorities at this time, in this place, in this cultural context. Hunter-gatherers are denied this trick; as we have seen, they cannot say no to sharing time or goods,

The polite language is designed to glide past deeper issues. I am also saying that my life at this moment is acceptable to me without making x, y, and z a higher priority. Shifting from the individual to the global, if x, y, and z

---

5 The New York Times, in a section designed for children (and their parents) facing college financial aid decisions, offers us examples of questions from the Advanced Placement tests in Economics administered by the College Board. The first question asks: "The basic economic problem of all countries is the existence of . . .?" Among five choices that point to a variety of issues surrounding government, taxes, industry, unemployment, and inflation, the answer is obvious: "limited resources and unlimited wants." "Econ 2009," *New York Times*, Paril 19, 2009, pp. 28–9.

happen to represent massive alienation, immiseration, and angry despondency by the vast majority of the planet's population, I am saying that I have other things that need my attention. Indeed, I imply that such immiseration is an acceptable cost given how the system of wealth creation we call capitalism benefits me/us.

Friedrich Hayek weighs such costs against capitalism's material benefits and its ethics.[6] Usually we are not as daring as the Hayekians; we rarely find the courage to admit that not just the material benefits but also the values of a competitive market society, what we have called the "culture of competition," are high on our priority list and are worth triaging the world's cultures and their populations. We lack this clarity. Nor do we usually have the courage to address their arguments head on. Most grievous, we lack the resolve to consider if, for everyday people, such libertarian arguments are a part of the ethical appeal of capitalism.

Rather than do the hard work of sorting out those attractions and appeals, we rely on the economist's trick of scarcity. We avoid this hard work not only because we consciously (sometimes loudly) reject the values of the Hayekians, but also because such work might lead us to our own hidden valorization of capitalism and the culture of competition. We would rather avoid our implicit and (partial) positive appraisal of the culture of capitalism and therefore our (partial) amenable complicity. Instead, we imagine that planetary poverty and immiseration exist not because we find it an acceptable cost of modernity and capitalism, but because of the "fact" of scarcity. In this way, the conjuring of scarcity is even more mesmerizing to left-leaning progressives than to our brothers and sisters on the right. Scarcity is the bandage on the wound we cannot properly dress; our pretense betrays our bad faith.

Why do we need economists? To short-circuit an encircling of the "real" by producing the *trick* of scarcity as science. Amen.

Inviting Indifference

If there are those that perpetrate capitalism, modernity, and the West, and if there are those who work to resist and counteract it, then we have been forced to admit that there must be those to whom capitalism, modernity, and the West are matters of indifference.[7] We don't mean that there is some pristine space outside of capitalism, modernity and the West. Such an outside no longer seems to exist. Rather, we are thinking of what Ashis Nandy calls the "non-player"—a space inside of each of us that is neither the "player"

---

6 See our discussion of Hayek and the citations therein in ch. 4, Inayatullah and Blaney, *International Relations*, especially pp. 132–45.

7 A recurring theme most recently provoked by discussion with Aida Hozic.

nor the "counter-player."[8] It's an aspect of ourselves that understands that part of the defense against modern imperialism is an enactment of some older, prior, other virtues and values that somehow continue to thrive. We are not sure what this is, how to access it, or even how to think it through. But let us try.

We return to a quotation from Eric Cheyfitz[9] for a third time:

> Indian kinship economics, which, I want to make clear, I understand not as pre-capitalist but as anticapitalist, constitute a powerful *and continuing* critique of the waste of an expansive, acquisitive capitalism that . . . [Europe] could not *afford* to entertain. The loss in social vision was, and is, incalculable.

We wonder whether the loss in social vision, which Cheyfitz refers to as "incalculable," might, nevertheless, be worth calculating. Even so, the "anti-capitalism" to which Cheyfitz refers is *his* use of Indian kinship economics. His work, like ours, wishes to use this kinship economics as something that resists and thwarts the act of temporal displacement perpetrated by the Scots, Hegel, and Marx within ourselves. It does not follow, however, that the practitioners of Indian kinship economics see themselves as "counter-players." As much as we would like to use them, following Cheyfitz, as counter-players and as anti-capitalists, we may want to regard them also as Nandy's "non-players." We imagine that part of their strength—a strength we want to find and locate in ourselves—is the ability to sustain a life that is warmly indifferent to capitalism, modernity, and the West. Could we need this as much as we need the critique of the counter-player? If we need an encounter that juxtaposes the putative temporally prior other with the modern self such that the implicit critique of the former is heard by the latter as an explicit critique, don't we also need the non-appearance of that encounter so that we can see how to go on living aspects of a non-capitalist, non-modern, non-Western life without the obsessions of the counter-player?

If we need capitalism, modernity, and the West to show us the power of a new mode of relating to nature, then we also need a critique of that same new mode to show us the limits of that vision. *And* perhaps we need Indian Kinship economics or the economics of hunter-gathers as a visionary otherness whose deeper resources we have yet to plumb.

8 Ashis Nandy, *The Intimate Enemy: Loss and Recovery of Self Under Colonialism*, Delhi: Oxford University, 1983, pp. xiii, 11.
9 Eric Cheyfitz, "Savage Law," in Amy Kaplan and Donald E. Pease (eds.) *Cultures of United States Imperialism*, Durham, NC: Duke University, 1993, p. 118.

Recursion

Sven Lindqvist writes that modernity is built on "a progress that presupposes genocide."[10] Perhaps it is only a small exaggeration to say that most of us are children of this massive injury. If Lindqvist is correct, can we be surprised at our inability to directly address this wound? Instead we convince ourselves that our treatment of the symptoms is somehow sufficient. Faith-healing we could call it. Or is it more accurate to call it bad faith?

Perhaps it is a necessary bad faith. For how easy is it to admit that we are all the progeny of genocidal ancestors? Perhaps the best we can do is to encircle the "real," refusing the ethical appeal of capitalism, modernity, and the West that sutures the "wound." Perhaps we need to acknowledge that appeal even as we face the fact that modernity was and is catastrophic for most of the cultures on this planet—cultures that were eradicated, assimilated, or temporally displaced. Nevertheless, and despite the prevalence of the politics of emergency—that other face of the coin of scarcity—no catastrophe is as final as we might imagine. The warm indifference of hunter-gatherers remains. It invites us to fashion IR/IPE as ethnology, as heterology.

---

10 Sven Lindqvist, *Exterminate All the Brutes*, New York: New Press, 1996, p. 88.

Bibliography

Ahmad, Aijaz, "Introduction," in Aijaz Ahmad (ed.) *On the National and Colonial Questions*, New Delhi: Left Word, 2001, 1–20.

Anderson, Gary M. and Robert D. Tolliver, "Sir James Steuart as the Apotheosis of Mercantilism and his Relation to Adam Smith," *Southern Economic Journal*, 1984, vol. 51, 456–68.

Armstrong, Susan, "A Feminist Reading of Hegel and Kierkegaard," in Shaun Gallagher (ed.) *Hegel, History, and Interpretation*, Albany: SUNY, 1997, 227–41.

Arthur, Christopher J., "Hegel on Political Economy," in David Lamb (ed.) *Hegel and Modern Philosophy*, London: Croom Helm, 1987, 102–18.

Ashley, Richard K., "Three Modes of Economism," *International Studies Quarterly*, 1983, vol. 27, 463–96.

Avineri, Shlomo (ed.) *Karl Marx on Colonialism and Modernization*, New York: Doubleday, 1968.

Avineri, Shlomo, *Hegel's Theory of the Modern State*, Cambridge: Cambridge University, 1972.

Balibar, Etienne, *The Philosophy of Marx*, London: Verso, 1995.

Ball, Terrence, "Marxian Science and Positivist Politics," in Terrence Ball and James Farr (eds.) *After Marx*, Cambridge: Cambridge University, 1984, 235–60.

Ball, Terrence, "History and the Interpretation of Texts," in Gerald Gaus and Chandran Kukathas (eds.) *Handbook of Political Theory*, London: Sage, 2004, 18–30.

Barber, Benjamin, *Strong Democracy: Participatory Politics for a New Age*, Berkeley: University of California, 1984.

Barkawi, Tarak and Mark Laffey, "The Postcolonial Movement in Security Studies," *Review of International Studies*, 2006, vol. 32, 329–52.

Barnard, Alan, *The Hunter-Gatherer Mode of Thought*, Buenos Aires: Anales de la Academis Nacional de Ciencias, 2000.

Barnard, Alan, "Hunting-and-Gathering Society: An Eighteenth-Century Scottish Invention" in Alan Barnard (ed.) *Hunter-Gatherers in History, Archaeology and Anthropology*, Oxford: Berg, 2004, 31–43.

Barnard, Alan, "Introductory Essay," in Alan Barnard (ed.) *Hunter-Gatherers in History, Archaeology and Anthropology*, Oxford: Berg, 2004, 1–14.

Barnard, Alan and James Woodburn, "Introduction," in Tim Ingold, David Riches, and James Woodburn (eds.) *Hunters and Gatherers: Property, Power and Ideology*, Oxford: Berg, 1988, 4–32.

Barnard, Alan and James Woodburn, "Property, Power and Ideology in

Hunter-Gathering Societies: An Introduction," in Tim Ingold, David Riches, and James Woodburn (eds.) *Hunters and Gatherers: Property, Power and Ideology*, Oxford: Berg, 1988, 4–31.

Becker, Carl L., *The Heavenly City of the Eighteenth-Century Philosophers*, New Haven: Yale University, 1971.

Behnke, Andreas,"Eternal Peace as the Graveyard of the Political: A Critique of Kant's *Zum Ewigen Frieden*," *Millennium*, 2008, vol. 36, 513–31.

Bellah, Robert et al., *Habits of the Heart: Individualism and Commitment in American Life*, New York: Harper and Row, 1985.

Benjamin, Jessica, *The Bonds of Love: Psychoanalysis, Feminism, and the Problem of Domination*, New York: Pantheon, 1988.

Benton, Ted. "Adam Ferguson and the Enterprise Culture," in Peter Hulme and Ludmilla Jordanova (eds.) *The Enlightenment and Its Shadows*, London: Routledge, 1990, 101–20.

Berger, Suzanne and Ronald Dore (eds.) *National Diversity and Global Capitalism*, Ithaca: Cornell University, 1996.

Berki, R.N., *Insight and Vision: The Problem of Communism in Marx's Thought*, London: J. M. Dent and Sons, 1983.

Bernard, Mitchell, "Ecology, Political Economy and the Counter-Movement: Karl Polanyi and the Second Great Transformation," in Stephen Gill and James H. Mittelman (eds.) *Innovation and Transformation in International Studies*, Cambridge: Cambridge University, 1997, 75–89.

Bernasconi, Robert, "Hegel at the Court of the Ashanti," in Stuart Brown (ed.) *Hegel After Derrida*, London: Routledge, 1998, 41–63.

Bernasconi, Robert, "The Invisibility of Racial Minorities in the Public Realm of Appearances," in K. Thompson and L. Embree (eds.) *The Phenomenology of the Political*, Dordrecht: Kluwer, 2000, 169–88.

Bernasconi, Robert, "With What Must the Philosophy of World History Begin? On the Racial Basis of Hegel's Eurocentrism," *Nineteenth-Century Contexts*, 2000, vol. 22, 171–201.

Bernasconi, Robert, "Hegel's Racism: A Reply to McCarney," *Radical Philosophy*, 2003, no. 119, 4–6.

Berry, Christopher J., *The Idea of Luxury: A Conceptual and Historical Investigation*, Cambridge: Cambridge University, 1994.

Berry, Christopher J., *Social Theory of the Scottish Enlightenment*, Edinburgh: Edinburgh University, 1997.

Best, Jacqueline, "Hollowing Out Keynesian Norms: How the Search for a Technical Fix Undermined the Bretton Woods Regime," *Review of International Studies*, 2004, vol. 30, 383–404.

Birchfield, Vicki, "Contesting the Hegemony of Market Ideology: Gramsci's 'Good Sense' and Polanyi's 'Double Movement,'" *Review of International Political Economy*, 1999, vol. 6, 27–54.

Bird-David, Nurit, "The Giving Environment: Another Perspective on the Economic Systems of Gatherer-Hunters," *Current Anthropology*, 1990, vol. 31, 189–96.

Bird-David, Nurit, "Beyond 'the Original Affluent Society': A Culturalist Reformulation," *Current Anthropology*, 1992, vol. 33, 25–47.

Bird-David, Nurit, "Sociality and Immediacy: Or, Past and Present Conversations on Bands," *Man*, 1994, vol. 29, 583–603.

Blaney, David L. and Naeem Inayatullah, "Prelude to a Conversation of Cultures in International Society? Todorov and Nandy on the Possibility of Dialogue," *Alternatives*, 1994, vol. 19, 23–51.

Blyth, Mark, *Great Transformations: Economic Ideas and Institutional Change in the Twentieth Century*, Cambridge: Cambridge University, 2002.

Bourdieu, Pierre, *The Social Structures of the Economy*, Cambridge: Polity, 2005.

Boyd, Richard, "Reappraising the Scottish Moralists and Civil Society," *Polity*, 2000, vol. 33, 101–25.

Brett, E. A., *Colonialism and Underdevelopment in East Africa: The Politics of Economic Change, 1919–39*, Farnham: Ashgate, 1992.

Brewer, Anthony, "Adam Ferguson, Adam Smith, and the Concept of Economic Growth," *History of Political Economy*, 1999, vol. 31, 237–54.

Brooks, Thom, "Hegel's Theory of International Politics: A Reply to Jaeger," *Review of International Studies*, 2004, vol. 30, 149–52.

Brown, Wendy, *Politics out of History*, Princeton: Princeton University, 2001.

Buchan, Bruce, "Civilisation, Sovereignty and War: The Scottish Enlightenment and International Relations," *International Relations*, 2006, vol. 20, 175–92.

Campbell, David, *Writing Security: United States Foreign Policy and the Politics of Identity*, Minneapolis: University of Minnesota, 1998.

Caporaso, James A., "Dependence, Dependency, and Power in the Global System: A Structural and Behavioral Analysis," *International Organization*, 1978, vol. 32, 13–44.

Caporaso, James A. and David Levine, *Theories of Political Economy*, Cambridge: Cambridge University, 1992.

Carrithers, David, "The Enlightenment Science of Society," in Christopher Fox, Roy Porter, and Robert Wokler (eds.) *Inventing Human Science: Eighteenth Century Domains*, Berkeley: University of California, 1995, 232–70.

Carver, Terrell, "Marx's Two-fold Character of Labour," *Inquiry*, 1980, vol. 23, 349–56.

Cassirer, Ernst, *The Philosophy of the Enlightenment*, Boston: Beacon, 1951.

Chakrabarty, Dipesh, *Provincializing Europe: Postcolonial Thought and Historical Difference*, Princeton, NJ: Princeton University, 2000.

Chamley, Paul E., "The Conflict between Montesquieu and Hume: A Study of the Origins of Adam Smith's Universalism," in Andrew S. Skinner and Thomas Wilson (eds.) *Essays on Adam Smith*, Oxford: Clarendon, 1975, 274–305.

Chandler, James, *England in 1819: The Politics of Literary Culture and the Case of Romantic Historicism*, Chicago: University of Chicago, 1998.

Chang, Ha-Joon, *Globalisation, Economic Development and the Role of the State*, London: Zed, 2003.

Cheyfitz, Eric, "Savage Law," in Amy Kaplan and Donald E. Pease (eds.) *Cultures of United States Imperialism*, Durham, NC: Duke University, 1993, 109–28.

Chinard, Gilbert, "Eighteenth Century Theories on America as Human Habitat," *Proceedings of the American Philosophical Society*, 1947, vol. 91, 27–57.

Cocks, Joan, "Hegel's Logic, Marx's Science, Rationalism's Perils," *Political Studies*, 1983, vol. XXXI, 583–603.

Cohen, Benjamin J., "The Transatlantic Divide: Why are American and British IPE so Different?" *Review of International Political Economy*, 2007, vol. 14, 197–219.

Cohen, Benjamin J., *International Political Economy: An Intellectual History*, Princeton: Princeton University, 2008.

Collingwood, R. G., *An Essay on Philosophical Method*, Oxford: Clarendon, 1933.

Cowen, Tyler, *Creative Destruction: How Globalization is Changing the World's Cultures*, Princeton: Princeton University, 2002.

Crang, Philip, "Cultural Turns and the (Re)Constitution of Economic Geography: Introduction to Section One," in Roger Lee and James Willis (eds.) *Geographies of Economies*, London: Arnold, 1997, 3–15.

Davie, G.E., "Anglophobe and Anglophil," *Scottish Journal of Political Economy*, 1967, vol. XIV, 291–301.

Davis, Mike, *Late-Victorian Holocausts: el Nino Famines and the Making of the Third World*, London: Verso, 2002.

de Certeau, Michel, "Writing vs. Time: History and Anthropology in the Works of Lafitau," *Yale French Studies*, 1980, Issues 59–60, 37–64.

de Certeau, Michel, *Heterologies: Discourse on the Other*, Minneapolis: University of Minnesota, 1986.

de Soto, Hernando, *The Mystery of Capital: Why Capitalism Triumphs in the West and Fails Everywhere Else*, New York: Bantam Press, 2000.

de Sousa Santos, Boaventura, "*Nuestra America*: Reinventing a Subaltern Paradigm of Recognition and Redistribution," *Theory, Culture and Society*, 2001, vol. 18, 185–217.

Deudney, Daniel, *Bounding Power: Republican Security Theory from the Polis to the Global Village*, Princeton: Princeton University, 2007.

deVries, Willem A., "The Dialectic of Teleology," *Philosophical Topics*, 1991, vol. 19, 51–70.

Diamond, Jared, *Guns, Germs, and Steel: The Fates of Human Societies*, New York: Norton, 1999.

Dickey, Laurence, *Hegel: Religion, Economics and the Politics of Spirit, 1770–1807*, Cambridge: Cambridge University, 1987.

Dirlik, Arif, "The Postcolonial Aura," *Critical Inquiry*, 1994, vol. 20, 328–56.

Doujon, Ruhdan, "Steuart's Position on Economic Progress," *The European Journal of the History of Economic Thought*, 1994, vol. 1, 495–519.

Dugger, William M. and James T. Peach, *Economic Abundance: an Introduction*, Armonk: M. E. Sharpe, 2009.

Duke, Michael I., "David Hume and Monetary Adjustment," *History of Political Economy*, 1979, vol. 11, 572–87.

Dussell, Enrique, "World-System and 'Trans'-Modernity," *Nepantla: Views from South*, 2002, vol. 3, 221–44.

Eagly, Robert V., "Sir James Steuart and the 'Aspiration Effect'," *Economica*, 1961 vol. 28, 53–61.

Easterly, William, *The Elusive Quest for Growth: Economists; Adventures and Misadventures in the Tropics*, Cambridge, MA: MIT, 2002.

"Econ 2009," *New York Times*, April 19, 2009, pp. 28–9.

Edkins, Jenny, *Poststructuralism and International Relations: Bringing the Political Back In*, Boulder: Lynne Rienner, 1999.

Edkins, Jenny, *Whose Hunger? Concepts of Famine, Practices of Aid*, Minneapolis: University of Minnesota, 2000.

Edkins, Jenny, *Trauma and the Politics of Memory*, Cambridge: Cambridge University, 2003.

Eliade, Mircea, *The Myth of the Eternal Return or Cosmos and History*, Princeton, NJ: Princeton University, 1971.

Ellingson, Ter, *The Myth of the Noble Savage*, Berkeley: University of California, 2001.

Elms, Deborah Kay, "New Directions for IPE: Drawing from Behavioral Economics," *International Studies Review*, 2008, vol. 10, 239–65.

Elster, Jon, "Historical Materialism and Economic Backwardness," in Terrence Ball and James Farr (eds.) *After Marx*, Cambridge: Cambridge University, 1984, 34–58.

Eltis, Walter, "Sir James Steuart's Corporate State," in R. D. Collison Black (ed.) *Ideas in Economics*, Totowa: Barnes and Noble, 1986, 43–73.

Escobar, Arturo, *Encountering Development: The Making and Unmaking of the Third World*, Princeton: Princeton University, 1995.

Escobar, Arturo, "Worlds and Knowledges Otherwise: The Latin American Modernity/Coloniality Research Program," *Cultural Studies*, 2007, vol. 21, 179–210.

Esteva, Gustavo, "Development," in Wolfgang Sachs (ed.) *The Development Dictionary: A Guide to Knowledge as Power*, London: Zed, 1993, 6–25.

Etzioni, Amitai, *The Spirit of Community: The Reinvention of American Life*, New York: Touchstone, 1993.

Euben, Roxanne L., *The Enemy in the Mirror*, Princeton: Princeton University, 1999.

Evans, Peter, *Embedded Autonomy: States and Industrial Transformation*, Princeton: Princeton University, 1995.

Fabian, Johannes, *Time and the Other: How Anthropology Makes its Object*, New York: Columbia University, 1983.

Fasolt, Constantin, *The Limits of History*, Chicago: University of Chicago, 2004.

Fatton, Robert Jr., "Hegel and the Riddle of Poverty: The Limits of Bourgeoisie Political Economy," *History of Political Economy*, 1986, vol.18, 579–600.

Fenton, William N. and Elizabeth L. Moore, "Introduction," Joseph François Lafitau, *Customs of the American Indians Compared with the Customs of Primitive Times*, Toronto: The Champlain Society, 1974, xxix–cxix.

Ferguson, Adam, *An Essay on the History of Civil Society*, Cambridge: Cambridge University, 1995.

Fink, Bruce, *The Lacanian Subject: Between Language and Jouissance*, Princeton: Princeton University, 1995.

Fleischacker, Samuel, *On Adam Smith's Wealth of Nations: A Philosophical Companion*, Princeton: Princeton University, 2004.

Forbes, Duncan, "Adam Ferguson and the Idea of Community," in Douglas Young et al. (eds.) *Edinburgh in the Age of Reason: A Commemoration*, Edinburgh: Edinburgh University, 1967, 40–7.

Forbes, Duncan, "Introduction" to G. W. F. Hegel, *Lectures on the Philosophy of World History*, Cambridge: Cambridge University, 1975, vii–xxix.

Foster, Martha Haroun, "Lost Women of the Matriarchy: Iroquois Women in the Historical Literature," *American Indians Culture and Research Journal*, 1999, vol. 19, 122–4.

Foster-Carter, Aidan, "The Modes of Production Controversy," *New Left Review*, 1978, no. 107, 47–77.

Fox, Christopher, "Introduction. How to Prepare a Noble Savage: The Spectacle of Human Science," in Christopher Fox, Roy Porter, and Robert Wokler (eds.) *Inventing Human Science: Eighteenth Century Domains*, Berkeley: University of California, 1995, 1–30.

Fraser, Ian, "Speculations on Poverty in Hegel's *Philosophy of Right*," *The European Legacy*, 1996, vol. 1, 2055–68.

Fraser, Nancy, *Justice Interruptus: Critical Reflections on the "Postsocialist" Condition*, New York: Routledge, 1997.

Friedman, Benjamin M., *The Moral Consequences of Economic Growth*, New York: Knopf, 2005.

Friedman, Jonathan, "Civilizational Cycles and the History of Primitivism," *Social Analysis*, 1983, no. 14, 31–50.

Friedman, Jonathan, "*Plus Ça Change*: On Not Learning from History," in Jonathan Friedman and Christopher Chase-Dunn (eds.) *Hegemonic Declines: Present and Past*, Boulder: Paradigm, 2005, 89–114.

Froebel, Folker, Jurgen Heinrich, and Otto Kreye, *The New International Division of Labor*, Cambridge: Cambridge University, 1980.

Fukuyama, Francis, *Trust: The Social Virtues and the Creation of Prosperity*, New York: Free Press, 1995.

Gallagher, Shaun, "Interdependence and Freedom in Hegel's Economics," in William Maker (ed.) *Hegel on Economics and Freedom*, Macon: Mercer University, 1987, 159–82.

Garrett, Aaron, "Anthropology: the 'Original' of Human Nature," in Alexander Broadie (ed.) *The Cambridge Companion to The Scottish Enlightenment*, Cambridge: Cambridge University, 2003, 79–93.

Geremek, Bronislaw, *Poverty: A History*, London: Blackwell, 1997.

Ghosh, Amitav and Dipesh Chakrabarty, "A Correspondence on *Provincializing Europe*," *Radical History Review*, 2002, vol. 83, 146–72.

Ghosh, Sunita Kumar, "Marx on India," *Monthly Review*, 1984, vol. 35, 39–53.

Gibson-Graham, J. K., *The End of Capitalism (as we knew it): A Feminist Critique of Political Economy*, Minneapolis: University of Minnesota, 2006.

Gilpin, Robert, *The Political Economy of International Relations*, Princeton: Princeton University, 1987.

Gilpin, Robert, *Global Political Economy: Understanding the International Economic Order*, Princeton: Princeton University, 2001.

Godelier, Maurice, *Rationality and Irrationality in Economics*, New York: Monthly Review, 1972.

Gould, Carol C., *Marx's Social Ontology: Individuality and Community in Marx's Theory of Social Reality*, Cambridge: MIT Press, 1978.

Gowdy, John, "Introduction: Back to the Future, Forward to the Past," in John Gowdy (ed.) *Limited Wants, Unlimited Means: A Reader on Hunter-Gatherer Economics and the Environment*, Washington, D. C.: Island Press, 1998, xv–xxxi.

Gowdy, John, "Hunter-Gatherers and the Mythology of the Market," in Richard B. Lee and Richard Daly (eds.) *The Cambridge Encyclopedia of Hunters and Gatherers*, Cambridge: Cambridge University, 1999, 391–9.

Granovetter, Mark, "Economic Action and Social Structure: The Problem of Embeddedness," *American Journal of Sociology*, 1985, vol. 91, 481–510.

Griswold, Charles L. Jr., *Adam Smith and the Virtues of Enlightenment*, Cambridge: Cambridge University, 1999.

Gudeman, Stephen, *Economics as Culture: Modes and Metaphors of Livelihood*, New York: Routledge, 1986.

Gwynne, Robert N., Thomas Klak, and Denis J. B. Shaw, *Alternative Capitalisms: Geographies of Emerging Regions*, London: Arnold, 2003.

Haakonssen, Knud, *Natural Law and Moral Philosophy: From Grotius to the Scottish Enlightenment*, Cambridge: Cambridge University, 1996.

Habib, Irfan, *Essays in Indian History: Towards a Marxist Perception*, London: Anthem Press, 2002.

Hall, Peter A. and David Soskice (eds.) *Varieties of Capitalism: The Institutional Foundations of Comparative Advantage*, New York: Oxford University, 2001.

Halperin, Rhoda H., *Cultural Economies Past and Present*, Austin: University of Texas, 1994.

Hamowy, Ronald, *The Scottish Enlightenment and the Theory of Spontaneous Order*, Carbondale: Southern Illinois University, 1987.

Hannaford, Ivan, *Race: The History of an Idea in the West*, Baltimore: Johns Hopkins, 1996.

Hannerz, Ulf, "Cosmopolitans and Locals in World Culture," *Theory, Culture, and Society*, 1990, vol. 7, 237–51.

Harvey, David, *The Condition of Postmodernity*, Oxford: Basil Blackwell, 1989.

Hay, Colin and David Marsh, "Introduction: Towards a New (International) Political Economy," *New Political Economy*, 1999, vol. 4, 5–22.

Hayek, Friedrich, *Prices and Production*, New York: Augustus M. Kelley, 1967.

Hayek, Friedrich, *Law, Legislation, and Liberty, volume 2: The Mirage of Social Justice*, Chicago: University of Chicago, 1976.

Hegel, G. W. F., *Reason in History: A General Introduction to the Philosophy of History*, New York: Bobbs-Merrill, 1953.

Hegel, G. W. F., *Lectures in the Philosophy of World History*, Cambridge: Cambridge University, 1975.

Hegel, G. W. F., *System of Ethical Life and First Philosophy of Spirit*, Albany: SUNY, 1979.

Hegel, G. W. F., *Elements of the Philosophy of Right*, Cambridge: Cambridge University, 1991.

Heiman, G., "The Sources and Significance of Hegel's Corporate Doctrine," in Z. A. Pelczynski (ed.) *Hegel's Political Philosophy: Problems and Perspectives*, Cambridge: Cambridge University, 1971, 111–35.

Helleiner, Eric, "Economic Nationalism as a Challenge to Economic Liberalism? Lessons from the 19th Century," *International Studies Quarterly*, 2002. vol. 46, 307–29.

Hettne, Björn, "The Double Movement: Global Market Versus Regionalism," in Robert W. Cox (ed.) *The New Realism: Perspectives on Multilateralism and World Order*, Tokyo: UN University, 1997, 223–42.

Hill, Lisa, "Adam Ferguson and the Paradox of Progress and Decline," *History of Political Thought*, 1997, vol. XVIII, 677–706.

Hirschman, A. O., *National Power and the Structure of International Trade*, Berkeley: University of California, 1945.

Hirschman, A. O., *The Passions and the Interests: Political Arguments for Capitalism before its Triumph*, Princeton: Princeton University, 1977.

Hirschman, A. O., "On Hegel, Imperialism, and Structural Stagnation," in *Essays in Trespassing: Economics to Politics and Beyond*, Cambridge: Cambridge University, 1981, 167–76.

Hodgen, Margaret T., *Early Anthropology in the Sixteenth and Seventeenth Centuries*, Philadelphia: University of Pennsylvania, 1964.

Hoffheimer, Michael, "Does Hegel Justify Slavery," *The Owl of Minerva*, 1993, vol. 25, 118–9.

Hoffheimer, Michael, "Hegel, Race, and Genocide," *The Southern Journal of Philosophy*, 2001, vol. XXXIX, 35–62.

Hont, Istvan, "The 'Rich Country-Poor Country' Debate in Scottish Political Economy," in Istvan Hont and Michael Ignatieff (eds.) *Wealth and Virtue: The Shaping of Political Economy in the Scottish Enlightenment*, Cambridge: Cambridge University, 1985, 271–316.

Hudson, Nicholas, "From 'Nation' to 'Race': The Origin of Racial Classification in Eighteenth-Century Thought," *Eighteenth-Century Studies*, 1996, vol. 29, 247–64.

Hudson, Nicholas, " 'Hottentots' and the Evolution of European Racism," *Journal of European Studies*, 2004, vol. 34, 308–33.

Hume, David, *The History of England from the Invasion of Julius Caesar to the Revolution of 1688. Volume II*, London: J. Mcreery, 1807.

Hume, David, "Of Money," in *Essays: Moral, Political, and Literary*, Indianapolis: Liberty Fund, 1985, 281–94.

Hume, David, "Of Refinement in the Arts," in *Essays: Moral, Political, Literary*, Indianapolis: Liberty Fund, 1985, 268–80.

Hutchings, Kimberly, *Time and World Politics: Thinking the Present*, Manchester: Manchester University, 2008.

Ilting, K.-H., "The Structure of Hegel's 'Philosophy of Right' " in Z. A. Pelzcynski (ed.) *Hegel's Political Philosophy: Problems and Perspectives*, Cambridge: Cambridge University, 1971, 90–110.

Ilting, K.-H., "The Dialectic of Civil Society," in Z. A. Pelczynski (ed.) *The State and Civil Society: Studies in Hegel's Political Philosophy*, Cambridge: Cambridge University, 1984, 211–26.

Ilting, K.-H., "Hegel's Concept of the State and Marx's Early Critique," in Z. A. Pelczynski (ed.) *The State and Civil Society: Studies in Hegel's Political Philosophy*, Cambridge: Cambridge University, 1984, 93–113.

Inayatullah, Naeem, "Theories of Spontaneous Order," *Review of International Political Economy*, 1997, vol. 4, 319–48.

Inayatullah, Naeem and David L. Blaney, "Realizing Sovereignty," *Review of International Studies*, 1995, vol. 21, 3–20.

Inayatullah, Naeem, and David L. Blaney, "Knowing Encounters: Beyond Parochialism in IR Theory," in Yosef Lapid and Friedrich Kratochwil (eds.) *The Return of Culture and Identity in IR Theory*, Boulder: Lynne Rienner, 1996, 65–84.

Inayatullah, Naeem and David L. Blaney, "Economic Anxiety: Reification, De-reification, and the Politics of IPE," in Kurt Burch and Robert Denemark (eds.) *Constituting International Political Economy*, Boulder: Lynne Rienner, 1997, 59–77.

Inayatullah, Naeem and David L. Blaney, *International Relations and the Problem of Difference*, New York: Routledge, 2004.

Isaak, Robert A., *Managing World Economic Change: International Political Economy*, Upper Saddle River: Prentice Hall, 2000.

Jackson, Peter, "Commercial Cultures: Transcending the Cultural and the Economic," *Progress in Human Geography*, 2002, vol. 26, 3–18.

Jackson, William A., "Culture, Society, and Economic Theory," *Review of Political Economy*, 1993, vol. 5, 453–69.

Jaeger, Hans-Martin, "Hegel's Reluctant Realism and the Transnationalisation of Civil Society," *Review of International Studies*, 2002, vol. 28, 497–517.

Jeffery, Renée, "Tradition as Invention: The 'Traditions Tradition' and the History of Ideas in International Relations," *Millennium*, 2005, vol. 34, 57–84.

Jessop, Bob, "Critical Semiotic Analysis and Cultural Political Economy," *Critical Discourse Studies*, 2004, vol. 1, 159–74.

Johnson, Chalmers, *MITI and the Japanese Miracle: The Growth of Industrial Policy, 1925–1975*, Stanford: Stanford University, 1982.

Jones, E. L., *The European Economic Miracle: Environments, Economies, and Geopolitics in the History of Europe and Asia*, Cambridge: Cambridge University, 1987.

Jones, Gareth Stedman, "Hegel and the Economics of Civil Society," in Sudipta Kaviraj and Sunil Khilnani (eds.) *Civil Society: History and Possibilities*, Cambridge: Cambridge University, 2001, 105–30.

Jones, Gareth Stedman, *An End to Poverty: A Historical Debate*, London: Profiles Books, 2004.

Karatani, Kojin, *Architecture as Metaphor: Language, Numbers, Money*, Cambridge, MA: MIT, 1995.

Kariel, Henry, "Becoming Political," in Vernon Van Dyke (ed.) *Teaching Political Science*, Humanities Press, 1977, 53–71.

Kaviraj, Sudipta, "Marxism and the Darkness of History," *Development and Change*, 1992, vol. 23, 79–102.

Kennedy, Paul, *The Rise and Fall of the Great Powers: Economic Change and Military Conflict from 1500–2000*, New York: Random House, 1987.

Kettler, David, *The Social and Political Thought of Adam Ferguson*, Columbus: Ohio State, 1965.

Kirshner, Jonathan, "Keynes, Capital Mobility and the Crisis of Embedded Liberalism," *Review of International Political Economy*, 1999, vol. 6, 315–37.

Klein, Naomi, *The Shock Doctrine: The Rise of Disaster Capitalism*, New York: Metropolitan, 2007.

Kordela, A. Kiarina, "Capital: At Least it Kills Time (Spinoza, Marx, Lacan, and Temporality)," *Rethinking Marxism*, 2006, vol. 18, 539–63.

Kordela, A. Kiarina, *Surplus: Spinoza, Lacan*, Albany: SUNY, 2007.

Kosselleck, Reinhart, *Futures Past: On the Semantics of Historical Time*, New York: Columbia University, 2004.

Krader, Lawrence, "Introduction," *The Ethnological Notebooks of Karl Marx*, Assen: Van Gorcum, 1972, 1–93.

Kuper, Adam, *The Invention of Primitive Society: Transformation of an Illusion*, London: Routledge, 1988.

Lafitau, Joseph François, *Customs of the American Indians Compared with the Customs of Primitive Times, Volumes I and II*, Toronto: The Champlain Society, 1974.

Landes, Joan B., "Hegel's Conception of the Family," *Polity*, 1981, vol. XIV, 5–28.

Lane, Robert, *The Loss of Happiness in Market Democracies*, New Haven: Yale University, 2001.

Larrain, Jorge, *A Reconstruction of Historical Materialism*, New York: Ashgate, 1992.

Latham, Robert, "Globalisation and Democratic Provisionism: Re-reading Polanyi," *New Political Economy*, 1997, vol. 2, 53–62.

Latouche, Serge, *In the Wake of the Affluent Society: An Exploration of Post-Development*, London: Zed Press, 1993.

Latour, Bruno, *We Have Never Been Modern*, Cambridge: Harvard University, 1993.

Layard, Richard, *Happiness: Lessons from a New Science*, New York: Penguin, 2005.

Leacock, Eleanor and Richard Lee, "Introduction," in Leacock and Lee (eds.) *Politics and History in Band Societies*, Cambridge: Cambridge University, 1982, 1–20.

Lee, Richard B., "Art, Science, or Politics? The Crisis in Hunter-Gatherer Studies," *American Anthropologist*, 1992, vol. 94, 31–54.

Le Goff, Jacques, *Time, Work, and Culture in the Middle Ages*, Chicago: University of Chicago, 1980.

Levine, David P., *Economic Studies: Contributions to the Critique of Economic Theory*, London: Routledge and Kegan Paul, 1977.

Lévi-Strauss, Claude, *Structural Anthropology*, New York: Basic Books, 1963.

Lindqvist, Sven, *Exterminate All the Brutes*, New York: New Press, 1996.

Lindqvist, Sven, *Terra Nullius*, New York: New Press, 2007.

Locke, John, *Two Treatises of Government*, Cambridge: Cambridge University, 1988.

Lovejoy, Arthur O., *The Great Chain of Being: A Study of the History of an Idea*, Cambridge: Harvard University, 1964.

MacIntyre, Alasdair, *After Virtue*, Notre Dame: Notre Dame University, 1981.

Maletz, Donald J., "History in Hegel's *Philosophy of Right*," *Review of Politics*, 1983, vol. 45, 209–33.

Manuel, Frank E., *The Eighteenth Century Confronts the Gods*, Cambridge, MA: Harvard University, 1959.

Manzer, Robert A., "The Promise of Peace? Hume and Smith on the Effects of Commerce on War and Peace," *Hume Studies*, 1996, vol. XXII, 369–82.

Marglin, Stephen and Juliet Schor (eds.) *The Golden Age of Capitalism: Reinterpreting the Postwar Experience*, Oxford: Clarendon Press, 1990.

Marx, Karl, *A Contribution to the Critique of Political Economy*, New York: International Publishers, 1970.

Marx, Karl, *Grundrisse: Foundations of the Critique of Political Economy*, New York: Vintage, 1973.

Marx, Karl, *Capital: A Critique of Political Economy. Volume I*, New York: Vintage, 1977.

Marx, Karl, *Theories of Surplus Value, Volume 3*, Moscow: Progress Publishers, 1979.

Marx, Karl, "British Rule in India," in Aijaz Ahmad (ed.) *On the National and Colonial Questions: Selected Writings*, New Delhi: LeftWord Book, 2001, 61–6.

Marx, Karl, "The Future Results of the British Rule in India," in Aijaz Ahmad (ed.) *On the National and Colonial Questions*, New Delhi: LeftWord Book, 2001, 70–5.

Karl Marx, "Marx to Sigfrid Meyer and August Vogt," in Aijaz Ahmad (ed.) *On the National and Colonial Questions*, New Delhi: LeftWord Book, 2001, 223–4.

Marx, Karl and Friedrich Engels, *The German Ideology, Part One*, New York: International Publishers, 1970.

Marx, Karl and Friedrich Engels, "The Manifesto of the Communist Party," in Robert C. Tucker (ed.) *The Marx-Engels Reader*, New York: W. W. Norton, 1978, 473–500.

Mbembé, J.-A., *On the Postcolony*, Berkeley: University of California, 2001.

McCarney, Joseph, *Hegel and History*, New York: Routledge, 2000.

McCarney, Joseph, "Hegel's Racism? A Response to Bernasconi," *Radical Philosophy*, 2003, no. 119, 1–4.

McCloskey, Deidre N., *The Bourgeois Virtues: Ethics for an Age of Commerce*, Chicago: University of Chicago, 2006.

McDowell, Linda, "Acts of Memory and Millennial Hopes and Anxieties: The Awkward Relationship Between the Economic and the Cultural," *Social and Cultural Geography*, 2000, vol. 1, 15–30.

Meek, Ronald L., "The Scottish Contribution to Marxist Sociology," in J. Saville (ed.) *Democracy and the Labour Movement*, London: Lawrence and Wishart, 1954, 84–102.

Meek, Ronald L., *Economics and Ideology: Studies in the Development of Economic Thought*, London: Chapman and Hall, 1967.

Meek, Ronald L., "The Rehabilitation of Sir James Steuart," in *Economics and Ideology and Other Essays: Studies in the Development of Economic Thought*, London: Chapman and Hall, 1967, 3–17.

Meek, Ronald L., *Social Science and the Ignoble Savage*, Cambridge: Cambridge University, 1976.

Mendell, Marguerite, "Karl Polanyi and Feasible Socialism," in Kari Polanyi-Levitt (ed.) *The Life and Work of Karl Polanyi: A Celebration*, Montreal: Black Rose, 1990, 66–77.

Merikoski, Ingrid A., "The Challenge of Material Progress: The Scottish Enlightenment and Christian Stoicism," *The Journal of the Historical Society*, 2002, vol. II, 55–76.

Miller, Daniel, *Capitalism: An Ethnographic Approach*, New York: Berg, 1997.

Mitchell, Timothy, "Fixing the Economy," *Cultural Studies*, 1998, vol. 12, 82–101.

Mitchell, Timothy, "The Stage of Modernity," in Timothy Mitchell (ed.) *Questions of Modernity*, Minneapolis: University of Minnesota, 2000, 1–39.

Montag, Warren, "Necro-Economics: Adam Smith and Death in the Life of the Universal," *Radical Philosophy*, 2005, no. 134, 7–17.

Moore, Stanley, "Marx and Lenin as Historical Materialists," in Marshall Cohen, Thomas Nagel, and Thomas Scanlon (eds.) *Marx, Justice and History*, Princeton: Princeton University, 1980, 211–34.

Mueller, John, *Capitalism, Democracy, and Ralph's Pretty Good Grocery*, Princeton: Princeton University, 1999.

Muldoon, James, *Popes, Lawyers, and Infidels: The Church and the Non-Christian World 1250–1550*, Philadelphia: University of Pennsylvania, 1979.

Muller, Jerry A., *Adam Smith, in His Time and Ours*, Princeton: Princeton University, 1993.

Murphy, Craig N., *Industrial Organization and Industrial Change: Global Governance Since 1850*, New York: Oxford University, 1994.

Murphy, Craig N. and Cristina Rojas de Ferro, "Introduction: The Power of Representation in International Political Economy," *Review of International Political Economy* 1995, vol. 2, 63–9.

Myers, Fred, *Pintupi Country, Pintupi Self: Sentiment, Place and Politics among Western Desert Aborigines*, Washington, D.C.: Smithsonian Institution, 1986.

Myers, Fred, "Burning the Truck and Holding the Country: Property, Time and the Negotiation of Identity among Pintupi Aborigines" in Tim Ingold, David Riches, and James Woodburn (eds.) *Hunters and Gatherers: Property, Power and Ideology*, Oxford: Berg, 1988, 52–73.

Nandy, Ashis, *The Intimate Enemy: Loss and Recovery of Self Under Colonialism*, Delhi: Oxford University, 1983.

Nandy, Ashis, *Traditions, Tyranny, and Utopias: Essays on the Politics of Awareness*, Delhi, Oxford University, 1987.

Nandy, Ashis, "Shamans, Savages and the Wilderness: On the Audibility of Dissent and the Future of Civilizations," *Alternatives*, 1989, vol. VIV, 263–77.

Nandy, Ashis, "The Savage Freud," in *The Savage Freud and Other Essays on Possible and Retrievable Selves*, Princeton: Princeton University, 1995, 81–144.

Nandy, Ashis, *Time Warps: Silent and Evasive Pasts in Indian Politics and Religion*, New Brunswick: Rutgers University, 2002.

Nandy, Ashis, *The Romance of the State and the Fate of Dissent in the Tropics*, Delhi: Oxford, 2008.

Nederman, Cary J., "Sovereignty, War and the Corporation: Hegel on the Medieval Foundations of the Modern State," *Journal of Politics*, 1987, vol. 49, 500–20.

Negri, Antonio, *Marx Beyond Marx: Lessons on the Grundrisse*, South Hadley: Bergin and Garvey, 1984.

Neocleous, Mark, "Policing the System of Needs: Hegel, Political Economy, and the Police of the Market," *History of European Ideas*, 1998, vol. 24, 43–58.

Nimtz, August, "The Eurocentric Marx and Engels and Other Related Myths," in Crystal Bartolovish and Neil Lazarus (eds.) *Marxism, Modernity, and Postcolonial Studies*, Cambridge: Cambridge University, 2002, 65–80.

Nurkse, Ragnar, *Problems of Capital Formation in Underdeveloped Countries and Patterns of Trade and Development*, New York: Oxford, 1967.

Onuf, Peter and Nicholas, *Nations, Markets, and War: Modern History and the American Civil War*, Charlottesville: University of Virginia, 2006.

Oz-Salzberger, Fania, *Translating the Enlightenment: Scottish Civic Discourse in Eighteenth-Century Germany*, New York: Oxford, 1995.

Oz-Salzberger, Fania, "The Political Theory of the Scottish Enlightenment," in Alexander Broadie (ed.) *The Cambridge Companion to the Scottish Enlightenment*, Cambridge: Cambridge University, 2003, 157–77.

Pagden, Anthony, *The Fall of Natural Man: The American Indians and the Origins of Comparative Ethnology*, Cambridge: Cambridge University, 1982.

Pagden, Anthony, *European Encounters with the New World: From Renaissance to Romanticism*, New Haven: Yale University, 1993.

Panter-Brick, Catherine, Robert H. Layton and Peter Rowley-Conwy, "Line of Enquiry," in Panter-Brick, Layton, and Rowley-Conwy (eds.) *Hunter-Gatherers: An Interdisciplinary Perspective*, Cambridge: Cambridge University, 2001, 1–11.

Paquette, Gabriel, "Hegel Analysis of Colonialism and Its Roots in Scottish Political Economy," *CLIO*, 2003, vol. 32, 415–32.

Pelczynski, Z. A. "Introduction: The Significance of Hegel's Separation of the State and Civil Society," in Z. A. Pelczynski (ed.) *The State and Civil Society: Studies in Hegel's Political Philosophy*, Cambridge: Cambridge University, 1984, 1–13.

Pinkard, Terry, *Hegel: A Biography*, Cambridge: Cambridge University, 2000.

Pittrock, Murray G. H., "Historiography," in Alexander Broadie (ed.) *The Cambridge Companion to the Scottish Enlightenment*, Cambridge: Cambridge University, 2003, 258–79.

Plant, Raymond, "Hegel and the Political Economy," in William Maker (ed.) *Hegel on Economics and Freedom*, Macon: Mercer University, 1987, 95–126.

Pluciennik, Mark, "Archaeology, Anthropology and Subsistence," *Journal of the Royal Anthropological Institute*, 2001, vol. 7, 741–58.

Pluciennik, Mark, "The Invention of Hunter-Gatherers in Seventeenth-Century Europe," *Archaeological Dialogues*, 2002, vol. 9, 98–151.

Pluciennik, Mark, "The Meaning of 'Hunter-Gatherers' and Modes of Subsistence: A Comparative Historical Perspective," in Alan Barnard (ed.) *Hunter-Gatherers in History, Archaeology and Anthropology*, Oxford: Berg, 2004, 17–29.

Pocock, J. G. A., *The Machiavellian Moment: Florentine Political Thought and the Atlantic Republican Tradition*, Princeton: Princeton University, 1975.

Pocock, J. G. A., "Intentions, Traditions and Methods: Some Sounds on a Fog-Horn," *Annals of Scholarship*, 1980, vol. 1, 57–62.

Pocock, J. G. A., *Virtue, Commerce, and History: Essays on Political Thought and History, Chiefly in the Eighteenth Century*, Cambridge: Cambridge University, 1985.

Polanyi, Karl, "The Economy as Instituted Process," in George Dalton (ed.) *Primitive, Archaic, and Modern Economies: Essays of Karl Polanyi*, Garden City: Anchor, 1968, 139–74.

Polanyi, Karl, "Aristotle Discovers the Economy," in George Dalton (ed.) *Primitive, Archaic, and Modern Economies: Essays of Karl Polanyi*, Garden City: Anchor, 1968, pp. 78–115.

Polanyi, Karl, *The Livelihood of Man*, New York: Academic Press, 1977.

Polanyi, Karl, *The Great Transformation: The Political and Economic Origins of Our Time*, Boston: Beacon, 2001.

Poovey, Mary, *A History of the Modern Fact: Problems of Knowledge in the Sciences of Wealth and Society*, Chicago: University of Chicago, 1998.

Porter, Roy, *The Creation of the Modern World: The Untold Story of the British Enlightenment*, New York: W.W. Norton, 2001.

Postone, Moishe, *Time, Labor, and Social Domination: A Reinterpretation of Marx's Critical Theory*, Cambridge: Cambridge University, 1993.

Pratt, Mary Louise, "Arts of the Contact Zone," *Profession*, 1991, vol. 91, 33–40.

Rahnema, Majid, "Poverty," in Wolfgang Sachs (ed.) *The Development Dictionary: A Guide to Knowledge as Power*, London: Zed Press, 1992, 158–76.

Raphael, D. D., "Adam Smith: Philosophy, Science and Social Science," in Stuart C. Brown (ed.) *Philosophers of the Enlightenment*, Atlantic Highlands: Humanities Press, 1979, 77–93.

Redman, Deborah, "Sir James Steuart's Statesman Revisited in Light of the Continental Influence," *Scottish Journal of Political Economy*, 1996, vol. 43, 48–70.

Ringmar, Eric, *Surviving Capitalism: How we Learned to Live with the Market and Remained Almost Human*, London: Anthem, 2005.

Robbins, Lionel, *An Essay on the Nature and Significance of Economic Science*, London: Macmillan, 1952.

Rosenberg, Justin, *The Empire of Civil Society: A Critique of the Realist Theory of International Relations*, London: Verso, 1994.

Rothschild, Emma, *Economic Sentiments: Adam Smith, Condorcet, and the Enlightenment*, Cambridge: Harvard University, 2001.

Rowley-Conwy, Peter, "Time, Change and the Archaeology of Hunter-Gatherers: How Original is the 'Original Affluent Society'?," in Catherine Panter-Brick, Robert Layton, Peter H. Rowley-Conwy (eds.) *Hunter-Gatherers: An Interdisciplinary Perspective*, Cambridge: Cambridge University, 2001, 39–72.

Ruggie, John Gerard, "At Home Abroad, Abroad at Home: International Liberalisation and Domestic Stability in the New World Economy," *International Studies Quarterly*, 1994, vol. 24, 507–26.

Sachs, Jeffrey, *The End of Poverty: Economic Possibilities for Our Time*, New York: Penguin, 2005.

Sahlins, Marshall, *Stone Age Economics*, New York: Aldine, 1972.

Sahlins, Marshall, *Culture and Practical Reason*, Chicago: University of Chicago, 1976.

Sahlins, Marshall, "The Sadness of Sweetness: The Native Anthropology of Western Cosmology," *Current Anthropology*, 1996, vol. 37, 395–428.

Sahlins, Marshall, "What is Anthropological Enlightenment? Some Lessons of the Twentieth Century," *Annual Review of Anthropology*, 1999, vol. 28, i–xxiii.

Sarkar, Sumit, "The Decline of the Subaltern in *Subaltern Studies*," in Vinayak Charurvedi (ed.) *Mapping Subaltern Studies and the Postcolonial*, London: Verso, 2000, 300–23.

Sayer, Andrew, "For a Critical Cultural Political Economy," *Antipode*, 2001, vol. 33, 687–708.

Sayer, Andrew, "(De)commodification, Consumer Culture, and Moral Economy," *Environment and Planning D: Society and Space*, 2003, vol. 21, 341–57.

Schor, Juliet, *The Overworked American: The Unexpected Decline of Leisure*, New York: Basic Books, 1992.

Schumpeter, Joseph A., *History of Economic Analysis*, New York: Oxford University Press, 1954.

Schumpeter, Joseph, *Capitalism, Socialism and Democracy*, New York: Harper Colophon, 1975.

Scott, Colin, "Property, Practice and Aboriginal Rights Among Quebec Cree Hunters," in Tim, Ingold, David Riches, and James Woodburn (eds.) *Hunters and Gatherers: Property, Power and Ideology*, Oxford: Berg, 1988, 35–51.

Scott, Helen, "Was There a Time Before Race? Capitalist Modernity and the Origins of Racism," in Crystal Bartolovich and Neil Lazarus (eds.) *Marxism, Modernity, and Postcolonial Studies*, Cambridge: Cambridge University, 2002, 167–84.

Sen, Amartya, *Poverty and Famine: An Essay on Entitlement and Deprivation*, Oxford: Oxford University, 1981.

Sen, Amartya, *Development as Freedom*, New York: Anchor, 1999.

Sen, S.R., *The Economics of Sir James Steuart*, Cambridge: Harvard University, 1957.

Serequeberhan, Tsenay, "The Idea of Colonialism in Hegel's Philosophy of Right," *International Philosophical Quarterly*, 1989, vol. XXIX, 301–18.

Serequeberhan, Tsenay, "Eurocentrism in Philosophy: The Case of Immanuel Kant," *The Philosophical Forum*, 1996, vol. 27, 333–56.

Shanin, Teodor, "Late Marx: Gods and Craftsmen," in Teodor Shanin (ed.) *Late Marx and the Russian Road: Marx and "the Peripheries of Capitalism"*, New York: Monthly Review, 1983.

Shapiro, Michael J., *Reading "Adam Smith": Desire, History, and Value*, Lanham: Rowman and Littlefield, 2002.

Shaw, William H., *Marx's Theory of History*, Stanford: Stanford University, 1978.

Shell, Susan M., "Kant's Concept of a Human Race," in Sara Eigen and Mark Joseph Larrimore (eds.) *The German Invention of Race*, Albany: SUNY, 2006, 55–72.

Shilliam, Robert, "The 'Other' in Classical Political Theory: Re-contextualizing the Cosmopolitan/Communitarian Debate," in Beate Jahn (ed.) *Classical Theory in International Relations*, Cambridge: Cambridge University, 2006, 207–32.

Siemens, Robert, "The Problem of Modern Poverty: Significant Congruences Between Hegel's and George's Theoretical Conceptions," *American Journal of Economics and Sociology*, 1997, vol. 56, 617–37.

Skinner, Andrew, "Sir James Steuart: Economics and Politics," *Scottish Journal of Political Economy*, 1962, vol. 9, 17–22.

Skinner, Andrew, "Economics and History—The Scottish Enlightenment," *Scottish Journal of Political Economy*, 1965, vol. 12, 1–22.

Skinner, Andrew, "Biographical Sketch," in Sir James Steuart, *An Inquiry into the Principles of Political Oeconomy. Volume One*, Chicago: University of Chicago, 1966, pp. xxi–lvii.

Skinner, Andrew, "Money and Prices: A Critique of the Quantity Theory," *Scottish Journal of Political Economy*, 1967, vol. 14, 275–90.

Skinner, Andrew, "Natural History in the Age of Adam Smith," *Political Studies*, 1967, vol. XVI, 32–48.

Skinner, Andrew, "Sir James Steuart: The Market and the State," *History of Economic Ideas*, 1993, vol. 1, 1–42.

Skinner, Andrew, "Economic Theory," in Alexander Broadie (ed.) *The Cambridge Companion to the Scottish Enlightenment*, Cambridge: Cambridge University, 2003, 178–204.

Skinner, Quentin, *Liberty Before Liberalism*, Cambridge: Cambridge University, 1998.

Skinner, Quentin, *Visions of Politics. Volume I: Regarding Method*, Cambridge: Cambridge University, 2002.

Smith, Adam, *An Inquiry into the Nature and Causes of the Wealth of Nations*, Chicago: University of Chicago, 1976.

Smith, Adam, *The Theory of Moral Sentiments*, Indianapolis: Liberty Fund, 1976.

Smith, Adam, "A Letter to the Authors of the *Edinburgh Review*," *Essays on Philosophical Subjects*, Indianapolis: Liberty Fund, 1980, 242–54.

Smith, Adam, "The History of Astronomy," *Essays on Philosophical Subjects*, Indianapolis: Liberty Fund, 1980, 33–105.

Smith, Adam, "Of the Nature of that Imitation which Takes Place in What are Called the Imitative Arts," *Essays on Philosophical Subjects*, Indianapolis: Liberty Fund, 1980, 176–209.

Smith, Adam, "Report of 1762–3," in *Lectures on Jurisprudence*, Indianapolis: Liberty Fund, 1982, 1–394.

Smith, Adam, "Report Dated 1766," in *Lectures on Jurisprudence*, Indianapolis: Liberty Fund, 1982, 395–554.

Smith, Adam, "Considerations Concerning the First Formation of Languages," in Adam Smith, *Lectures on Rhetoric and Belles Lettres*, Indianapolis: Liberty Fund, 1985, 23–8.

Smith, Paul, "Conjecture, Acquiescence, and John Millar's History of Ireland," *The European Legacy*, 1996, vol. 1, 2227–48.

Smith, Roger, "The Language of Human Nature," in Christopher Fox, Roy Porter, and Robert Wokler (eds.) *Inventing Human Science: Eighteenth Century Domains*, Berkeley: University of California, 1995, 88–111.

Smith, Steven B., "Hegel's Discovery of History," *Review of Politics*, 1983, vol. 45, 163–87.

Smith, Steven B., "Hegel on Slavery and Domination," *Review of Metaphysics*, 1992, vol. 46, 97–124.

Stepan, Nancy, *The Idea of Race in Science: Great Britain 1800–1960*, Hamden: Archon Books, 1982.

Steuart, Sir James, *An Inquiry into the Principles of Political Oeconomy: Being an Essay on the Science of Domestic Policy in Free Nations*, Chicago: University of Chicago, 1966.

Stewart, Dugald, "An Account of the Life and Writings of Adam Smith, L.L.D." in *Essays on Philosophical Topics*, Indianapolis: Liberty Fund, 1982, 269–351.

Stillman, Peter G., "Partiality and Wholeness: Economic Freedom, Individual Development, and Ethical Institutions in Hegel's Political Thought," in William Maker (ed.) *Hegel on Economics and Freedom*, Macon: Mercer University, 1987, 65–93.

Stocking, George W. Jr., "Scotland as the Model of Mankind: Lord Kames' Philosophical View of Civilization," in Timothy H. H. Thoresen (ed.) *Toward a Science of Man: Essays in the History of Anthropology*, The Hague: Mouton, 1975, 65–89.

Stocking, George W. Jr., *Victorian Anthropology*, New York: Free Press, 1987.

Strange, Susan, "Wake up Krasner! The World *has* Changed," *Review of International Political Economy*, 1994, vol. 1, 209–19.

Swanson, Jacinda, "Recognition and Redistribution: Rethinking Culture and the Economic," *Theory, Culture and Society*, 2005, vol. 22, 87–118.

Szasz, Margaret Connell, *Scottish Highlanders and Native Americans: Indigenous Education in the Eighteenth Century Atlantic World*, Norman: University of Oklahoma, 2007.

Teichgraeber, Richard E. III., *"Free Trade" and Moral Philosophy: Rethinking the Sources of Adam Smith's Wealth of Nations*, Durham: Duke University, 1986.

Thrift, Nigel, "Pandora's Box? Cultural Geographies or Economies," in G. Clark, M. Feldmann, and M. Gertler (eds.) *The Oxford Handbook of Economic Geography*, Oxford: Oxford University, 2003, 689–702.

Todorov, Tzvetan, *The Conquest of America: The Question of the Other*, New York: Harper and Row, 1984.

Torrence, Robin, "Hunter-Gatherer Technology: Macro- and Microscale Approaches," in Catherine Panter-Brick, Robert Layton, and Peter Rowley-Conwy (eds.) *Hunter-Gatherers: An Interdisciplinary Perspective*, Cambridge: Cambridge University, 2001, 73–98.

Trautmann, Thomas R., "The Revolution in Ethnological Time," *Man*, 1992, vol. 27, 379–97.

Tribe, Keith, G*overning Economy: The Reformation of German Economic Discourse 1750–1840*, Cambridge: Cambridge University, 1988.

Trouillot, Michel-Rolph, "Anthropology and the Savage Slot," in Richard G. Fox (ed.) *Recapturing Anthropology: Working in the Present*, Santa Fe: School of American Research, 1991, 17–44.

Uchitelle, Louis, *The Disposable American: Layoffs and their Consequences*, New York: Vintage, 2007.

Urquhart, Robert, "Reciprocating Monads: Individual, *The Wealth of Nations*, and the Dream of Economic Science," *Scottish Journal of Political Science*, 1994, vol. 41, 294–415.

Urquhart, Robert, "The Trade Wind, the Statesman and the System of Commerce: Sir James Steuart's Vision of Political Economy" *The European Journal of the History of Economic Thought*, 1996, vol. 3, 379–410.

Vernon, Raymond, "International Investment and International Trade in the Product Life Cycle," *Quarterly Journal of Economics*, 1966, vol. 80, 190–207.

Viner, Jacob, *Studies in the Theory of International Trade*, New York: Harper, 1937.

Viner, Jacob, *The Role of Providence in the Social Order: An Essay in Intellectual History*, Princeton: Princeton University, 1972.

Vogel, Jeffrey, "The Tragedy of History," *New Left Review*, 1996, no. 220, 36–61.

Vrasti, Wanda, "The Strange Case of Ethnography and International Relations," *Millennium*, 2008, vol. 37, 279–301.

Walker, R.B.J., *Inside/Outside: International Relations as Political Theory*, Cambridge: Cambridge University, 1993.

Walton, A. S., "Economy, Utility and Community in Hegel's Theory of Civil Society," in Z. A. Pelczynski (ed.) *The State and Civil Society: Studies in Hegel's Political Philosophy*, Cambridge: Cambridge University, 1984, 244–61.

Walsh, W.H., "Principle and Prejudice in Hegel's Philosophy of History," in Z. A. Pelczynski (ed.) *Hegel's Political Philosophy: Problems and Perspectives*, Cambridge: Cambridge University, 1971, 181–98.

Warren, Bill, *Imperialism: Pioneer of Capitalism*, New York: Verso, 1981.

Wartenberg, Thomas, "Poverty and Class Structure in Hegel's Theory of Civil Society," *Philosophy and Social Criticism*, 1981, vol. 8, 168–82.

Waszek, Norbert, *The Scottish Enlightenment and Hegel's Account of "Civil Society,"* Dordrecht: Kluwer Academic, 1988.

Watson, Matthew, *Foundations of International Political Economy*, Houndsmill: Palgrave, 2005.

Weinstein, Jack Russell, "Sympathy, Difference, and Education: Social Unity in the Work of Adam Smith," *Economics and Philosophy*, 2006, vol. 22, 79–111.

Wendt, Alexander, "Why a World State is Inevitable," *European Journal of International Relations*, 2003, vol. 9, 491–542.

West, E.G., *Adam Smith: The Man and his Works*, New Rochelle: Arlington House, 1969.

Wheeler, Roxann, *The Complexion of Race: Categories of Difference in Eighteenth Century British Culture*, Philadelphia: University of Pennsylvania, 2000.

White, James D., *Karl Marx and the Intellectual Origins of Dialectical Materialism*, New York: St. Martin's, 1996.

Wiessner, Polly, "Risk, Reciprocity and Social Influence on !Kung San Economics," in Leacock and Lee (eds.) *Politics and History in Band Societies*, Cambridge: Cambridge University, 1982, 61–84.

Williams, Raymond, "Culture is Ordinary," in Robin Grable (ed.) *Resources of Hope: Culture, Democracy, Socialism*, London: Verso, 1989, 2–18.

Williamson, Arthur H., "Scots, Indians and Empire: The Scottish Politics of Civilization 1519–1609," *Past and Present*, 1996, no. 150, 46–83.

Winch, Donald, *Adam Smith's Politics: An Essay in Historiographic Revision*, Cambridge: Cambridge University, 1978.

Winch, Donald, *Riches and Poverty: An Intellectual History of Political Economy in Britain, 1750–1834*, Cambridge: Cambridge University, 1996.

Winfield, Richard Dien, "Hegel's Challenge to the Modern Economy," in William Maker (ed.) *Hegel on Economics and Freedom*, Macon: Mercer University, 1987, 29–63.

Winfield, Richard Dien, "Postcolonialism and Right," in Robert R. Williams (ed.)

Beyond Liberalism and Communitarianism: Studies in Hegel's Philosophy of Right, Albany: SUNY, 2001, 91–109.

Winterhalder, Bruce, "The Behavioural Ecology of Hunter-Gatherers," in Catherine Panter-Brick, Robert Layton, and Peter Rowley-Conwy (eds.) *Hunter-Gatherers: An Interdisciplinary Perspective*, Cambridge: Cambridge University, 2001, 12–38.

Wokler, Robert, "Anthropology and Conjectural History in the Enlightenment," in Christopher Fox, Roy Porter, and Robert Wokler (eds.) *Inventing Human Science: Eighteenth-Century Domains*, Berkeley: University of California, 1995, 31–52.

Wolf, Eric, *Europe and the People without History*, Berkeley: University of California, 1982.

Woo-Cumings, Meredith (ed.) *The Developmental State*, Ithaca: Cornell University, 1999.

Wood, Alan W., *Hegel's Ethical Thought*, Cambridge: Cambridge University, 1990.

Woodburn, James, "Hunters and Gatherers Today and Reconstruction of the Past," in Ernest Gellner (ed.) *Soviet and Western Anthropology*. New York: Columbia University, 1980, 95–117.

The World Bank, *Attacking Poverty: World Development Report 2000/2001*, New York: Oxford University, 1999.

Wyatt-Walter, Andrew, "Adam Smith and the Liberal Tradition in International Relations," *Review of International Studies*, 1996, vol. 22, 5–28.

Xenos, Nicholas, *Scarcity and Modernity*, New York: Routledge, 1989.

Youngs, Gillian, "The Knowledge Problematic: Richard Ashley and Political Economy," Nottingham Trent University: manuscript, 1994.

Zein-Elabdin, Eiman O. and S. Charusheela, "Introduction: Economics and Postcolonial Thought," in Eiman O. Zein-Elabdin and A. Charusheela (eds.) *Postcolonialism Meets Economics*, New York: Routledge, 2004, 1–18.

Zizek, Slavoj, *The Plague of Fantasies*, London: Verso, 1997.

Zizek, Slavoj, *On Belief*, New York: Routledge, 2001.

Index